FV_

WHY
MEN
RULE

WHY MEN RULE

A Theory of Male Dominance

STEVEN GOLDBERG

OPEN COURT

Chicago and La Salle, Illinois

© 1993 by Open Court Publishing Company

First printing 1993

Library of Congress Cataloging-in-Publication Data

Goldberg, Steven, 1941–
    Why men rule : a theory of male dominance / Steven Goldberg.
      p.   cm.
    Rev. ed. of: The inevitability of patriarchy. 1977.
    Includes bibliographical references (p.   ) and index.
    ISBN 0-8126-9236-5 (cloth).—ISBN 0-8126-9237-3 (paper)
    1. Sex role. 2. Men—Psychology. I. Goldberg, Steven, 1941–
Inevitability of patriarchy. II. Title.
HQ1075.G64 1993
305.31—dc20   93-23346
                                               CIP

For My Father

בני היקרים
ובניהם שניים יהיו
לאשר ובאשה
היתום לי ותהניהם

and
For My Mother

Numquam naturam mos vinceret;
est enim ea semper invicta . . .

(Custom will never conquer
nature, for it is always she who
remains unconquered.)

—Cicero, *Tusculanae Disputationes*

Contents

Acknowledgments

There have been so many people who have made suggestions, answered technical questions, and helped in a host of other ways that giving all the thanks they deserve is impossible. However, in addition to the many I cannnot mention here, to specialists mentioned in the book, and to my parents (to whom the book is dedicated), I am particularly grateful to:

Joan Downs, Carol Saltus, Michael Cooperstein, and Robert Sheaffer;

Elizabeth and Michael Mayers, Alan Goldberg, Helen Hans, William Helmreich, Faith Scheer, and Jack Winter;

Ibtihaj Arafat, Pnina Bright, Neil Epstein, William Fishbein, Willie Flower, Ernest van den Haag, and Ruth Wolff;

Jane B. Alexander, editor of *Human Nature,* were it not for whom this book would never have seen the light of day;

Rabbi Robert Gordis for his rendering of my dedicatory line, "may the answer to the final question lead him finally home to peace";

David Ramsay Steele, who holds that the pursuit of truth is more important than pleasing everybody, and Open Court, which once again lives up to its distinguished name by providing a platform for the exposition of views that displease a few vocal people most intensely.

Steven Goldberg
New York, New York

Introduction

1. This book has only one purpose: to demonstrate the universality—the presence in every society—of certain social institutions and to provide a *sufficient* explanation of this universality.

There is nothing in this book that attempts to explain the variation that one finds within the limits that define and make universal these institutions. Thus, for example, this book does not address the question of why one society's patriarchy (domination of hierarchies by males) is so different from another's. This book is concerned only with the question of why all societies are patriarchal (and with analogous questions relevant to attainment of non-maternal status and to dominance in male-female encounters and relationships).

Likewise, there is nothing in this book concerned with the desirability or undesirability of the institutions whose universality the book attempts to explain. For instance, this book is not concerned with the question of whether male domination of hierarchies is morally or politically 'good' or 'bad'. Moral values and political policies, by their nature, consist of more than just empirical facts and their explanation. 'What is' can never entail 'what should be', so science knows nothing of 'should'. 'Answers' to questions of 'should' require subjective elements that science cannot provide. Similarly, there is no implication that one sex is 'superior' in general to the other; 'general superiority' and 'general inferiority' are scientifically meaningless concepts.

There is an asymmetry between empirical analyses of the sort this book represents and analyses supporting moral or political systems, policies, or programs. Empirical analyses need not address moral-political issues. And even if they do address moral-political issues, empirical analyses alone cannot find the 'answers' to moral-political questions. Moral-political analyses, on the other hand, must take into account the empirical realities that they hope to affect if they are to be relevant to anything other than unattainable utopias.

Thus: all that is written here could not, for example, commit one to be either for or against equal pay for equal work, an equal rights amendment, co-ed (or separate) schools, or any other policy.

One could agree with everything in this book and argue that this indicates the crucial importance of an equal rights amendment that limits as much as possible a male advantage in attaining positions, an advantage that often has nothing to do with performance in those positions. On the other hand, one could agree with everything in this book and argue that this indicates the need, in a time when role models are so hard to come by, for our emphasizing differences between male and female tendencies and their ability to form the nuclei of strong roles and role models. On issues such as these, empirical science must be silent.

I realize that, in this politicized time, the distinction between the correctness of an explanation and its political utility has evaporated for many people. Such people argue that all analyses are 'moral' (or 'immoral') and 'political' in that they have moral and political effects. I think that this view tends to absurdly exaggerate the importance of ideas in determining the realities of social life. But whether or not this is true, the relevant point here is that the consequences of an acceptance of an empirical explanation have nothing to do with the correctness of that explanation. This is so obvious that for thousands of years the attempt to refute an explanation by citing the (putative) bad effects of an acceptance of that explanation has been recognized as fallacious. Even if acceptance of the belief that the world is round somehow threatened our species' survival, that would not make the earth flat. Truth is independent of consequences.

2. Because no scientific explanation can ever determine value or policy, one might think that nothing I write here could elicit the powerful emotions that greet works arguing for a value or policy. However, one would think this only in the absence of any experience with human beings. In reality, people often react to empirical analyses as if they are recommendations for values or policies they abhor, and this no doubt accounts for the fact that, for a decade, my first work on this subject was listed in *Guinness* as the book rejected by the most publishers before final acceptance (69 rejections by 55 publishers).

This sort of resistance has infused most of the criticism of my work on the subject of men and women. In *Why Men Rule* I respond to the past criticisms of my work, and I hope that the reader will attempt to produce better criticisms than most critics have managed to supply so far.

3. The reader who remembers that all statements about males and females are *statistical* statements will avoid wasting time on criticisms that ignore this fact and render all discussion of males and females incoherent. Virtually all male-female differences are statistical and it is only on the social level of institutions that, as a result of the effects and concretizations of 'the law of large numbers', we may speak of universalities.

Indeed, it is a good practice for the reader who believes that he has found an error in the reasoning presented in this book to ask whether the point that he or she is making would also be true of the height difference between males and females. If it is, then the criticism fails to find an error in the reasoning. One would not, for example, deny the claim that men are taller than women (and that the best basketball teams are likely to be male) on the basis of the fact that some women are taller than some men. Some women are, of course, taller than some men, but this fact is not in conflict with the statistical claim that 'men are taller than women' (in other words, the male mean is greater and the tallest people are virtually all male) or that they are so for innate physiological reasons.

Stated so bluntly this may all seem insultingly obvious. I hope the reader will agree, after reading my discussion of the past criticisms of my work, that there were many for whom this *wasn't* so obvious.

4. When I first wrote on male-female differences over 20 years ago, nearly all people who described themselves as 'feminists' subscribed to the view that behavioral differences between men and women were entirely due to environmental factors and that tendencies associated with males and females were purely social or cultural in origin. I followed this usage and employed the term 'feminist' as a convenient term to refer to arguments that deny the determinativeness of neuro-endocrinological differences between men and women for an explanation of the universality of the institutions I attempt to explain.

Today, however, nearly everyone—even most people describing themselves as 'feminists'—understands that physiological differentiation plays some part in differentiating male and female behavior. While I would like to believe that my arguments had something to do with the change, no doubt a more important reason is that most of those who once found intolerable the explanation I offered have now had children. Very few people could be so dogmatic in outlook as to ignore the differences that their small sons and daughters exhibit daily, or believe these differences to be primarily the results of such influences as the colors of boys' and girls' pajamas.

Hence, readers who consider themselves 'feminists' for any reason other than a denial of the importance of physiology (such as a belief in equal pay for equal work, a belief that women [whatever they are] are *better* than men [*whatever* they are], or any other belief that does not deny the role of physiology in explaining what I try to explain) should not suppose that the argument of this book is inimical or hostile to feminism.

Accordingly, I have changed the wording of numerous passages, so that 'environmentalists', rather than 'feminists', are my designated targets. It's unfortunate that nowadays 'environmentalist' conjures up ozone holes and global warming. In this book I employ the term exclusively in its older sense, to denote the position that inborn qualities are of little or no importance in explaining human behavior.

However, an acceptance of the role of neuro-endocrinology is not satisfied by mere lip service; an explanation that claims to accept the importance of the neuro-endocrinological, but which implies its unimportance—for example, an attempt to explain the male-female ratio in governing bodies primarily in terms of environmental factors—implicitly denies the theory I present and no protestation that it doesn't can immunize the explanation against the criticism that it ignores the neuro-endocrinological.

5. My original work on this subject was titled *The Inevitability of Patriarchy*. I also liked *Why Men Rule*, but—and this is an interesting example of how the subtle overtones of words can change in a short time—in 1970 everyone would have interpreted 'Why Men Rule' to mean 'why those men who rule, rule, and why those men who don't rule, don't rule'. Today, people more readily understand that the meaning is 'why men—and not women—rule'. (About 85 percent of *Why Men Rule* is new material, either responding to criticism of *The Inevitability of Patriarchy* or reworking the original argument for better clarity and precision.)

The original title did have one great virtue: it made clear in the very title that the theory presented did what a scientific theory is supposed to do: it specified the conditions—the discovery or development of a single society lacking the institutions I attempt to explain—that, should they come to exist in reality—would demonstrate the theory to be incorrect.

Both the old and the new titles have the virtue of making it clear in the very title that the *purpose* of this book is to demonstrate and explain the existence of certain universal institutions. Most of that which is written in the area of sex differences is infused with such confusion and fallacy that it is impossible to say what is supposed to be being explained (to say nothing of what would count as refutation).

6. A few readers may notice that I here stress, more strongly than I did before, the fact that a society that lacked hierarchies would not refute the theory I present.

In practice, we need not worry about societies lacking patriarchal hierarchies. There has never been a society that lacked such hierarchies or their less-formal equivalent, and, for reasons mentioned in the book, it seems unlikely there could be one as long as a society has values and people differ in their ability to meet the requirements of those values.

But even if such societies did exist they would not be refutory. They lack the cue (the hierarchy) to which males, for neuro-endocrinological reasons, respond more easily, a response manifested in the behaviors that lead to the domination of the hierarchies. Such societies would not—even if they existed—demonstrate the possibility of a society that *has* hierarchy, but in which the hierarchy is not dominated by males. (A past, present, or future society *with* hierarchies, but in which upper hierarchical positions are not held overwhelmingly by males, *would*, of course, immediately refute the theory.)

To be quite candid, my reason for stressing this point despite the fact that not even one primitive society lacks an obvious male dominance is my disinclination to waste more time tracking down obscure ethnographies in order to demonstrate that the ethnographies do not describe an exception to the universalities we discuss. Perhaps the knowledge that a society lacking hierarchies would not refute the theory will limit the number of authors (never the ethnographer who wrote the ethnography) willing to misrepresent evidence on primitive societies and will save me the time required to expose the misrepresentation. But I doubt it.

7. On a number of occasions I have taken the risk of repetitiveness and for this I apologize to the reader in advance. Experience indicates that such repetition is justified: many people will consult this book for a particular discussion (for example, a particular part of the argument or a response to a particular criticism). Such people will not have read, or will not remember, a specific point that is crucial to the material that interests them. Since any cross-referencing system would soon become incomprehensible, restatement of the point is the only reasonable alternative.

8. No doubt the tone of this book will correctly strike some readers as stronger than one usually finds in a scientific work. I use a strong tone only when dealing with gross misrepresentation of fact or logical fallacy that should have been obvious to any author not willfully blind. I cannot see how any serious person can react otherwise to such a narcissistic attempt to subordinate the truth to one's personal view of the good, or how any responsible person could take seriously a moral or political view that requires denial of truth.

To readers who come to this book prepared to think for themselves and to listen to reasoned argument: I hope you find this trip illuminating and enjoyable and remember that nothing here commits you to any moral or political view that you do not like.

Part I

The Inevitability of Patriarchy

Chapter *I*

A Question and Some Ground Rules

The Question of Male and Female

Perhaps at the core of our certainty there are only questions. We can tolerate our lives, and our societies can endure, because we are rarely forced to encounter the uncertainty that underlies so many of our beliefs. But to acknowledge the unrest we feel when such uncertainty is exposed is not to prove that our beliefs were founded on incorrect assumptions. The introduction of doubt serves a powerful function, but it is one of raising questions, not of providing answers. That is the job of those for whom ideas are central to existence; if such people are rendered no less uncomfortable than anyone else when their most basic assumptions are challenged, at least they are forced to remember why society tolerates them at all. At this point they must leave the security of their esoteric studies and reconsider the questions that are integral not only to those studies but to the beliefs and practices of all mankind.

Until recently few had even questioned the assumptions on which our conceptions of man and woman were based. Until recently, we tended to accept masculinity and femininity, and male and female functions, as somehow springing from our male and female natures, and were satisfied to allow the strength of our beliefs to compensate for the depth of our ignorance. If for no other reason, the biologist, the anthropologist, the psychologist, and the sociologist are in debt to the feminist movement. For if there is any single question at the center of all artistic and much scientific thought (to say nothing of our daily lives), it is this: what are men and women, and to what degree must male-female differences be manifested in societies' expectations, values, and institutions? It is to this question that I addressed myself and it is from the answers I found that the theory presented here has developed.

Superiority and Inferiority

It seems that we have a penchant for perceiving differences in subjective terms. This is understandable, and perhaps necessary for daily life, but it is the bane of science. The scientist may observe the attitudes of others in an attempt to explain them, but if he allows his own subjective attitudes to color his work, then it will be worthless. Therefore it is necessary to bear in mind throughout this book that at no point am I intimating that science can ever lead one to the *general* conclusion that one sex is superior or inferior to the other. It is as meaningless to say that one sex is superior to the other as it is to say that one society is superior to another, and for the same reason: a general judgment of superiority or inferiority has meaning only in the context of a subjective value system. It is not surprising that one's estimation of superiority will usually reflect one's sex or society, but, for whatever reasons, some will view the other sex or another society as *superior*. In neither case are we dealing with science. We can, however, speak of superiority in specific areas. Men are superior at lifting heavy weights, while women are superior at singing the upper register. American society is superior to that of the Mbuti Pygmy in the ability to produce consumer goods, while Mbuti society is superior to American society in the ability to inculcate hunting skills in its members. Scientific objectivity is lost only if one says that men are superior in general or that the United States is superior in general, for to do this, one must *subjectively* select a set of criteria.

Most men and women in every society realize this intuitively. Anthropologists have written at length about the areas in which women are unquestionably superior to men. It is through these abilities that the world's women have always fulfilled themselves, just as men have emphasized their singular abilities and identified with their manhood.

Indeed, while an essay on patriarchy must emphasize the factors that are emphasized here, and while societies would be patriarchal even if women were nothing more than less-masculine men, the likelihood is overwhelming that feminine behavior and the institutions that are related to it are as inevitable as patriarchy and for the same reasons.

Possibly someone who wished to examine woman's universal role of creator and keeper of society's emotional resources (rather than patriarchy and male dominance) could invoke a line of reasoning complementing that used in this book. The author of such an examination could demonstrate that women will inevitably have the powers necessary for directing emotionality in the members of every society and to a great extent, determining the very kind of people the society is to produce.

Even if one limits oneself to the issue of 'power' (in male-female and familial relationships), neither male dominance nor the other male characteristics we shall discuss necessarily imply that male behaviour is more effective than female behaviour. Although the factor that engenders political patriarchy does render impossible a political authority system not ruled by men (for reasons that we shall examine), male dominance does not necessarily mean that males will achieve their goals more often than females in dyadic and familial relationships. (A dyadic relationship is between two people—in this book a male and a female.) One could make an interesting case that, on a dyadic or familial level, women are more successful at utilizing feminine abilities to achieve their goals than men are at utilizing masculine abilities to achieve theirs. Indeed, the women of every society possess the emotional skills necessary to 'get around' men and to 'get their way', while acknowledging the authority of the male even on a dyadic level. However, a woman's feeling that she must 'get around' a man (who is acknowledged by individual emotions and societal values to be dominant) is, as we shall see, the hallmark of male dominance.

Some sociologists have defined *power* in these terms and have suggested that—even in societies and subcultures such as the Shtetl that maintain a high degree of male dominance—women are more powerful in familial and dyadic situations than the men, in whom authority is invested. The line of reasoning supporting this hypothesis would not necessarily conflict with any statement in this book. An analysis of dyadic or familial groups which considers that 'real' power is exercised through women's superior emotional power is the virtual opposite of that put forward by radical environmentalists. *For such an analysis emphasizes the positive, power-engendering aspects of femininity, and implies that the reduction in feminine behavior desired by the older generation of feminists would force women to deal with men on male terms, which would inevitably lead to a reduction in women's real dyadic power.* The old-style feminist who denies the physiological basis of femininity and the likelihood that femininity is women's greatest strength for attaining dyadic or familial power is left with the conclusion that the women of every society have acted in a feminine way out of stupidity. I think not. Though an analysis which emphasized the informal, real power of femininity might take on Strindbergian overtones, it could proceed without theoretical contradiction or obvious factual inaccuracy. This cannot be said of the extreme environmentalist line of reasoning, which we shall discuss.

I appreciate that those who define the qualities and roles associated with the male as somehow better than those associated with the female will find no solace in the inherent impossibility of the scientist ever declaring one sex superior to the other. I realize too that, because this book concentrates on patriarchy and male dominance, anyone who reads it through feminist eyes may feel that the book is biased in a male direction and may react against it. This is because we are focussing on the very areas which have been emphasized by those feminists who value masculine qualities more highly than feminine ones. If a woman feels that it is better to be relatively tall and muscular than relatively short and elastic, she may be tempted to ignore the evidence presented by the physiologist who demonstrates that height and muscularity will be associated with the man whether she likes it or not. The feminist can argue that when a society is endangered the women 'get' the men to risk their lives while they remain safely at home, and she can argue that the woman's longevity is superior to the male's dominance. But if she believes that it is preferable to have her sex associated with authority and leadership rather than with the creation of life, then she is doomed to perpetual disappointment.

In any case, to make judgments of what is good and what is bad, what should be and what should not be, is outside the realm of science; science can never validate or invalidate subjective appraisals. Science speaks only of what is.

Chapter II

Anthropology and the Limits of Social Variation

The Approach of This Study

Reassessing formerly unquestioned assumptions is a challenge to any one discipline's modes of inquiry; the analytic methods which have been developed to investigate successfully one large area of reality are often taxed when forced to deal with another. This applies to some extent when the sociologist tries to investigate the nature of patriarchy and male dominance, and is faced with the strong possibility that these may be inevitable social manifestations of human physiology. For in nearly all his investigations the sociologist deals with social behavior that falls within the limits of biological possibility, and he is rarely forced to examine the limits of human possibility or the forces that set these limits. In his study of political behavior, for example, he has always assumed that leadership in any society will be male dominated, and has concentrated on developing the methods of inquiry necessary for investigation within that theoretical framework. As a result, in our investigation of patriarchy, we will have to use the methods and findings of a number of disciplines.

This is not a sociological, anthropological, or economic analysis *per se.* It is a theory which tries to show the limitations which are imposed on social possibility, and the impossibility of a society's failing to conform its institutions to these limitations. Within these limitations, considerable variation is possible. A sociological, anthropological, or economic analysis would attempt to describe and explain the configurations of factors that differ from one society to another in order to discover the differing etiologies of differing institutions in terms of methods of socialization, the social meanings attached to behavior by individuals, economic necessities, the structures of various systems within the various social systems and the connections between them, and all the other considerations which are the concern of the sociologist, the anthropologist, and the economist. The theory presented here is important to these kinds of analyses in that—if this theory of limits is correct—any analysis that hypothesizes elements that fall outside the limits of possibility described here, or implies that such elements could exist in a real society, would have to be incorrect. Since every society that has ever existed comes within the limits described by this theory, no analysis of any *particular* society is demonstrated to be incorrect by this theory. Furthermore, if the theory presented here is correct it demonstrates that no theoretical analysis that limits itself to the sociological, cultural and anthropological, or economic level can ever hope to explain the primary *causation* of the behavior and institutions we shall discuss.

Patriarchy Defined

The definitions of patriarchy and male dominance used in this book, while similar to the orthodox anthropological definitions, mean no more than is stated here. *Patriarchy* is any system of organization (political, economic, industrial, financial, religious, or social) in which the overwhelming number of upper positions in hierarchies are occupied by males. Patriarchy refers only to suprafamilial levels of organization: authority in familial and dyadic relationships is a manifestation of the psychophysiological reality that is referred to in this book as *male dominance.*

In order to avoid the confusion that could arise from the fact that the terms *patriarchy* and *matriarchy* are used in a number of ways, it is necessary to enumerate the alternative definitions. None of these is inherently superior to the others, though agreement would be convenient. The reader is free to favor any of the alternative pairs of definitions as long as he appreciates that the terms will then be irrelevant to this book, so he will be forced to appropriate or invent other terms to substitute for *patriarchy* and *matriarchy* as I use the terms. The point is that authority and leadership are, and always have been, associated with the male in every society, and I refer to this when I say that patriarchy is universal and that there has never been a matriarchy.

The British and some American anthropologists use the terms *patriarchate* and *matriarchate* where I use the terms *patriarchy* and *matriarchy,* and all agree that there has never been a matriarchate. They use *patriarchy* and *matriarchy* to refer to lineage and residence, a matriarchy being a society that is both matrilineal and matrilocal. It is this usage, combined with the mistaken belief that there have been *prehistoric matriarchies* and *Amazonian societies* (discussed below), which accounts for the widespread misconception that there have been societies in which suprafamilial authority was not associated with the male. In matrilineal-matrilocal societies, as in all others, authority is associated with the male even within the family, though occasionally with the mother's brother, rather than with the father.

Sociologists often use *patriarchy* and *matriarchy* to refer to various aspects of familial authority. As we shall see, the ethnographic evidence demonstrates that, even if we use the terms in this sense, there has never been a matriarchy. The American press occasionally uses the term *black matriarchy* to describe a situation in which certain economic factors (such as welfare regulations that prohibit welfare for families in which the male lives in the household) force a minority of black women to assume authority in the home. This situation is not *matriarchy* in the sense we use the term (black political and religious leaders are nearly always male) nor is it even female familial dominance: the term *female dominance* would have meaning only if the family included a male adult but vested authority in the female. Obviously if there is no male in the household, authority will have to be vested in a female. The question we are dealing with is why no society or group anywhere ever associates authority with a female when an equivalent male is available. Finally, the term *gynecocracy* has occasionally been used to describe an (imaginary) society in which government is run by women.

The Universality of Patriarchy

Patriarchy is universal. For all the variety different societies have demonstrated in developing different types of political, economic, religious, and social systems, there has never been a society which failed to associate hierarchical authority and leadership in these areas with men. Indeed, of all social institutions there is probably none whose universality is so totally agreed upon. Although most anthropologists consider the family, marriage, and the incest taboo universal—and believe that, while it is easy to *imagine* societies without one or more of these institutions, no real society could survive without them—with each of these institutions they will debate problems of definition and borderline cases. There is not, nor has there ever been, any society that even remotely failed to associate authority and leadership in suprafamilial areas with the male. There are no borderline cases.

There have, of course, been queens in a small number of societies, but the existence of patriarchy even in such societies is demonstrated by the fact that—as in England—queens rule only when there is no equivalent man available (just as there have been a few societies in which the royal families have ignored their societies' incest taboos in order to maintain the purity of the blood line). There have been 'Queen Mothers' in a few African societies such as the Lovedu (see the Appendix), but, while these had a measure of autonomy denied other women in their societies and some authority in secondary areas, in every case they were subordinate to a male king or chief in whom the society vested the highest authority. Again, there have been societies in which there were hierarchies from which men were excluded, but in every case these were subordinate to *exclusively male hierarchies*[1]

In the Appendix I give quotations from every ethnography I have ever seen invoked—never by the ethnographer, but always by a third party who has usually clearly not consulted the ethnography he invokes—as describing an exception, a non-patriarchal society. Included among these are a few tiny primitive societies in which virtually everyone knows everyone else, and which are comprised of relatively independent, relatively 'nomadic' groups of a few families. In these few societies, while there is always at least seminal hierarchy, decision-making is primarily a function of a less-formal male dominance in dyadic and familial situations. (A group of twenty or thirty adults and children does not need to create a Senate and House; informal decision-making is sufficient.)

The Appendix demonstrates that all of these few societies exhibit male dominance. It is worth reiterating, however, that, if there *were* a society lacking both hierarchy and male dominance, this would not refute the theory of patriarchy presented here. The theory claims that hierarchies elicit more strongly from those with male neuro-endocrinological systems the behavior (discussed below) responsible for the fact that the hierarchies are dominated by males. If there are no hierarchies, there can, of course, be no patriarchy. However, since there are no societies totally lacking hierarchy, and since there is clear male dominance in the few that have little formal hierarchy, we can ignore the theoretical possibility of a society without hierarchy. (A society that lacked hierarchy *and* male dominance *would* refute the claim that male dominance

---

1. Perhaps the closest approximation to a non-patriarchal society was Iroquois society, in which women did serve in an important role, analogous to that of nominating the male leader. We shall discuss male dominance in Iroquois society later: here I wish merely to make the point that one cannot argue that the Iroquois were non-patriarchal when women were not even permitted to hold positions in the leadership hierarchy.

arises merely from the mingling of males and females. But there is no record of any such society.)

The Evolutionary Fallacy

Before this century the dearth of ethnographic studies enabled some theorists to maintain that all societies developed along a single evolutionary line. This belief in universal societal evolution, particularly when it confused the economic functions of an institution with its cause, made at least vaguely credible the argument that those institutions which had existed 'all through history' owed their existence to economic and *temporary* social necessities and that they would decay when economic and technological change rendered them anachronistic. Some evolutionary theory could not pass even the test of internal logicality. For example, theories postulating that before males learned of their biological importance to conception there was a 'matriarchal stage' of history were unable to explain what enabled men to 'take over' once they had learned about their own biological role. Since women automatically understand their own importance, the males' discovery of the mechanisms of conception should have enabled them merely to share power equally if knowledge of biological role had been the determining factor. However, while there seems to be no reason for believing that paternity is relevant to patriarchy once one has been forced to invoke some other factor, it must be admitted that one could, logically if not credibly, argue that knowledge of biological importance is a precondition for the attainment of power, but that once this has been met *then* some other factor—such as physical strength—becomes the determining factor. As long as there was little relevant ethnographic data, the question of evolution was forced to remain on this theoretical level. Evolutionary theory was not doomed until ethnographic studies demonstrated that every institution was either, like slavery, absent from some societies and therefore not evolutionarily necessary (unless one presupposes an unrecorded earlier stage in which every institution occurred in every society—in which case such evolutionary theory has no evidence) or, if universal, like patriarchy, was found even when its supposed cause was absent. The ethnographers found a number of societies in which males did not know of their biological importance, *yet these societies were as patriarchal as all others*. This shows that knowledge of paternity has nothing to do with patriarchy.

There are other problems with social evolutionary theory: unless one is merely attempting to explain a particular characteristic, evolutionary theory is by its very nature ethnocentric and often racist. Deciding which factors constitute advancement is subjective—with the possible exception of the factor of survival, in which case all surviving societies are equal.[2]

It is not accidental that few evolutionary theorists saw any society but their own as the most advanced. Perhaps one could defend this by saying that the ability to propose evolutionary theory is a measure of advancement, but this criterion is most obviously based in the value system of the theorist. Lastly, it should be noted that the power of matriarchal social evolutionary theory to convince is not increased when we observe that primates demonstrate behavior that seems not unlike that which we refer to as male dominance, and that certain institutions have resisted every political attempt to change them and every theoretical attempt to explain their etiologies in terms of environment and economic function.

The 'Prehistoric Matriarchies', the 'Amazons', and Engels

Likewise, theories that hypothesized a matriarchal form of society at 'an earlier stage of history' made a certain, if tortuous, sense until the findings of the past 50 years failed to include a single shred of evidence that such matriarchies had ever existed, and demonstrated the inability of all such theories to deal with reality.

Hundreds of the societies we have studied in this century are infinitely more primitive—by any measure—than the Classical societies occasionally alleged to be 'matriarchal' or 'Amazonian'. Without exception these societies have been patriarchal.

One constructs imaginary elements only when such a hypothesis helps to explain an observed reality better. For example, it made sense to hypothesize a male 'aggressive instinct' before the discovery of the male hormone because this made it possible to explain an observed reality (men rule in every society) in a way that was more plausible and logically tighter than any theory that had preceded it. There is no reason whatsoever for hypothesizing the existence of an as yet undiscovered matriarchy. Observation of empirical reality not only gives

---

2. It is legitimate to speak of social evolution *with reference to a specified criterion* as long as there is no implication that this criterion represents some general evolutionary or moral advance or that a society must reach the specified evolutionary stage. For example, one may say that a literate society is more advanced than a non-literate society when discussing urbanization—literacy being a necessary condition for urbanization—as long as one does not imply that urbanization is an inevitable stage in a society's evolution, that it represents some objective moral advance, or that it is a sign of some *general* evolutionary advancement.

no reason to construct such a hypothesis, but indicates that it would be incorrect. I have consulted the original ethnographic materials on every society I have ever seen associated with matriarchy, female dominance, or the association of high-status, non-maternal roles with women. Like the authors of the compilations cited in this chapter, I have been unable to find one which represents any of these (see the Appendix): But it must be admitted that one cannot *prove* that matriarchy or anything else has never existed. If one wants to show that there has never been a centaur one can refer to the evidence of physiology and evolution to indicate the biological improbability of its ever having existed and demonstrate that the evidence to the contrary is worthless. If the reader insists on maintaining a belief in a once-existent matriarchial society, all we can do is demand evidence more convincing than his desire that there should have been one.[3]

For the reasons we have discussed it is not surprising that, until their recent resurrection by feminists, the totally discredited matriarchal and evolutionary theories of Lafitau, Ward, Bachofen, McLennan, and Briffault (and a host of popularizations of their theories by Helen Diner and others) had long been deservedly forgotten. There is no reason to detail yet once again the innumerable factual errors and logical fallacies particular to each of these works; suffice it to say that they all share the contradictions and lack of empirical evidence we have discussed, and to reiterate Panos Bardis's observation that ". . . these theories were soon rejected by all social scientists."[4]

This is not to say that matriarchal myths and legends have not served valid exaggerative and metaphorical purposes for writers from Homer, Diodorus, Herodotus, and Plutarch to Robert Graves. As literary devices they have often been used with devastating effect to ridicule men in societies in which male dominance was less institutionalized than in that of the authors. As myths they may well reflect male fears—every infant does indeed live in a matriarchy. As symbols they represent the matrilineal society in which the woman does 'carry the throne' that will hold succeeding generations of men. But as anthropological descriptions of real societies they are nonsense. When such descriptions are

---

3. The fact that from 1860 to 1890 many anthropologists—Victorian anthropologists no less—accepted the idea of matriarchy and devised unnecessary theories to explain it casts doubt on the charge sometimes made that male anthropologists refuse to admit that there were once matriarchies because they are threatened by the possibility.

4. Panos Bardis, 'Synopsis and Evaluation of Theories Concerning Family Evolution', *Social Science*, 38:50 (January 1963). Interested readers might further consult virtually any introductory text in anthropological theory and M.F. Ashley Montagu's introduction to *Marriage Past and Present: A Debate Between Robert Briffault and Bronislaw Malinowski* (Boston: Porter Sargent, 1956. The debate took place in 1931).

not so metaphysical as to be unfalsifiable, they prove, without exception, to be without foundation.

These myths and legends provide the 'evidence' advanced in a number of books that imply the former existence of matriarchies for the (usually unstated) purpose of casting doubt on any physiological explanation of sexual differentiation in social institutions.[5] The authors of these books rarely, of course, name a society that was not patriarchal or whose institutions did not conform to male dominance. They are aware that when they do, mere reference to any history book, to say nothing of the original source materials which these authors avoid as if they were contaminated, would immediately demonstrate that the society in question was ruled by men, that expectations and institutions conformed to male dominance, and that males occupied the high-status, non-maternal roles. Instead these authors advance evidence so selective that it would be dishonest were it not so ineptly handled. A marriage contract from one society is advanced along with a female holiday from a second and a goddess from a third. One could equally well use myths to prove the existence of a society of centaurs. With this approach one need not even select evidence from more than one society; the story of Jack and the Beanstalk and the celebration of Mother's Day would be enough to 'prove' that America was a society ruled by giant women.

Yet more serious than their totally uncritical mixtures of myth and isolated facts about real societies is the fact that such books do not make even theoretical sense—which makes it unnecessary for us to demonstrate the inadequacy of the empirical evidence provided by each individual book. The arguments advanced are, often without the authors being aware of it, based on the three assumptions which are implicit in Engels's fallacious and empirically refutable evolutionary theory: if any one of the three is incorrect, then Engels's analysis is incorrect. These assumptions are that matrilineality precedes and must precede

---

5. As we shall see in our discussion of cultural variation, serious Marxist scholars like Kathleen Gough have acknowledged that no matriarchy has ever existed. While such anthropologists place far greater emphasis on the economic factor than I do, there is no direct conflict between their work and the theory presented here; they do not maintain that there has ever been a society that lacked patriarchy, male dominance, or male attainment of high-status suprafamilial roles and positions. I am bothering to discuss the presentations of works alleging the former existence of matriarchies not because they deserve discussion on their intellectual merit—they are uniformly inaccurate and incompetently done—but because they are occasionally invoked by laymen. The works are: Elizabeth Gould Davis, *The First Sex* (London: Dent, 1973); Helen Diner, *Mothers and Amazons* (New York: Julian Press, a 1965 translation of a work originally published around 1930); M. and M. Vaerting, *Dominant Sex* (London: Doran, 1923); Nancy Reeves, *Womankind* (Chicago: Aldine, 1971); Evelyn Reed, *Is Biology Woman's Destiny?* (New York: Pathfinder Press, 1972); Phyllis Chesler, *Woman and Madness* (London: Allen Lane, 1973); and Emanuel Kanter, *The Amazons* (Chicago: Charles Kerr, 1926).

patrilineality, that the transformation from matrilineality to patrilineality is engendered by the advent of private property and class differentiation, and that the early stages of societal development are not merely matrilineal, but matriarchal. The matrilineality we find in various societies is alleged to be not only a residue of an earlier matrilineality, but of an earlier matriarchal stage. This matriarchal stage is seen by some as a reversal of patriarchy and by others as an equalitarian situation in which women received high status. We have seen that the former is simply incorrect; there is no evidence that at any time there has ever been any society in which men did not rule, and there is great reason, as we shall see, to believe that none could have ever existed. The latter is not necessarily incorrect (so long as it merely asserts that maternal roles received high status and does not imply that the universals we discuss in this book were not present), but it is irrelevant to patriarchy, male dominance, and male occupation of high-status, non-maternal roles. As we shall see, it is true that certain matrilineal societies allow women very high status by giving very high status to roles that men are incapable of playing. This is of far greater significance to those who would put less emphasis on the female role than it is to our discussion of institutions, to which the status given to female roles is irrelevant. The ideological component of this reasoning is illustrated by the fact that, rather than referring to a matrilineal society which at least gives women high status by giving their female roles high status, these authors continue to invoke Lewis Henry Morgan's Iroquois as a roughly equalitarian society despite the fact that, as we shall see, Morgan states that not only do the Iroquois prohibit women from ruling, but that they also consider them 'servants'.

Some of these authors have not even considered the ethnographic materials that are available; if they had, they would have seen the absurdity of looking to *our* antecedent societies for a matriarchy when none can be found among the thousands of societies to which we are not related and which are at 'earlier stages of development' (whatever the yardstick) than those invoked and invented by these authors. They would not have even had to refer to the original ethnographic studies. George Murdock's definitive cross-cultural analysis[6] exposes Engels's three assumptions as not merely unjustified by the evidence, but as inarguably incorrect. Murdock demonstrates that there are a great many patrilineal societies for which there is no evidence that patrilineality was preceded by matrilineality; in other words even an evolutionary theory of lineage that does not imply the accompanying evolution of some second variable is unsupported by the evidence. More importantly, matrilineality is not

---

6. See George Murdock, *Social Structure* (New York: Free Press, 1949), 184–207.

dependent on any other variable; and such dependence gives meaning to Engels's evolutionary theory. Matrilineality is found in thriving societies with highly developed rights of private property, with elaborate stratification systems, with extensive political integration, and even with systems of feudal land tenure, as well as in societies in which these institutions are as minimally developed as possible. All of this can be said of patrilineality also. Most crucial, of course, is the fact that no change in any direction of any variable renders any society significantly less patriarchal than any other society.

As it has become increasingly indisputable that there is no evidence of a non-patriarchal society, some have resorted to arguing that: it "is as foolish to postulate masculine dominance in prehistory as to postulate female dominance."[7] This makes about as much sense as saying, 'it is as foolish to postulate one-headed people in prehistory as to postulate two-headed people.' It is surely more likely that that which is universal now was true of human groups earlier than it is that earlier groups exhibited behavior for which there is no evidence, past or present. If today's stone-age societies exhibit the universals, there is no reason to think that any society in the Stone Age failed to do so.

The fact that none of the alleged Amazonian societies has ever existed has been demonstrated by a number of anthropologists,[8] but it is nonetheless

---

7. Sarah Pomeroy, quoted in Carol Tavris, *The Mismeasure of Women*, 77.

8. "Since the Amazons never existed, but are a mythical group first mentioned by Herodotus and soon doubted by Strabo, their social organization need not further detain us except perhaps as an enduring example of the will to believe." (Montagu, *op. cit.*, 88.) "The fabled Amazon women are just that—a fable. Even in societies which are organized about women, in societies which follow matrilineal descent and inheritance and matrilocal residence, power tends to be held by males in the female lineage. Power is usually held by the mother's brother from the viewpoint of ego, by the maternal uncle. Male dominance, or at least a tendency towards it appears to be one of those basic features of human existence that culture cannot completely contradict. A minority of societies are organized around female lineage, but even among them, power, status and property tend to be held by males." Gerald Leslie, *The Family in Social Context* (New York: Oxford University Press, 1967), 52. Marvin Harris (*Culture Man, and Nature*, New York: Crowell, 1971) writes: (328) ". . . certainly there was never any matrilineal 'stage' in this general evolution of culture. The basic reason for this is that men have always been politically and economically dominant over women . . . Despite the persistent popular notion that the presence of matrilineal descent groups reflects the political or economic domination of men by women, it is the men in these societies no less than in patrilineal societies who control the corporate kin group's productive and reproductive resources", and (582) "Matriarchy has never existed", and (585) ". . . anthropology lends no support to the view that there are no innate differences between males and females." Lastly we should note that Kathleen Gough, a leading anthropologist who certainly looks favorably upon the feminist movement, has written ". . . matriliny does not involve 'matriarchy' or female dominance, either in the home or in society, as Engels tended to believe. Matriarchy, as the reverse of patriarchy, has in fact almost certainly never existed . . . men predominate as heads of households, lineages and communities in matrilineal as in patrilineal societies, and women experience greater or less authority from their

interesting to examine the internal logic of a report of "the first Amazons" that appeared in a popular magazine[9] On the evidence of a few ideograms, a photographer developed a theory that an all-woman Lesbian society had existed long ago in the wilds of Brazil. It was supposed to have perpetuated itself by periodically raiding neighbouring tribes, mating with captured males, and killing all the males and all male offspring. The theory is not taken seriously by any anthropologist, but let us for the moment imagine that this 'society' did exist. If it is advanced as evidence for the possibility of a non-patriarchal society, certain questions arise. Why did these women have to hide in caves? Why did they not merely attain positions of authority in the societies from which they came in the same manner as men have done in every society? More generally, we might ask all those who claim that there has ever been a matriarchy or an Amazonian society of any type why they cannot provide a single example from ethnographic evidence drawn from societies of virtually every conceivable type at virtually every conceivable stage along virtually every conceivable line of development; if socialization alone explains why societies are patriarchal, there should be any number of societies in which leadership and authority are associated with women, and one should not have to invoke examples of non-patriarchal societies that exist only in myth and literature:[10]

Modern Societies

In the United States the female percentage of Senators, Representatives, or Governors has never approached ten. In the business world, the ratio of

---

mother's brothers, elder brothers, or even their grown sons. Some degree of male dominance has, in fact, been universal to date in human society, although matrilineal systems are usually kinder to woman." 'An Anthropologist Looks at Engels', in Nona Glazer Malbin and Helen Youngelson Waehrer, eds., *Women in a Man-Made World* (Chicago: Rand McNally, 1972), 115.

9. *Time*, 27th December 1971, 54.

10. However, one may perhaps speak meaningfully of 'masculine' and 'feminine' societies or 'masculine' and 'feminine' periods in a particular society's development, if one uses these merely as relative terms, describing aggressive values as 'masculine' and relatively nurturant values as 'feminine'. We shall come close to doing this when we discuss the factors that determine the extent to which male aggression is manifested in any given society. But such relative terms are applicable only within the limits described in this book. No society was ever so 'feminine' that authority and dominance were not associated with males, and no society was ever so 'masculine' that child-rearing was primarily the responsibility of males (except, as with the Marquesan Islanders, who practised female infanticide, when there was a great shortage of women). Some historians, using this terminology, have referred to societies which would be 'feminine' as 'matriarchies'. Since they do not imply that the societies were not patriarchies (in my terms) or that they did not exhibit male dominance, this does not conflict with the analysis presented here.

men to women is greater: a recent study of the top four thousand executives at the *Fortune* 500 companies found that men outnumbered women 3,993 to 19.

In every nation that permits women in hierarchial political positions, the further down one goes from the top, the higher is the percentage of women. This suggests that, as we shall see in our discussion of status attainment, the higher the status—the more competitive the position—the lower will be the percentage of women.

In the United States there has certainly been some increase at lower levels (for instance, women have more than doubled their numbers over the past twenty years in state legislatures, to about 19 percent). Time will tell what this implies for the future of the sex ratio at the upper level, but societies that have long had higher percentages of women in the equivalent of state legislatures have never seen this translated into significant percentages at the higher levels. Thus, there is no reason to expect that the increase in women at the lower levels will translate into even a similar increase at the higher levels. Given the enormous expenditure of energy, time, money, and skill by the women's movement, followed by a representation of women in politics lower than has long existed in some other societies, the lower-level increase in the United States does not make one sanguine about the likelihood of significant increases at the higher levels.

The increase that has taken place already is certainly significant in the sense that, to the woman who wishes to enter politics (or join the police or serve in some other previously nearly all-male role), even a ten percent figure probably represents a 90 percent decrease in the toll the woman must pay for entering the area. The woman who wishes a career in politics is no doubt much better off when the female politician is not a rare breed and when, as a result, the woman avoids much of the negative sanction that the pioneer political women had to face.

However, in the context of the cross-cultural universality that is the empirical question we address, the increase in the number of women at the state legislative level, even if it were manifested in a similar increase at the highest levels, would not be significant. The question we address is why suprafamilial authority is always overwhelmingly male in every society. Whether the percentage of males is 80 or 100, while no doubt important for one wishing to discover what conditions maximize the percentage of women in government, is unimportant to an explanation of why the male percentage is always much higher than the female. For the female increase to be relevant to the subject of this book, there would have to be some evidence that increases already accomplished give reason to suggest the possibility of a society not describable as 'patriarchal'. Despite unsupported claims to the contrary, there is just no evidence that this is happening.

In the broad terms relevant to the universality of patriarchy we discuss, the political distribution of the sexes is no different in any other society. Occasionally a woman will attain the highest position in a democratic society, but this is the unusual event in every such society (as unusual as in many non-modern societies; there were more female heads of states—queens—in the first two-thirds of the sixteenth century than in the first two-thirds of the twentieth. More important, when this does occur, it is always the case that—as in Golda Meir's Israel, Indira Gandhi's India, and Margaret Thatcher's England—the vast majority of other upper hierarchical positions are held by males. A government may claim an ideological commitment to hierarchical equality, and even that this commitment has been met. But the reality is always that the claim of achieved equality is not true; in China, for example, 67 of the ministries are headed by males and the other five positions are vacant. One may choose any society that has ever existed anywhere and he or she will find the same thing. There is slight variation as power lessens: the percentage of males tends to be somewhat greater in the upper houses of bicameral systems (such as, the Senate) than in the lower houses and unicameral houses, and somewhat greater in small unicameral houses than in large unicameral houses. But in no case do such differences approach a reduction of male percentages that would cast doubt on the presence of patriarchy.

Norway, for example, which has a higher percentage of women in its unicameral house than does any other nation, places an unusual degree of power in the hands of its municipal councils; 443 of 454 municipal council chairpersons are men. Males outnumber females at the judicial level 15:3 (Supreme Court), 63:7 (Appellate Court), and 182:25 (district city courts). In general, "the large disparity in the distribution of women and men in political bodies continues to apply" and, in the Parliament, "the greatest numbers of women are to be found in committees that deal with matters relating to the family, education, and social welfare" (areas with relatively low status). "The predominance of men is far greater in committees within major economic sectors such as commerce, industry, and oil."[11]

---

11. *Norway Information* (June 1984) and *Royal Norwegian Ministry of Foreign Affairs Information* (February 1981)

Likewise, in Sweden, where the percentages of women in the unicameral Parliament is higher than that found in any nation other than Norway, "men dominate nearly all of the policy-making bodies." Men dominate "senior positions in employer and employee organizations as well as in political and in other associations. In senior management in the private sector there is an even lower percentage." Only five of 82 directors of government agencies, nine of 83 chairpersons of agency boards, and nine percent of judges are women. In short, "a clear pattern emerges: the higher up the hierarchy, the fewer the women. Among the appointments studied, 251 were of senior rank; only 25 of them were held by women."[12]

The Scandinavian nations raise an interesting point that I consider below in Chapter 5 in the section entitled "Three Methodological Observations". I have assumed (probably correctly) that the property of the hierarchical position that attracts males is primarily the position itself, not its status. It is conceivable, however, that it is the status that is the primary attractant. If this is the case, and if, as has been suggested, national office in Norway has somewhat less status than it does elsewhere, we might expect male interest in such position to decrease. The evidence here is far from clear: Norway is still "patriarchal" by any reasonable definition, it is unclear that upper hierarchical position *can* lose much status, and—in all likelihood—the opportunity to rule inherent in upper hierarchical positions renders upper positions attractive to males even if the positions somehow lose status. But the possibility that a loss of status of the positions would reduce male interest, resulting in a significant increase in the percentage of women is an interesting—if unlikely—one. (Note that the point would not be that the position would lose status *because* males became less interested in them; males would become less interested because the positions lost status—for whatever reason.)

The ten countries in which women have recently held the highest percentage of national legislative seats were all either Communist or Scandinavian countries, in which an unusually high percentage of the real power resided in the hands of (overwhelmingly male) alternative entities (such as the Politbureau and the non-parliamentary entities mentioned above[13]). We may expect to see the percentage fall in the former Soviet-bloc countries, now that elected bodies have real power. As we shall see, this is analogous to the situation that obtains with nonhierarchical status roles: As status increases, males are

---

12. The Swedish Institute, *Equality Between Men and Women in Sweden* (May 1987).
13. *Inter-Parliamentary Union*, 1989.

increasingly drawn to those roles. In general, the greater the status of hierarchical or (non-maternal) non-hierarchical roles, the greater the percentage of males in such roles. The failures of the kibbutzim and every other Utopian attempt to alter sex-role differentiation in this area merely reinforces the conclusions indicated here.[14] (A number of sub-societal groups have attempted not only to explain reality in terms that assume that logic is the only factor defining social possibility, but to implement this view by developing new 'societies'. Because logic is not the only limitation which defines social possibility, every such experiment had to fail completely or, like the kibbutz, fail in just those areas where the inexorable pull of sexual and familial biological forces eventually overcame the initial thrust of nationalistic, religious, ideological, or psychological forces that had made possible the temporary implementation of Utopian ideas. This is not to say that particular social factors did not cause the demise of any particular Utopian experiment before the biological factors had a chance to come into play, but that eventual doom was as inherent in these Utopian experiments as it was for the Shakers.)

No doubt one can devise separate and different explanations for each of these societies' failure to deviate from the near-total male occupation of positions of political authority. Each explanation could be made in terms of the particular social values and economic conditions of the society whose failure is being explained and in terms of the residual strength of its 'patriarchal' values (values common to every society) rather than in terms of an inevitable manifestation of biological reality. Let us disregard the fact that viewing each society only in its specific terms tends to demonstrate *not* why equalization has not been achieved, but rather why there has been any increase at all in the number of women in positions of authority, in those cases where there was any increase at all.[15] A far more important point is that anyone who attempts to explain these failures in this manner is in the same position as someone who tries to explain patriarchy in four thousand different societies with an equal

---

14. Readers interested in the failure of the kibbutz to challenge the universal sex-role distinctions we have discussed might consult: Melford Spiro, 'Is The Family Universal: The Israeli Case' (particularly the addendum) in *The Sociological Perspective*, Scott McNall, ed. (Boston: Little, Brown, 1971) and A.I. Rabin's 'Ideology and Reality in the Israeli Kibbutz' in *Sex Roles in a Changing Society*, Georgene Seward and Robert C. Williamson, eds. (New York: Random House, 1970).

15. For example, the devastation of the Soviet Union in World War II created such a dearth of qualified people in every area that the competitive aspects of the attainment of position were reduced.

number of different explanations, each in terms particular to that society rather than in terms which could explain all four thousand cases. As we shall see, this is preposterous even if theoretically defensible. The failure of these societies to alter political patriarchy does not, of course, 'prove' that patriarchy is inevitable any more than the universality of patriarchy 'proves' it. I have mentioned the failures of these disparate societies, with very different economic systems, value systems, and traditions, only as presumptive evidence—very strong presumptive evidence, I believe—that there is a physiological factor that renders a non-patriarchal society impossible to achieve.

Male Dominance Defined

Up to now we have been discussing patriarchy, a reality that is easily defined and revealed in terms of the percentages of males in dominant positions in hierarchies. Because patriarchy can be so defined and revealed, the definition need not include the psychophysiological sexual differentiation of which it is a manifestation. Male dominance, the second societally universal reality that this book attempts to explain, is somewhat more difficult to define and reveal because the *formal* and *legal* manifestation of the psychophysiological differentiation is only *almost* universal, rather than universal. There is much evidence for the universality of the psychophysiological differentiation; the songs, stories, jokes, proverbs, and expressions of every society recognize (with favorable attitudes in some societies and unfavorable in others) the male and female emotional *expectations* of male dominance. However, while the informal presence of male dominance is always demonstrable the formal and legal expression of male dominance is not quite universal; chivalrous societies and societies whose laws ignore sex prevent our including in our definition formal authority with the psychophysiological differentiation and its manifestation in informal authority.

In all but a very few societies, evidence of male dominance is apparent from the customs of deference so well documented by the anthropologists; there is no difficulty in discussing dominance in terms of its manifestation in customs rather than the emotional differentiation of which the customs are manifestations. Dominance and deference refer not to the customs but to the feelings when one is examining the ten or twelve 'chivalrous' societies, in which women *seem* to receive deference, or American society, in which customs of deference are minimal when compared to those of virtually any other society. Examination of the ethnographic materials on these 'chivalrous' societies demonstrates that chivalrous male deference is seen in these societies as a complement to feminine fragility rather than as a reversal of male dominance. In American society, for example, a man's holding a door for a woman symbolizes masculine strength rather than female authority: a man's walking nearer to the curb acknowledges the male's feeling that the woman is to be protected rather than the female's dominance. Such male 'deference' is, clearly, not an acknowledgment of female authority equivalent to the acknowledgment of male authority that female deference in non-chivalrous societies represents.

We can observe the feelings of male dominance most clearly during an argument, because it is in times of conflict that the emotional acknowledgment of male authority comes into male and female consciousness. Most of the time, when men and women are performing different roles which they and their society define as male and female roles, there is no conflict, and feelings of authority will not come into play. It is only when there is conflict that this feeling will be apparent to the male, who makes use of it, and to the female, who must get around it.[16]

The voluminous writings of many feminists attest to the fact that the same feelings and emotional expectations that underpin the customs of every other society affect our behavior as surely as they affect that of the men and women of every other society. Thus the author of a feminist essay complains that she feels that she has somehow lost an argument with her husband, that somehow she was wrong, even when she knows intellectually that she had the better argument, that she was right, and that her husband was being emotionally dishonest. Thus the feminist novelist objects to the fact that it is somehow the male who 'takes the lead' in endless situations as varied as crossing streets and choosing friends. The husband tends to 'tell' ('my husband told me to take the TV to the repair shop') while the wife tends to 'ask' ('my wife asked me to take the TV to the repair shop'). To be sure, women do, as these novelists acknowledge, have a great deal of power in that they make decisions in many areas, but it is the *feeling* that the husband *lets* them make such decisions (that

---

16. For the sake of convenience I shall occasionally use the term *male dominance* to refer not merely to the feelings of the members of a society, but also to those dyadic and familial institutions in which these feelings are manifested. Thus when I speak of one society's exhibiting more male dominance than another, I mean that its institutions emphasize or utilize these feelings more than those of another. Furthermore, it should be noted that 'male dominance' is a relative term. One might be tempted to introduce the hypothesis that differing social conditions have resulted in the women of one society becoming more dominant than the men of another. Such a hypothesis would be meaningless. *Dominance* and *deference* are relative terms that refer to the feelings and institutions relevant to dyadic and familial relationships in a *single* societal context.

he delegates authority, that he 'allows') that annoys the feminist and that is the evidence of the presence of male dominance. Likewise feminists have pointed out that nearly all women (and men) associate authority with the father, save those few who begrudge their fathers their refusal to invoke male authority. Our acceptance of the feminist's description of her feelings and observations does not require that we attach a judgment to these feelings and observations or that we accept any assumption that this manifestation of sexual difference has its roots in social factors only.

The customs of deference have made it simple to identify the presence of male dominance in the vast majority of societies. It is quite likely that such customs will disappear from modern societies with their need for women in the labor force and increasing mixing of the sexes in the marketplace. It is important to remember, therefore, that such customs are merely convenient identifiers of male dominance and are not the feelings of male dominance or the behavior in which male dominance is manifested. Just as male dominance is easily uncovered even in chivalrous societies, it is easy to demonstrate— through observation of behavior and reports of feelings by both men and women—even when the customs are absent.

It should be repeated that I am not rejecting the possibility that in dyadic relationships women using female means may attain their ends more often than men using male means (either universally or in some societies, perhaps the chivalrous ones), nor am I denying the obvious fact that, whatever qualities one considers masculine or feminine, every member of each sex will occasionally exhibit the behavior of the other. I am saying only that every society recognizes a particular emotional difference between men and women, and that this difference always works in the same direction (no society feels that it is the *woman* who 'allows'). In other words, the male strength and dominance and the female gentleness and endurance portrayed in our novels and movies mirror not merely *our* society's view of the emotional natures of men and women, but the views of every society that has ever existed.

For our purposes, one's attitude towards male dominance is irrelevant; it does not matter whether the reader enjoys the idea that the male dominates and protects the female or detests it. The men and women of every society feel this way and acknowledge this feeling in their societies' institutions. Why this is the case and why, if male dominance does not result from some fact- or that is either suprasocial or inherent in the very nature of society, does no society reverse this or alternatively fail to manifest any sexual dominance at all?

The Universality of Male Dominance

Cross-cultural compilations of ethnographic materials demonstrate the universality of male dominance with the same conclusiveness with which they demonstrate that of patriarchy. While the greater subtleties of definition and discovery have led some of the anthropologists responsible for such compilations to use slightly qualified terms ('universality for all intents and purposes') when referring to the universality of male dominance, this scientific tentativeness does not indicate a belief that there is any society in which the members do not demonstrate the feelings relevant to male dominance or in which authority in dyadic relationships is not associated with the male. With one exception, all the authors indicate quite definitely that there is no exception to male dominance (as we define it).[17]

The exception is Dr William Stephens, who does not deal directly with male dominance, but with authority in specific areas relevant to the household and the rearing of children. However, even if we accept Dr Stephens's focus on the familial rather than the dyadic, the universality of male dominance is not brought into question. Dr Stephens suggests five possible exceptions to universality (in his terms): the Tchambuli (the society which is most often invoked and which we shall look at more closely), the people of Modjokuto (Java), the Berbers, the Jivaro, and the Nama Hottentot. Recourse to the original materials on which Dr Stephens bases his assessment supports his contention that these societies delegate to women a certain authority in specific matters concerning the home and children, but by no stretch of the imagination could the men and women of these societies be said to fail to demonstrate the feelings relevant to male dominance. In every case the same ethnographic study that is used to support the assessment of 'exception' explicitly states this. For example, the study of the Modjokuto people of Java states that the father "is expected to be, above all, patient and dignified (*sabar*) with his wife and children: he should lead them with a gentle though firm hand . . ."[18]

Similar acknowledgments of male dominance can be found in every

---

17. For extended discussion of the anthropological data relevant to the universality of male dominance, the reader might wish to consult: Gerald Leslie, *op cit:* M.F. Nimkoff, *Comparative Family Systems* (Boston: Houghton-Mifflin, 1965); Ira L. Reiss, *The Family System in America* (New York: Holt, Rinehart, and Winston, 1971); and William N. Stephens, *The Family in Cross-Cultural Perspective* (New York: Holt, Rinehart, and Winston, 1963).

18. Hildred Geertz, *The Javanese Family* (New York: Free Press, 1961), 107.

ethnographic study claimed to demonstrate the absence of male dominance in a particular society. For example, one often hears it claimed that Lewis Henry Morgan's work on the Iroquois demonstrated that, while patriarchy in Iroquois society is apparent from the fact that women were not permitted to fill positions of leadership, the Iroquois failed to manifest male dominance. That this was not the case is clear when Morgan writes: "The Indian regarded women as the inferior, the dependent, and the servant of man, and from nurturance and habit, she actually considered herself to be so."[19]

In the Appendix the reader will find similar ethnographic quotations on every alleged exception. The point is neither that male dominance makes it necessary for women to consider themselves inferior (while this may be the case with the Iroquois, it is not with many other societies) nor that male dominance is only attributable to 'nurturance and habit'. We shall discuss causation later. Here I am interested merely in noting the universality of male and female feelings of male dominance.

Moreover, whatever can be said about any alleged societal exception to the universality of male dominance can also be applied to American society. Indeed, it is doubtful whether any other society delegates to women the same degree of authority even in the home—and those feminists who are also extreme environmentalists are hardly anxious that American society should increase women's authority and responsibility in the home. In our society men show chivalrous deference to women (by standing when a woman enters the room, for example), acknowledge female authority in most decisions concerning the household to such an extent that many women complain that the American male has abdicated his role as father in order to concentrate on suprafamilial pursuits, give women equal rights in selecting the leaders of the society and equal rights in reaching positions of leadership, and, with a few exceptions which are of primarily symbolic importance, equal *rights* of ownership and participation in economic life. Moreover, with the exception of land ownership in certain matrilineal societies—which does not lessen male control of suprafamilial or dyadic situations—no society gives women authority in any area in which she is not given authority in the United States.

It is unnecessary to examine the evidence from each of Dr Stephens's societies in order to make the point that he has not discovered any exception to

---

19. Lewis Henry Morgan, *League of the Ho-dě-No-Sau-Nee or Iroquois* (New York: Dodd, Mead and Co., 1901), 315.

male dominance as we use the term here (though the reader who desires to do so will find the relevant material in the Appendix). Speaking of wives in American society, Dr Stephens states that "If there are any exceptional societies (in which each family may freely choose—or fight it out—to determine who does what), our own society probably comes as close as any"[20] and that, "In the allocation of power and privilege, our society—compared with other societies —treats its wives most generously."[21]

The environmentalist who wishes to demonstrate that male dominance is not universal need not even mention Dr Stephens, but if he does not he is left with only cross-cultural compilations that do not offer even a hint of an exception. In that case, he must find an exception on his own and this, we shall see, he will not be able to do. If the environmentalist does invoke one of Dr Stephens's societies as an exception to the universality of male dominance, he not only faces the fact that none of these societies are exceptions (see the

---

20. Two interesting points emerge when we examine those societies in which there is a relatively low degree of male dominance. The first is one that we would expect if we view dyadic relationships in the terms of this book: women in these societies are successful because they make use of 'feminine' abilities to counter the societal expectations which conform to male aggression or, to use Dr Stephens's words, "In the face of . . . [the male advantage] . . . a wife—if she wishes to fight back—must employ characteristically female weapons." The second point of interest is that a low degree of male dominance seems to occur when there is a strong societal emphasis on some suprafamilial male functions. This is not to say that societies that emphasize some such factor will necessarily demonstrate a relatively low male dominance (i.e. give the women authority in certain familial areas, Dr Stephens's 'exceptions'), but that societies which *do* demonstrate a relatively low male dominance, which *do* give women authority in these familial areas, will place an unusually strong emphasis on some suprafamilial area. For example, the male obsession with work and career in the United States has been documented by sociologists since Weber; the Jivaro male sees warriorship as the purpose of life. Perhaps this implies that a relatively low degree of familial male dominance and authority may occur where the paternal role is not thought to contribute to high status, with a resulting male lack of interest in the paternal role. This is analogous to a situation we will observe shortly: when a suprafamilial position is given high status by a society, men will occupy it; when it is given low status, men will attempt to attain other (high status) positions. This would explain the fact that the relatively low degree of familial male dominance in the American family is combined with a moderately high degree of patriarchy in the political and economic areas. A decrease in the strength of the work ethic and a resulting increase in the American male's interest in the paternal role may lead to an increase in familial male authority, with the male invoking dominance in an area he had formerly ignored in favor of his work. In other words, it is likely that the increased emphasis on women's filling suprafamilial roles, and the reduced emphasis on maternal roles urged by many feminists, may combine with a weakening of the male work ethic *not* to increase women's authority in suprafamilial areas (where the positions of authority will be attained by males as they have been in every society—even those without a strong emphasis on suprafamilial male functions), but only to increase the degree of male dominance at home.

21. All references to Dr Stephens's work refer to Stephens, *op. cit.,* 300–06.

Appendix), but that, as Dr Stephens's words suggest, he must invoke the United States (because none of Dr Stephens's societies manifest male dominance any less). But if the environmentalist does so his cause is lost at once: to invoke the United States as an exception is to assert that it does not have male dominance and to admit the incorrectness of the environmentalist premiss. Since he will obviously not want to do this, he must acknowledge that none of Dr Stephens's societies fail to acknowledge male dominance.

It is worth considering briefly the Tchambuli of New Guinea, not only because of all Dr Stephens's societies it is the one for which the strongest case can be made for its being a society which fails to acknowledge male dominance, but because a number of popular writers have repeated Margaret Mead's questionable conclusions to her study of the Tchambuli without repeating her qualifying statements. While Dr Mead did not claim that the Tchambuli failed to acknowledge male dominance, she did imply that sex roles and sexual temperament for these people were so different from those exhibited in every other society that the study caused something of an uproar.[22] The excellent ethnographic data Dr Mead presents enable the careful reader to see that her conclusions about the plasticity of sex roles do not follow from the observations she describes. For example, she points out that the Tchambuli boy's initiation consisted of his killing a victim and hanging the head in the ceremonial house as a trophy; it is difficult to see this as indication of 'male femininity'. Indeed, in response to one of her critics Dr Mead wrote, "Nowhere do I suggest that I have found any material which disproves the existence of sex differences. . . . This study was not concerned with whether there are or are not actual and universal differences between the sexes, either quantitative or qualitative."[23] More recently, in a review of the first edition of this book, Dr Mead acknowledged that

---

22. See Margaret Mead's *Sex and Temperament in Three Primitive Societies* (New York: Morrow, 1935).

23. Letter, *The American Anthropologist*, 39 (July–September 1937) 558–561. The reader who wishes further evidence that Dr Mead's implication (that the Tchambuli sex roles do not conform to the limits demonstrated by every other society) is supported only by her own choice of adjectives, and not at all by the data she presents, should consult the following analyses of *Sex and Temperament*: Jessie Bernard, 'Observation and Generalization in Cultural Anthropology', *The American Journal of Sociology*, 50 (January 1945), 284–291; Richard Thurnwald, 'Oceania and Africa', *The American Anthropologist*, 38 (October-December 1936) pp. 663–67; Victor Barnouw, *Culture and Personality* (Homewood, Ill.: Dorsey Press, 1963), pp. 85–91; and Marvin Harris's brief criticism in *The Rise of Anthropological Theory* (London: Routledge, 1969) 413–14.

It is true . . . that all the claims so glibly made about societies ruled by women are nonsense. We have no reason to believe that they ever existed. . . . men everywhere have been in charge of running the show. . . . men have been the leaders in public affairs and the final authorities at home.[24]

Those who so frequently invoke the Tchambuli (and occasionally the Mundugumor, also studied by Dr Mead) as societies that do not exhibit the institutions under discussion must explain why the ethnographer who studied them does not consider them to be exceptions.

In this chapter we are considering only empirical realities, in this case the universality of male dominance, and not the explanation of these realities. The explanations offered vary greatly from society to society. Thus, the Gahuku-Gama observe male dominance in their society and explain it as resulting from an initial male physiological inferiority.[25] Other societies have other explanations. These are of great interest in other anthropological contexts, but they are irrelevant here, as are the attitudes towards male dominance. For observation of the empirical reality we must look to the society; for an explanation of it we need not.

Indeed, parsimony and plausibility demand that we seek a single explanation of a universal institution, even when different societies have hundreds of different explanations of the universal institution and even when different societies attach hundreds of different meanings to the institution. After all, different societies offer us hundreds of explanations of, and meanings of, the fact that it is the woman who gives birth, but we are satisfied with the explanation that explains this universality in terms of female physiology.

The Universality of Male Attainment

One often hears the Bamenda, the Hopi, the Iroquois, the Mbuti Pygmies, the Nayar, certain Philippine groups, the people of the kibbutz, or even the fictitious Amazons invoked as exceptions to the universality of male dominance.[26] These alleged exceptions are, aside from the Amazons, societies that

---

24. *Redbook*, October 1973, 48.

25. Kenneth E. Read, 'Nama Cult of the Central Highlands, New Guinea', in I.L. Langness and John C. Weschler, eds., *Melanesia: Readings on a Culture Area* (Scranton: Chandler, 1971).

26. For a more extended discussion of alleged exceptions to male dominance see the Appendix.

associate with women *tasks* or *functions* that *we* associate with men. They are not exceptions to the universality of male dominance, for male dominance in no way precludes the possibility that any task or function which we may choose to emphasize may be associated with women in one society or another. What is important here is the association of high-status (non-maternal) roles with males. The reason why role A may have a high status in society X and a low status in society Y, while role B has a low status in society X and a high status in society Y, is irrelevant. What is relevant is that role A in society X and role B in society Y tend to be male roles, while role B in society X and role A in society Y tend to be female roles.

This, then, is the third universal that this book attempts to explain: male attainment. *Every society gives higher status to male roles than to the non-maternal roles of females.* To put it in another, and I believe more illuminating, way: *in every society males attain the high-status (non-maternal) roles and positions and perform the high-status tasks, whatever those tasks are.* Margaret Mead has written:

> In every known human society, the male's need for achievement can be recognized. Men may cook, or weave or dress dolls or hunt hummingbirds, but if such activities are appropriate occupations of men, then the whole society, men and women alike, votes them as important. When the same occupations are performed by women, they are regarded as less important.[27]

Professor Mead goes further than I do, and the difference is important. The correct and important point made by Mead is that high-status, non-maternal roles are male. However, it is not true that low-status roles are rarely male. Ditch-digging is male and low-status. This is important because it indicates that it is not primarily the maleness of a role that gives the role high status, but the high status that attracts males to the role. Males who cannot attain such roles may become ditch-diggers, but their maleness does not serve to raise the status of ditch-digging.

It should be clear that the roles filled by males are, *in reality,* not necessarily more important to the society's survival—or whatever criterion one uses to measure importance. (Obviously, no male role is more important than the female's reproductive role.) We are speaking here of the view held, the status accorded, by the society, rather than by the sociologist. Business executives are not more important than nurses, but they are given higher status and are usually

---

27. Margaret Mead, *Male and Female* (London: Penguin, 1970), 168.

male. In the Soviet Union, practising (as opposed to research) medical doctors tended to be women, but the role of doctor in the Soviet Union had a lower status than in the United States. If being a practising doctor had been given high status in the Soviet Union, doctors would have been men; as it was, men directed their energies towards other, higher-status, roles.[28]

The Soviet Union was often put forward as the society which most closely approached sexual occupational equality—though China, which had far less such equality, despite constant declarations to the contrary, was also a fashionable incorrect example. In the Soviet Union there was "an almost perfect *negative* correlation between the average wage for a given sector of the economy and the proportion of women workers in that sector. The worst-paid sector, public health and physical education (listed as a single category in Soviet statistics), is the sector with the highest proportion of women, 85 per cent."[29] The same relationship between status-wage and sex will be found in any society the reader wishes to examine: for example, in France the chefs are men.

Two vitally important points must be made here. First, nothing I have written so far implies that males *perform* better or have a greater aptitude for, male roles. Everything I have written concerns *attainment* of position and role, not performance in it. I do not argue that females cannot perform high-status roles as well as males, but only that they are not, for psychophysiological reasons we shall discuss, as strongly motivated to attain the upper hierarchical positions and high-status roles. Second, *male roles, whatever they are in a given society, are not given high status because they are male roles; males occupy roles because high status motivates the male more strongly, with the result that society comes to associate such roles with males.* We shall see that this distinction is of great theoretical importance when we discuss the psychophysiological differentiation of the sexes. It may or may not be true that there is a second and different tendency for the members of society to, for whatever reason, increase the status given a role once the role becomes associated with males simply on account of the associatiation of the role with males. However, since the greater attraction that the high-status role holds for males by virtue of its high status is sufficient

---

28. For data relevant to status in the Soviet Union see 'The Social Evaluation of Occupations in the Soviet Union' in *Slavic Review* (28,4); 'Soviet Women and Their Self-Image in Science and Society' (39,3) and Dodge, *op. cit.* With the move to an economy in which individuals' incomes correspond more closely to what others are willing to pay for their services, it is likely that the profession of physician in the former Soviet Union will gradually become predominantly male.

29. Victor Baras, 'Contemporary Soviet Society', *Current History* (October 1974), 174.

to explain the higher status of male roles, the question of whether the second tendency exists is irrelevant here.

A woman who is older, wealthier, from a higher class or 'better' family, more intelligent, or more educated than a particular male may be given authority over him, and may even feel dominance over him, but she will have less status and authority than an equivalent male, and will feel some deference towards him. Thus in some societies an older woman whose husband has died rules the family, and the presence of an educated, wealthy woman may make the less wealthy and educated male feel insecure. *But whatever variable one chooses, authority, status and dominance within each stratum rest with the male in contacts with equivalent females.*

Men do not merely fill most of the roles in high-status areas, they also fill the high-status roles in low-status areas. The higher the level of power, authority, status, prestige, or position—whether the area be economic, occupational, political, or religious—the higher the percentage of males. Thus the percentage of women in the workforce in the United States has risen by 75 percent since 1900, but the percentage of women in the high-status area of medicine has declined during this period. In the Soviet Union, where, as we have seen, medicine has a far lower status than in the United States, the majority of all doctors are women, but as one rises from the level of practical medicine to that of authority the percentage of males rises, until, at the top, males constitute the overwhelming majority.[30]

Of all the *tasks* one might think of or choose to emphasize, virtually every one, with the exception of those related to protection, fighting, and political authority, is associated with women in one society or another,[31] but in every society the roles filled by men are given higher status. None of this, of course, denies that in every society women are responsible for the care and rearing of the young, the single most important function served in any society or in nature itself. Just as patriarchy, male dominance, and male attainment of high-status roles and positions are universal, so the association of nurturance and emotional

---

30. See William J. Goode, *World Revolution and Family Patterns* (New York: Free Press of Glencoe, 1963), 57–66.

31. While there are no exceptions in these three spheres (every society's military and leadership functions are served primarily by men), it should be noted for the record that in the mid-nineteenth century the army of Dahomey included a corps of female warriors (different authors estimate their percentage of the total number of warriors as being between 5 and 15 per cent) and that at one time Iroquoian women served a vital political function in selecting male leaders (though women were not permitted to lead). Contrary to popular misconception, Israeli women do not serve in combat roles.

socialization with the woman is universal, and these female roles are, in some societies, given very high status.

The Hunt for 'Exceptions' to Universality

There is not a single exception to the universality—the presence in every society, past and present, on which we have any evidence—of patriarchy, male attainment, and male dominance.

The mere assertion that there are such exceptions, unaccompanied by even an attempt at specifying an exceptional society, is the most common of the 'methods' invoked by those who would deny the universality of the institutions we discuss. This unsupported assertion has as its purpose the denial of the possible determinativeness of physiological differentiation to the differentiations of male and female behaviors and institutions we discuss.

However, in ignoring or denying universality these critics render their criticisms irrelevant; it is the universality—be it a function of physiology, the inherent nature of society, or mere temporary social factors that have always been present but may not be in the future—that is the empirical reality whose existence it is this book's purpose to demonstrate and explain.

In their *Not In Our Genes*, Richard Lewontin, Steven Rose, and Leon Kamin adopt this stratagem of heroic, unsupported denial. Summarizing their presentation of the cross-cultural evidence, they write:

> [Cross-cultural universals] appear to lie more in the eye of the beholder than in the social reality that is being observed.[32]

With reference to the behaviors and institutions I discuss, this statement is utterly untrue. If it were true, Lewontin, Rose, and Kamin would have had merely to name a society lacking the institutions we discuss and that would have settled the issue. They cannot do so, hence they simply refuse to address the empirical reality this book addresses. In so refusing, Lewontin, Rose, and Kamin render irrelevant their entire discussion of sex differences, most of which purports to be a refutation of my argument.

Lewontin, Rose, and Kamin present the reader with a *pot-pourri* of biological facts (about longevity, disease rates, and the like) that are irrelevant to the theory they attempt to refute. Moreover, it is not clear what these facts are

---

32. Richard Lewontin, Steven Rose, and Leon Kamin, *Not In Our Genes* (New York: Pantheon, 1984), 138.

meant to be relevant to, because the authors never say what it is they are trying to explain.

Lewontin, Rose, and Kamin do not even attempt to refute the universality of the three institutions we attempt to explain. In their only reference to the three universals, the authors point out that most family doctors in the Soviet Union are women, and "of course, there family doctoring has a lower status and lower pay than in the United States, *but that is a different point*" (emphasis added).[33] This point is "different" from the others the authors raise in that it is relevant to the argument they claim to be criticizing. Lewontin, Rose, and Kamin do not ask themselves *why* there is a universal correlation between non-maternal high-status roles and being male. They hint that the answer is economic, but they do not even attempt to give such an answer.

Indeed, they couldn't. The fact that high-status, non-maternal roles in every society—from the most primitive to the most modern—are male mocks all economic explanations and supports my claims that a. the 'motivational' differences between males and females is rooted in the male's physiologically-based lower threshhold for the release of dominance and status-attainment behavior, and b. this physiologically-rooted sexual difference gives direction to social systems and social values and sets limits of possibility on social variation.

The demonstrable fact of universality has not prevented a host of critics from attempting to specify exceptions. Had they bothered to consult the ethnographies, rather than depend on second-hand sources, they would have seen that the societies they claim to be exceptions were in no way exceptions.

Every time one looks at the sources claimed for these exceptions, one finds societies so obviously not exceptions that even those who invoked them are forced to acknowledge the fact. Like the believer in unicorns who acknowledges that the last claimed unicorn turned out to be a horse with a party hat, but who still expects a unicorn to appear at any moment, one who wants to believe in societies without the realities we discuss can always come up with another 'exception' to invoke. In this text and in the Appendix the reader will find refutory quotations from every ethnography I have ever seen suggested as representing an exception to universality. It is clear that in nearly every case the critic did not consult the original ethnography, but merely accepted the claim

---

33. *Ibid.*, 136.

of another who also did not consult the original ethnography. (It is hardly necessary to add that no ethnographer has claimed to have observed a society lacking the institutions we discuss.)

More than mere sloppiness is at work here. About a decade ago I wrote a letter to *Contemporary Sociology,* perhaps the most widely-read sociological journal. In the letter I made clear—as I have above—that Margaret Mead had for 40 years denied that the Tchambuli demonstrated a sex-role reversal or that they demonstrated the possibility of such a reversal. I did this because I had discovered that 30 of 32 introductory sociology texts—as well as an astonishing number of allegedly high-level sociological and feminist works—began their chapters on sex roles with the claim that the Tchambuli did reverse sex roles and were, therefore, evidence of the social causation of the differentiation of male and female behavior.

In the years since the publication of that letter, I have three times checked recently-published introductory sociology texts. The percentage of textbooks invoking the Tchambuli has not significantly diminished. In fairness, however, it should be said that about a third of those invoking the Tchambuli now acknowledge that the view they attribute to Mead is "controversial" ('controversy' seeming to mean that those who looked at the evidence all believe one thing while some of those who did not believe another). More hopeful is the claim of a number of publishers that the *next* generation of texts will acknowledge the universality of the institutions we discuss. Even the publishers admit that the texts will all assume a social etiology of the institutions and will either ignore opposing analyses or will dismiss them without argument. But at least they will not invoke the non-existent evidence claimed to be provided by Mead and that is an advance of sorts.

Some of the authors of current texts have admitted to me in private that they know that the Tchambuli are not an exception, but argue that 'it is important to stress the social over the biological'. We used to call this 'lying'. For some other authors, carelessness is more to blame than ideological dogmatism. Many authors of introductory texts merely follow earlier texts and accept without question claims made in these texts, more out of a desire to complete their books quickly than out of ideological demands.

Occasionally an author will make the sincere mistake of confusing a societal reversal of tasks (for instance, a society that considers secretarial work a 'male' task) with a reversal of the roles relevant to the institutions we discuss. However, as we have just seen, since such task reversals never, as a matter of empirical fact, include those relevant to hierarchical or dyadic dominance or to status attainment they are never able to show that a genuine and relevant 'exception' has been found. The author most prone to commit this and analogous errors is William King Whyte.

Whyte claims that his coders uncovered a number of exceptions to the universalities I discuss. I have written at length on this elsewhere, but it is worthwhile giving a few examples here for the reader who is tempted to believe that a mere claim of exceptionality necessarily confers some likelihood of exceptionality. Let us look at Whyte's two variables that would indicate exceptions if there were exceptions.

There are four societies that Whyte claims to be exceptions to the universality of male dominance. In each case I give a quotation from the *same* ethnographic source on which Whyte bases his claim.[34]

The Iban:	"Typically, every *bilek* family has as its head a man who is responsible for the general management of the farm." (81)
The Semang:	"In each family the father alone is a respected person." (226)
	"The head of a Semang local group is first of all the eldest, if he has any ability at all for leadership. Nevertheless it may happen—and not rarely—that another man is leader of the group." (225)
The Marquesans:	"Theoretically, women could hold the highest rank, but in practice few women were actual household heads." (184)
The Kenuzi Nubians:	"The subservient position of women was determined by the Islamic religion." (133)
	"Women influence their husbands, but [their husband's] decisions are decisive." (89)

The other variable that could provide an exception if there were one

---

34. William King Whyte, *The Status of Women in Pre-Industrial Society* (Princeton: Princeton University Press, 1978). Bibliographical information on the ethnographies cited will be found in Whyte. Page numbers refer to the pages of the ethnography where the quotations occur.

concerns "evidence of rough equality". Whyte fails to name the 19 societies supposedly showing such evidence. However, this causes us no problem because Whyte names two societies alleged to give *dominance,* rather than mere equality, to the female (the wife). Thus, Whyte implicitly acknowledges that these two of the 21 societies he alleges to be exceptions are the strongest cases he can make for the existence of exceptions and that these two are qualitatively stronger cases than the other 19. If these two fail, so presumably do the other 19.

| The Javanese (Modjokuto): | "(The father) is expected to be, above all, patient and dignified (*sabar*) with his wife and children: he should lead them with a gentle firm hand . . ." (107) |
| The Bribri: | "(The brother) . . . or in the default of a brother, a cousin or uncle, [has a ruling voice in any family council or discussion]." (p. 497)[35] |

All of the rest of Whyte's 'exceptions' concern variables consistent with my argument (for example: two societies with women leaders at male levels, but few of them) or irrelevant to it (infant care). Thus, we need not consider these here.

In other cases, the claim that there is an exception is more difficult to attribute entirely to an innocent blunder. In an article written for Alice Schlegel's feminist anthology, *Sexual Stratification: A Cross-Cultural View,* Albert S. Bacdayan describes at length the Bantoc, a Tanowong/Tanulong culture that, he contends, exhibits sexual equality.

Now, a close reading of Bacdayan makes clear that this does not follow even from the evidence he provides in this very article. But we need not examine this article here. For when he describes this same culture for a serious anthropological journal, Bacdayan writes:

> As is typical of the Bantoc . . . the Tanowong are organized into different *dap-ay* groups. . . . The *dap-ay* . . . is the men's house. The *dap-ay* are the religious, social, and political centers of village life, where major decisions are made. . . . While each *dap-ay* theoretically has a council of old men who make the decisions, in actual fact, especially at present, every mature man participates in the deliberations of the council.[36]

---

35. Gabb (To whom Stone and Skinner attribute relevant material).
36. Albert S. Bacdayan, in *Ethnology: 1974.* For discussion of Bacdayan's Schlegel contribution, see my response to critics in *Society* (September-October, 1986).

The misleading influence of writings such as Bacdayan's contribution to Schlegel's anthology is not limited to readers of the original. The misrepresentation is accepted by other authors who accept the article at face value and repeat the misrepresentation. At this point the misrepresentation becomes 'widely-known fact', a robust legend, and is repeated endlessly.

Take, for example, Rae Lesser Blumberg's entry in *Sociological Theory: 1984,* which presents a theory attempting to correlate divergence from sexual egalitarianism with economic factors. To the extent that Blumberg considers only variation that really does exist cross-culturally, her work is irrelevant to my argument. I have not offered a general explanation of societal variations that are observed to exist, other than to make the elementary point that when there is very little stratification, there are few cues eliciting male dominance and a small arena in which that dominance can formally manifest itself; as we shall see, this is concordant with Blumberg's empirical evidence.

However, Blumberg (25–26) comes close to implying that five societies have virtually egalitarian conceptions of male and female dominance—that, in other words, actual variation comes much closer to covering the range of imaginable variation than is, in my view, the case. The societies she names are: The Bantoc, Tasaday, !Kung, Iroquois, and Mbuti.

We have seen that a glance at Bacdayan's serious work on the Bantoc refutes any argument that this group exhibits a sexual equality casting doubt on the presence of the institutions we discuss.

Argument has raged over the true status of the Tasaday, originally hailed as an untouched Stone Age tribe, then apparently exposed as a virtual hoax, a completely fraudulent society 'constructed' for purposes of profit and publicity by a malevolent government minister.[37] Some now claim that the truth lies somewhere in between: the Tasaday may be a very small group which has led a semi-isolated existence for a century or two, before being exploited by an unscrupulous politician. At the time of their discovery, the Tasaday were a tiny group, barely a 'society' at all. Nonetheless, such evidence as we have fails to support the claim that the Tasaday are in any way exceptional in their male-female relationships (see the Appendix).

The !Kung, in the same source cited by Blumberg, are described as being comprised of "male-centered groups" (75) in which men "have power and can exercise their will in relation to women" (277). Elsewhere in this book I

---

37. See *New York Times* (Letters), January 9th, 1988, and *Newsday,* November 18th, 1986.

give citations from the same sources invoked by Blumberg, demonstrating the clear presence of patriarchy and male dominance among the Iroquois and Mbuti.

In short: I have read many claims of societies that are exceptions to the universals we discuss. In not one case is the claim made by the anthropologist who actually studied the society in question. In every case, I have consulted the *same* ethnographic work cited by the person contending that the ethnography indicates that the society is an exception. Every such contention is as refutable as those offered by Whyte, Bacdayan, and Blumberg. Every such claim is addressed and countered in the text of this book or in the Appendix.

The perhaps unpalatable truth is that the social sciences have discovered precious few institutions that are universal and whose universality is best explained by direct physiological evidence, yet whose explanation is not—like those for women's giving birth or everyone's eating—so obvious as to be trivial. When a universal is uncovered, it demands explanation.

Two Hypotheses Tested

There are two major works of social science[38] which, while their purpose is to test other theoretical constructs, shed considerable light on universal manifestations of sex differences in society. While each of these calls into question certain aspects of the theory it is testing, both indicate the correctness of the description of sexual role distinctions discussed here.

Sigmund Freud and Bronislaw Malinowski agreed that in Western cultures male children harboured a rage against their fathers. The theorists disagreed on the cause of the rage. Freud saw the son's anger as an envy of the father's sexual rights to the mother; Malinowski believed this to be of little importance and saw the anger as a response to the father's authoritarian role and the limitations it

---

38. Bronislaw Malinowski, *Sex and Repression in Savage Society* (London: Routledge, 1927), and Morris Zelditch, 'Role Differentiation in the Nuclear Family: A Comparative Study', in Talcott Parsons and Robert F. Bales, eds., *Family, Socialization, and Interaction Process* (London: Routledge, 1956). Dr Zelditch's definition of 'instrumental role' differs in some respects from our definition of 'male dominance'. As a result he lists the Manus (alone among 56 societies) as giving the father a slightly less instrumental role than the mother. That this does not indicate that the Manus male is not dominant is apparent when Zelditch writes (337): "Father holds the authority in the family, but it is through the mother evidently that he disciplines the child—that is he disciplines the mother and she is responsible for the child's behaviour."

set on the son's autonomy. In Freud's Vienna, as in most societies, both of these roles were played by the father. Among the people Malinowski studied, however, the mother's brother played the authoritarian role to his sister's son and *he*, not the son's biological father, was, according to Malinowski, the recipient of the son's rage.

Likewise, a theory of Talcott Parsons suggests that all possible societies will give the father an 'instrumental' role (solving the problems of society at large, serving as source of authority and discipline, receiving respect and hostility) and to the mother an 'expressive' role (as a source of care and guardian of emotional development, and a receiver of warmth). Morris Zelditch found that in ten out of a sample of 56 societies the instrumental role was played by a *male* other than the father (though even in these the father seemed relatively 'instrumental' and the mother relatively 'expressive').

The Freud-Malinowski 'debate' and the Parsons-Zelditch works are still the subject of much argument, and I apologize for any oversimplification. I raise all of this only to indicate that, whatever other disagreements these theorists may have, their data have led them all to the conclusion that, if a male is included in the family, the dominant role will be played by a male even when it is not played by the father. If even matrilineal and matrilocal societies pass over the obvious selection of the mother as an authority figure in favor of her brother, is it not likely that there is some underlying imperative associating authority with the male?

I am not at any point in this chapter saying that every society includes a male in the family unit. I think that this is the case, but it does not matter for our purposes if there exist societies in which the family consists of only the mother-child dyad. My point is only that if a male *is* included in the family, authority will be associated with him by both male and female feelings and societal expectations. Male dominance can manifest itself only when males and females come into contact. If there is no adult male in the family unit then, obviously, there will be no male dominance. If a role does not give males high status or some other reward (or if a high-status role is one for which males are at a biological disadvantage) then the role will not attract males and, since there will be no males, there will be no male dominance. One need not even look to a society with a dyadic family; a number of matrilineal societies and American society indicate that when male time and energies are devoted to the pursuit of suprafamilial status the role of familial disciplinarian (the familial authority role) will in practice be delegated to the mother, who will fill this role in addition to her expressive role; in the matrilocal family type which marks such societies the male familial role may be relatively unimportant, but male dominance will nonetheless be manifested whenever males and females *do* meet.[39]

Does Any Society Reverse Childhood Socialization?

In an article in the *Journal of Abnormal and Social Psychology*, Barry, Bacon, and Child compared the socialization of boys and girls in a number of societies.[40] Two judges assessed the relative degrees of socialization in various areas of behavior in an attempt to discover to what extent these varied among different societies. In the area that is relevant to my argument—socialization towards achievement—they found that 87 percent of the 31 societies under consideration socialized boys more strongly towards achievement, 3 percent socialized girls more strongly towards achievement, and 10 percent socialized boys and girls equally. One critic suggested that this implies that 3 percent of all societies socialize girls more strongly than boys towards hierarchical attainment, but it would be incorrect to draw such a conclusion even on a literal reading of the article, since the authors do not define socialization towards achievement in terms of socialization towards hierarchical attainment. Moreover, it would stretch one's belief to argue that in a society in which males occupy the vast majority of hierarchical positions (as they do in every society), females are more strongly socialized towards the behaviour that is necessary for hierarchical attainment and towards hierarchical attainment itself. *Most importantly, if we accept the dubious premiss that there are societies that socialize females more strongly than males towards hierarchical attainment, we must then conclude that, since males actually attain the hierarchical positions in these societies, socialization plays no part in the attainment of hierarchical position.* In any case, the actual behavior of role models is a far more important aspect of socialization than any

---

39. I make this point in response to R. T. Smith's suggestion that the family in British Guiana begins as a nuclear family, but soon develops into just the mother-child dyad. For reasons too numerous to go into here I do not consider that Dr Smith's illuminating study refutes the argument that a permanent, stable society must be built around a family consisting of at least mother, child, and one adult male; but even if one accepted the possibility of a society's family system being based on only the mother-child dyad, such a society would cast no doubt on the universality of male dominance in male-female encounters and relationships. See R.T. Smith, *The Negro Family in British Guiana: Family Structure and Social Status in the Villages* (London: Routledge, 1956).

40. Herbert Barry III, Margaret K. Bacon, and Irvin L. Child, 'A Cross-Cultural Survey of Some Sex Differences in Socialization', in *Journal of Abnormal and Social Psychology*, 55 (November 1957), 327–332.

stated social values. Children see the father play the dominant role and the mother the nurturant role; this observation of what actually occurs would be far more important than any stated social values, even if such values did not conform to the observation.

The Meaning of Universality

An institution is universal if it prevails in every society of which we have any knowledge, the total number of which is between approximately twelve hundred (societies that were relatively isolated from other societies and have been studied directly by anthropologists) and over five thousand (groups that are definitely known to exist, or to have existed, but that have not been studied directly by anthropologists).

An institution is not universal if there is (or ever has been) a single society in which it does not (or at one time did not) occur. Universality need not, indeed usually does not, mean that every individual in every society exhibits the behavior that leads to (or is generated by), and is regulated by, the institution in question. Marriage is a universal institution (if we allow the anthropologists to worry about the one or two societies which some consider exceptions), even though some members of every society remain unmarried. Universality means that the general population of every society bases its behavior and expectations on the universal institution. It means that thousands of 'experiments' for which we could have imagined a great number of other results, all turned out the same way.[41]

---

41. If this book were about the universality of marriage, family, or incest taboo, I would not, of course, cavalierly dismiss possible exceptions to universality. I would, as I have done with patriarchy, attempt to demonstrate either that alleged exceptions are not exceptions or that the institution is not universal. Since, in this section, I am concerned merely with the meaning of universality, and not with demonstrating that any particular institution is universal, I do not involve myself with alleged exceptions to the universality of marriage, family, or incest taboo. The reader who is interested in the universality of any of these institutions will find an enormous literature on the subject. Those who question the universality of marriage and family emphasize the difficulty we have in defining these terms in such a way that they describe the societies that are suggested as exceptions; no anthropologist doubts the universality of the family if all that is meant by 'family' is (at the very least) mother, child, and an adult male (either the father, or mother's brother). While a few authors have suggested specific societies as lacking the incest taboo, and while it is clear that some very high-status individuals in a few societies have escaped the restrictions of the incest taboo under certain conditions, I think it fair to say that very few, if any, anthropologists believe that we have evidence that there has existed a society that did not prohibit nuclear incest for the general population.

Universality Does Not Imply Inevitability

Let me make it clear beyond the possibility of misunderstanding that I am not suggesting that because an institution is universal it is necessarily inevitable. It would be ridiculous to argue that because an institution has been present in every society it must, therefore, always be so in the future. However, it is equally fatuous to ignore the question of what factor is responsible for the universality and to assert away the possibility that, if this factor is a function of human physiology, or of the very nature of society, the emotional, behavioral, and—ultimately—social-institutional manifestations of this factor may be inevitable for as long as we are physiologically constituted as we are now.

There are different reasons for universality, and by no means do they all imply inevitability. Perhaps the most obvious reason for universality, and the one for which no reasonable argument for its inevitability could be made, is technological ignorance or economic scarcity; certainly no one would argue that because no society has a two-hour work week such a work week could never be achieved by any society. However, while universality can never, by itself, prove inevitability, there are times when it combines with other evidence to strongly suggest it. The inevitability may flow from the nature of society in general, as opposed to the particular nature of a particular society, or from the very nature of human physiology. An example of the former is the incest taboo. One can imagine a society in which parent-child incest is a common form of sexual activity, but what we know about the effects of incest on social structure has led us to conclude that these effects alone would preclude the survival of such a society even though it is logically and (let us agree for argument's sake) biologically possible that such a society could survive. Even when we deal with the most basic limitations on societal possibility, those imposed by human physiology, universality alone does not *prove* inevitability. One would not say that in every future society (composed of men and women who are biologically constituted as they are now, and disregarding for now the possibility of new forms of childbirth) women will be the ones to give birth *because* they have always been the child bearers in every society in the past, but here the physiological factor is so apparent that the implication of inevitability cannot reasonably be questioned. Universality indicates that there has never been an exception. An exception would, of course, immediately disprove inevitability. Given the *seemingly* unlimited plasticity of human beings and the *seemingly* endless variety of their societal institutions, the universality of an institution alerts the investigator to the possibility that there is an underlying factor which would explain this universality, and that if this factor is inseparable from the general nature of society or of human biology, the institution *may be* inevitable.

The oft-made criticism that this reasoning would force us to suspect that, say, slavery might be a manifestation of physiological tendencies misses the point entirely. Most societies have never had slavery and even one society lacking slavery is sufficient to prove that slavery is not inevitable. Likewise, a single society lacking patriarchy would refute both claims of universality and physiological determinativeness. (Moreover, there is no direct physiological evidence relevant to slavery analogous to that relevant to the institutions we discuss; there could not be, for if there were, slavery would be found universally—or at least universally in heterogeneous societies—rather than in just a relatively small percentage of past and present heterogeneous societies.)

If there were no physiological evidence relevant to patriarchy, male dominance and male attainment, then one might argue that the inevitability of these institutions was merely a fairly likely probability. I suspect that the anthropologist, who is impressed by the cultural diversity he finds and still more impressed when he discovers an institution which over-rides this diversity, tends very strongly to believe that there is an as yet undiscovered factor that makes these institutions universal. An explanation of these institutions in terms of the specific values of a specific society may be fairly satisfactory if one is only studying a single society or a few related societies, but it loses its persuasive powers as more and more unrelated societies with unrelated, highly varied value systems all demonstrate only *one* of a number of logically possible institutional alternatives. On the other hand, sociologists, who more often concern themselves with societies in the Western tradition and who, I believe, too often see themselves as having a vested interest in a totally environmentalist approach to social reality, would hold out more strongly for an explanation that did not imply inevitability. But universality is only part of the evidence for the argument which sees patriarchy, male dominance, and male attainment as inevitable. It is important because it demonstrates that there has been no exception to disprove the inevitability of these institutions, because it points the way to other kinds of evidence that may explain such universality, because universality represents an astonishing regularity in a world of variation, and because it is for the explanation of such regularity that the scientist searches.

For the cultural anthropologist nothing is lost when an admirable scientific conservatism leads him to describe in slightly qualified terms the universality of a universal institution. However, I am advancing the hypothesis that patriarchy, male dominance, and male attainment are inevitable, and it is important to emphasize that the conservatism of some anthropologists does not indicate that they believe that there are any clear exceptions to total universality. Throughout this book I accept that one need find only one societal exception to the universality of an institution to show that not only is the institution not inevitable, but that its presence in all other societies is probably not related to physiological factors. I do this to reinforce the correctness of the theory, and I can do so because there is not a single exception to the universality of patriarchy, male attainment, and male dominance.

The Relevance of Cultural Variation

All social scientists agree that there are unchanging preconditions that must be met by any society that is to survive, as well as great variations from one society to another. Whether a social scientist is more impressed by similarities or variations may reflect his own personality—whether he sees the glass as half empty or half full. If he sees the glass as half empty, he will be sustained by the fact that no society has ever failed to develop games; if he sees the glass as half full, he will stand in awe of the wonderfully varied types of games the members of different societies have developed. If he sees the glass as half empty, he will note that man's emotions and the biological materials that underlie them have changed only very slightly, if at all, since our species first evolved. If he sees the glass as half full, he will devote his attentions to the ingenuity societies have demonstrated in developing the various institutional mechanisms for satisfying the emotional needs of their members. The reality is that the glass contains water equal to half its capacity; the correctness of an analysis is threatened only when someone who considers it to be half empty (or half full) argues that it is less than (or more than) half full. This is what many social scientists do when discussing the institutions discussed in this book.

The nature of sociology is such that the sociologist often sees the glass as half full and emphasizes variation among societies; he analyses these in social and economic contexts in an attempt to explain cross-cultural variations relevant to particular institutions. He might, for example, study women's roles in America and India in order to discover the differing etiologies of differing roles and the differing mechanisms that sustain them. This approach is justified because the differences discussed in the analysis of these two societies reflect real empirical differences. There is a danger, however, that this customary sociological perspective may lead to overestimating the variation that is found from society to society, to seeing the glass as more than half full. Indeed, many

sociologists who are not aware of the universality of patriarchy, male dominance, and male attainment invoke 'cultural variation' as 'proof' that these
institutions could not be inevitable.

As we have seen, when patriarchy is considered, there is very little variation.
The number of women in the highest positions of leadership and authority
varies from zero to perhaps six or seven percent as one spans the entire range of
human societies—including those societies in which women comprise half the
work force. Calculation of the exact upper figure depends on how far down
from the top one considers 'leadership' to extend (state legislatures and
unicameral legislatures may on occasion have considerably higher percentages
than six or seven percent while the highest political positions and the more
competitive houses of bicameral legislatures rarely approach these figures);
whether appointed positions are considered; and the relative status given politics
(when politics is given low status relative to industrial, financial, and other
hierarchical areas we might find that the percentages of women in political
positions rises somewhat). In any case, the point is abundantly clear: no society
fails to associate suprafamilial authority with males or fails to fill its authority
positions overwhelmingly with males. There is even some empirical and, if the
theory presented here is correct, strong theoretical evidence that modernization
(specialization, division of labor, bureaucratization, and the removal of hereditary barriers to mobility) restricts the possibility of women reaching positions of
leadership even within the slight variation that is possible. There were, for
example, more female heads-of-state in the first two-thirds of the sixteenth
century than in the first two-thirds of the twentieth.

Likewise, with reference to the variation among societies in the high degree
to which males attain/occupy the non-maternal roles that are given high status
(whichever these may be in any given society), there is nowhere near the
variation that would be required to cast doubt on the universality of this 'male
attainment'. If male attainment is, in a few primitive societies, less apparent
than are patriarchy and male dominance, it is merely because, as we see in our
discussion of the Mbuti, the simple societies have few high-status roles to attain,
hence fewer cues to elicit male dominance tendencies and a smaller arena in
which these can be manifested. Even in these societies, it is clear that those
non-maternal, high-status roles that do exist are associated with males.

Since we have defined 'male dominance' in terms of the feelings of males
and females, it is difficult to specify in a general way degrees of cross-cultural
variation in these feelings. What we can say without qualification is that the
ethnographies of all societies without exception show clearly that both males

and females associate dominance with the male in male-female relationships. The attitudes of the societies towards this reality vary dramatically, but the reality is always present.

If we examine variations in the extent to which such feelings are manifested in dyadic and familial institutions, we may well get bogged down in subjective considerations over which aspects to emphasize. I have suggested that the extent to which male dominance will be manifested will be lowest when a society's males are most preoccupied with high-status suprafamilial pursuits and when the paternal role is given low status. Even in such societies authority within the family will be invested in the male (usually the father, but the mother's brother in the case of some matrilineal-matrilocal societies), but male lack of interest and female ability to 'get around' males by 'feminine means' will serve to give women a great deal of real power, though not authority, within the family. But beyond that, almost all we can say about variations from society to society in the degree to which male dominance is manifested in dyadic and familial institutions is to repeat that male dominance is present in every society. The societies that least manifest male dominance are the United States and a few matrilineal societies. If one believes that male dominance in the United States is extreme, then one must agree that there is very little variation in the degree to which different societies manifest male dominance (relative to the logically possible variations), because nearly all other societies manifest it to a greater degree. Nor can one argue that, within the variations that we do find, industrialization necessarily decreases manifestations of male dominance, because the other two or three societies that least manifest male dominance are primitive societies. While it is true that modernization has tended to reduce the manifestation of male dominance in the past two centuries in America, it would no doubt increase it in a matrilineal-matrilocal primitive society whose starting point is low male dominance.

We can now consider a point that is not only central to the question of alleged cultural variation, but also enables us to avoid the endless and needless confusion engendered by the phrase *status of women,* a phrase we shall try to avoid in this book. Confusion develops because this term is used to include two or more factors that are not only not necessarily positively correlated, but which, if the above suggestions are correct, will often be inversely correlated. Some authors use this phrase to refer to *rights,* and find that there is a great deal of variation from society to society in the rights given to women; some societies give women virtually no rights at all, while in modern societies such as America women have virtual equality of rights. The feminist may abhor the few remaining laws that differentiate between the sexes, but she will admit that they are not a major cause of the disparity in the numbers of men and women in positions of power, and they are not the primary focus of her criticism of contemporary society. If all authors referred to *rights* when they used the phrase *status of women*, there would be no problem: we could admit that there is great variation here, but that it is irrelevant to this book because it has no bearing on patriarchy, male dominance, or male attainment.

However, a number of anthropologists have suggested that the 'status of women' is highest in certain, though by no means all, matrilineal-matrilocal societies. Here they are referring to the *respect* given to women. If we focus on respect, we see, once again, that variation from society to society is very great. But once again this is irrelevant to our purposes because the great respect given to women does not reduce the degree of patriarchy, male dominance, or male attainment of high-status suprafamilial positions; it reflects the high status of maternal and female lineage-related roles, and is perfectly compatible with the suggestion that male dominance will be somewhat subdued in societies in which male time and energies are directed towards suprafamilial pursuits to an unusual degree. In these societies men are typically outsiders in the matrilineal household, and interaction between the sexes is far less frequent than in our society. When these societies give high status to women's female roles, women's position is, in a very real sense, quite strong. Women are given great respect and a considerable degree of familial power. It is important to note, however, that these are made possible by the male suprafamilial orientation and emotional detachment from the family. Women have few suprafamilial rights, patriarchy is as strong as in any other society, males attain all the suprafamilial high-status positions, and male dominance, while it may be somewhat subdued because of the male's 'visitor' status and the infrequency of male-female encounters, is unmistakably present in both the feelings of men and women and the expectations of the society.

The reader can no doubt already see the confusion that ensues when one uses the phrase 'status of women' to include two separate factors, rights and respect. Women receive great respect in certain matrilineal societies that give them few rights; the respect derives from the fact that they fill high-status roles that men are incapable of filling. There is nothing in the theory presented here that precludes the possibility that a society will give higher status to female roles that men are incapable of filling than to the roles occupied by males. Women receive equality of rights in some societies in which they compete with men and in which the female roles men are incapable of playing are given relatively *low* respect. In both societies female attainment of high-status, suprafamilial positions is insignificant, so which society gives women 'higher status'?

Were this the limit of the confusion engendered by the phrase 'status of women', the problem would be irrelevant to the universal institutions we discuss; we could merely suggest that those authors who are interested in the rights or the respect granted to women should discard the confusing phrase and specify the variable they wish to discuss. However, the problem is more serious than this. Some anthropologists acknowledge that there has never been a matriarchy, but, invoking variations of Engels's arguments, imply that there were once societies in which women's position was far higher than it has been in any of the thousands of societies that have existed since the dawn of history.[42]

It is not clear from these authors' writings exactly what they imagine prehistoric societies were like. If they only mean that they were like the matrilineal societies we have just discussed, then there is no necessary conflict between the theory presented here and their claims; for if we are willing to admit that such societies now exist, we lose nothing by admitting that they existed long ago as well. The problem derives from their implication, quite possibly unintentional, that these societies did not manifest male attainment of high-status, non-maternal roles and positions of male dominance. This is not only incorrect, but leaves the impression that matrilineal societies are somehow closer to the present-day feminist ideal than the modern industrial societies in which we live. A non-feminist woman might well prefer life in a matrilineal society, but such a society is a feminist's nightmare. A technological society that was matrilineal could not, in my view, develop for a number of reasons, but if one did exist and resembled 'prehistoric matrilineal societies' or contemporary matrilineal societies, it would differ most notably from our society in the total separation of male and female roles and prohibitions against women even entering the areas from which men derived their status, the impossibility of women's attaining status in any way but through maternal and lineage-related roles, and the lesser extent to which men would even think about women. It is true that male dominance would be somewhat diminished, but only to the extent that males were absent from the family setting. This would still be dominated by a male, though he might be the mother's brother. This might all be satisfactory for the woman who did not care that the society manifested

---

42. See Kathleen Gough, *op. cit.*, 107–118, and Eleanor Burke Leacock's introduction to Engels's *The Origin of the Family, Private Property, and the State* (New York: International Publishers, 1972), 7–67.

patriarchy, male attainment, and male dominance provided it gave her female roles high status, but it would be dreadful for the woman who sees women's value in terms of the suprafamilial high-status roles and positions that males attain.

The real lesson to be learned from societies that give women equality of rights and from those that give women great respect is twofold: 1. males attain the positions of authority and high status no matter what rights are given to women; 2. *a reduction of the status and respect given to roles which only a woman can fill forces women who desire status to compete in areas in which the males' greater motivation is a precondition for attainment, and reduces the respect given to them.* As we shall see, this means that a reduction of the status given to the roles which only a woman can fill changes the situation in which most women find themselves from one in which they cannot lose to one in which they cannot win.

In every stratum of every society the status of women is derived in part from the status accorded the roles only a woman can play and in part from the status of the husband or, in the few polyandrous societies, the primary husband.[43]

This is not to deny that in many societies there are individual women who attain status by virtue of sheer ability and accomplishment. Nor is it to deny the theoretical possibility that maternal roles only a woman can fill could be given higher status than any male role. It is simply to make the point that the rule in every society is that women derive their super-familial status from lineage or husband. In no society do many women attain high-status roles and positions by successfully competing with men.

There is, of course, much more variation within a society in male status and in the status derived by women from male status than there is in the status derived by women from the roles only women can fill (for example, a janitor's wife derives much lower status from her husband than does a doctor's wife, but as much status from the maternal role as does the doctor's wife). Thus a decrease in the status accorded the roles only a woman can fill will result in a situation in which: a. there will be a net loss of status accorded women; b. males will, for all the reasons we shall discuss, continue to be the attainers of status and positions of authority; c. the wives of such attainers (whose feminine abilities are primarily responsible for their attaining the marital positions from

---

43. I include in 'roles only a woman can play' both the high-status, lineage-determined roles for which males are at a physiological disadvantage—for example, high-status maternal roles in a matrilineal society—and lineage-determined roles for which there is no available male—such as the woman who becomes queen because there is no royal male.

which they derive high status) will continue to be the highest status females: d. other women will see their status lowered to the degree that the status accorded the roles only a woman can play is lowered.

In any case, numerous anthropologists, sociologists, psychologists, and even psychoanalysts have attempted to invoke cultural variation to reject the possibility of a physiological basis of the universal institutions under discussion. They are free to invoke cultural variation in order to refute a physiological explanation of institutions that *do* vary, and to argue that the theory proposed here is incorrect, which would mean that someday there could exist a society that failed to manifest one of the universal institutions. But if they attempt to invoke variation among societies that exist or have existed—or the real variation that exists at the superficial level of tasks performed—in order to counter the implications of an analysis based on the absence of variation found in the universal realities under discussion—then they are really ignoring the evidence. By focussing on patriarchy, male dominance, and male attainment of high-status suprafamilial roles and positions, three criteria that avoid the confusion engendered by vague and misleading paradigms like 'the status of women', we discover that there is not now, nor has there ever been, any variation large enough to cast the slightest doubt on the universality of these institutions or on the *possibility* that they represent three inevitable manifestations of psychophysiological sexual differentiation. This book is an attempt to discover why these three institutions are universal and to assess the possibility of their being inevitable.

Grounds for an Empirical Refutation

The theory that I shall present in the following chapters assumes three, and only three, universal realities: patriarchy, male attainment, and male dominance. The discovery or development of a single society that lacked one of these realities would be sufficient to refute the theory on two grounds.[44]

First, since the empirical reality that the theory attempts to explain is the *universality*, a single exceptional society would demonstrate that the claimed

---

44. As I explain a number of times in this book, this is a slight oversimplification, but one that is justified for the sake of comprehensibility; a society without hierarchy would not demonstrate the possibility of a society with hierarchies not dominated by males. This oversimplification is permissible because there are no known societies altogether lacking patriarchal hierarchy and those few, small societies with little hierarchy all exhibit an informal male dominance that is pretty much all that is required in such societies.

universality did not exist, in which case there would be nothing to explain. Second, the psychophysiological differentiation of males and females that the theory considers determinative is the same in every society, and therefore could not explain why the exceptional society lacked the institutions.

It is important to emphasize, however, that empirical refutation can result from the discovery or development *only* of *a society that lacks one of the three institutions we discuss here.* I stress this because a number of American critics invoked cultural variation in some *other* reality. Such an approach can never refute the theory presented here because I am perfectly willing to grant, for argument's sake, that there is variation in every other area and institution and that the universals discussed here are the only universals. For instance, *attitudes* vary tremendously from society to society and from era to era in a single society. Patriarchy and male dominance were valued by the American people a hundred years ago, while today many Americans dislike these empirical realities. But the critic cannot invoke variation in attitudes as evidence for the possibility of variation in the *realities* that are the objects of the attitudes. Indeed, the very fact that patriarchy and male dominance are as well represented in societies whose members dislike these institutions as in societies that value them indicates the irrelevance of attitudes.

Similarly, the critic cannot invoke societies in which women have special areas of autonomy or in which there is a reciprocity of male and female roles somewhat different from that found in our society; he cannot allude to historical development, or cite the fact that many *other* aspects of male and female roles (and many male and female tasks) are reversed in other societies.

No matter how peaceful or unassertive a society's values, it will manifest patriarchy, male attainment, and male dominance. Women have areas of autonomy in every society and in every society male and female roles are reciprocal; but in no society are women autonomous to the extent that the vast majority of women do not come under the authority of a husband or brother, and in no society does this fail to represent a reciprocity between males in whom authority is vested and females in whom it is not. (There are societies in which *laws* do not reflect this, but the expectations of the members of the society and the values of the society always do.) There are many societies in which women do tasks that are more strenuous and of objectively greater economic importance, many in which kinship and residence are determined through the female, and many in which the women are nominal owners of most of the property; but in none of these do men fail to attain the upper hierarchical positions, the high-status roles and tasks, or dominance and authority in male-female relationships. In no society, anywhere or at any time, have these realities been absent. It is the great variation in other areas and institutions that makes the universality of patriarchy, male attainment, and male dominance so astonishing, and it is this which the next three chapters attempt to explain.[45]

Because every society—even those primitive societies that are least hierarchical—clearly exhibits the institutions whose universality it is our purpose to explain, I stake the correctness of the theory on the absence of even a single societal exception (past, present, or future). I grant that a single societal exception—a single society clearly lacking patriarchy, male attainment, or male dominance—would serve to demonstrate the incorrectness of the theory.

This is the test of the most extensive version of the theory and, since the theory can pass this test, it is the test I have in mind as I write.

However, it is possible that my emphasis on absolute universality might divert attention from a more important issue: because even the most radical environmentalist does not argue that there is a modern exception to universality, attention is focussed on small, low-hierarchy primitive societies and environmentalist attempts to find an exception among primitive societies. While it is easy to demonstrate that even these societies are not exceptions, this demonstration draws our attention away from the (perhaps more important) issue of the inherent tendency of societies with extensive hierarchies to offer the cues and arenas, just discussed, for the male tendency to attain and dominate.

Perhaps many readers would find the book more interesting if I granted—incorrectly and for argument's sake alone—the possibility, or actual existence, of primitive societies that lacked patriarchy or male attainment because they lacked the hierarchy and role differentiation of the more-hierarchical society. This approach would simply grant, falsely: 1. the possibility of primitive societies without hierarchy and, therefore, without the cues to elicit the male behavior, and 2. the absence of an informal male dominance that would substitute for the lack of hierarchies when decisions were made for male-female groups. The theory in this weaker form would still state the conditions under which it could be shown to be incorrect (a society with considerable hierarchy

45. As we shall see in the Chapter 4 section entitled 'The Irrelevance of Exceptions', one cannot invoke as refutation *individuals* who are exceptions, for example, the woman who has an exceptionally strong dominance tendency. The theory proposed here is a theory of *societies*—it predicts that there could not be a non-patriarchal *society*—and it is only on this level that it is claimed to hold absolutely. The theory is statistical on the level of individuals; a refutory exception on this level is not the exceptional woman, or thousand women. An exception on this level would be a society in which there were as many women with strong dominance tendencies as men; such a society would be non-patriarchal, and the theory would therefore be refuted on both levels.)

and status differentiation that was not dominated by males). It would focus on the *inherently hierarchical* tendency of modern society and the resulting tendency of modern society to elicit male behavior and to give it an arena not present in those primitive societies that have low hierarchy. However, such a theory, while perhaps more relevant to the interests of many readers (few of whom are from primitive societies) would understate the ease with which the male tendencies are elicited and the impossibility of even a primitive society in which they are not manifested in institutions.

Let us consider, for example, the Waorani of Ecuador. (We could also consider the much-cited Mbuti in this connection.) The Waorani are a society of about 600 in which the males hunt and the females pursue agricultural activities. Popular accounts of the Waorani (including two books, a 'Nova' television show, an article in *Natural History,* and numerous newspaper articles) tend to imply a sexual equality, though even these accounts, when they give examples of leadership, show that such leadership is associated with males: "Kaempaede [a male] was, in short, the patriarch"[46] and "It is true that leadership does exist, but it is situational by nature. A man becomes a leader for a specific event, and when that event has passed, his cloak of leadership disappears."[47] This certainly sounds as if, to the extent that leadership is informal, male dominance fills in where the slightly-developed patriarchy leaves a void.

More telling is a paper given to a symposium on women's roles by the anthropologist who was consultant on one of the popular works and author of the others.[48] Despite the fact that the paper clearly presented its evidence in such a way as to make it most acceptable to its primarily feminist audience, it shows more clearly than do the popular works that the Waorani do not demonstrate sexual equality. It describes the Waorani as permitting polygyny; practicing infanticide, nearly always of females; allowing men to agree to exchange sisters; and requiring that a male be the head shaman ("the Jaguar father"). While the Waorani, like the Mbuti (whose small, isolated bands render extensive social structure as unnecessary as it is for the Waorani), may live within a less-formalized social structure than do the members of larger

---

46. John Man (James A. Yost, consultant), *Jungle Nomads of Ecuador: The Waorani* (Amsterdam: Time-Life Books, 1982), 65.

47. James A. Yost, 'People of the Forest: The Waorani', in *Ecuador Ediciones* (Libri Mundi, 1981), 109.

48. James A. Yost and C. Roderick Wilson, 'The New Amazons', paper delivered to symposium on 'Women's Roles in Traditional and Modernizing Societies', 78th Annual Meeting of the American Anthropological Association in Cincinnati, Ohio, November 27th–December 1st, 1979.

societies, it is clear that an informal male dominance prevails. In this respect, these societies can be interestingly compared to small, informal groups within a modern society, groups in which informal male dominance also prevails in a relative lack of formal hierarchy.

But let us for the moment ignore all this and pretend that the Waorani *do* exhibit a real sexual equality. What this would demonstrate is that, for groups so small that they represent not much more than a number of extended families, it is possible to form a society that can survive without formal hierarchy. This would *not* imply that any modern society—or, indeed, any society large enough to require hierarchical structure—could exhibit the same sort of sexual equality. For it is the hierarchy itself that elicits, much more strongly from males than from females, the behavior whose social resolution is patriarchy. In other words, even if it were true—which it is not—that some small, primitive societies maintained a sexual equality, this would not indicate that a large society, with the hierarchies it requires for social stability—could do so.[49]

---

49. Blumberg (*op. cit.*, 27) finds that "Once societies develop complex political economies and stratification systems extending beyond the community, these are dominated by men". As we have seen, Blumberg is incorrect in believing that the most simple of societies demonstrate an absence of male political and dyadic dominance. But even she acknowledges that increases in hierarchy and specialization increase the manifestations of male dominance and attainment tendencies (compared to those exhibited in the simple societies she discusses). Blumberg might disagree with my explanation of the increase as resulting from the complex society's stronger hierarchical pull on male physiology. But her empirical data are consistent with this explanation.

Chapter *III*

Differentiation of Dominance Tendency

The Need for a Simple Explanation

In the preceding chapter I have not attempted to explain anything, but merely to demonstrate an empirical fact:[1] that in every society that has ever existed one finds patriarchy (males fill the overwhelming percentage of upper hierarchical positions in political and other hierarchies), male attainment (males attain the high-status roles, whatever these may be in any given society), and male dominance (both males and females feel that dominance in male-female encounters and relationships resides in the male, and social expectations and authority systems reflect this). To discover why these realities are universal is the purpose of this book.

The answer must be simple, if by simple we mean parsimonious. I make this point because I am well aware that any explanation which sees physiology as the determining factor will automatically be criticized as simplistic or reductionist. To attempt to explain cultural *variation* by physiology (assuming there is no correlated physiological variation) *is* simplistic and reductionist (as it would be, for example, to try to explain the fact that the British political system is parliamentary rather than congressional by physiology). But if one is attempting, as I am, to offer a *sufficient* explanation of universality, of the limits to which all societies conform, rather than of differences and variations within those limits, then the explanation must be simple. The simplicity lies in the empirical reality we wish to explain, and our explanation must reflect that simplicity; a more complex explanation of universality would not be superior,

---

1. Some would prefer to term patriarchy in a given society an 'empirical fact' and to term the universality, the fact that every society is patriarchal, an 'empirical generalization' (a generalization of 'empirical facts'). The distinction is unimportant here.

but inelegant. Good sense forces one to reject an explanation of patriarchy that 'explains' patriarchy in the United States in terms of capitalism, in China in terms of socialism, in Watusi society in terms of the superiority that size gives to males in a hunting society, in Great Britain in terms of British historical tradition, and in thousands of other societies in hundreds of other terms. Such an explanation would be unacceptable even if we did not have one that possessed the desired simplicity, and that explained the fact that all societies are patriarchal in terms of one causal factor. (We shall examine possible alternative parsimonious explanations of universality—explanations that do not invoke physiological differentiation—at length later.)

Similarly, some critics have accused my theory of 'biological determinism'. If by this they mean that it is reductionist, this section will serve as a response to their criticism; if they do not mean that the theory is reductionist, then I would accept their assessment, but without seeing it as a criticism. Sometimes biological determinism is correct. A theory that predicted that because males are taller than females, the best basketball teams in every society will be comprised of males and that socialization will conform to this reality, and will increase the male-female difference in basketball ability, is 'biological determinism': it is also correct.

A Short Summary of the Theory Presented in This Book

Stated a bit loosely, this book attempts to demonstrate and explain the universality (the presence in every society that has ever existed) of three institutions: 1. patriarchy: males occupy the overwhelming numbers of upper hierarchical positions; 2. male attainment, the association of high-status roles—whichever they happen to be in any given society—with males; and 3. male dominance, the association of dominance in male-female encounters and relationships with the male, an association made in every society by the emotions of men and women and reflected in most societies in the formal authority system.)

It is argued that these institutions are manifestations of neuro-endocrinological differences between men and women. The neuro-endocrinological differences are such that the presence of hierarchy (any hierarchy), high-status role, or member of the other sex elicits from the male, more readily, more often, and more strongly than from the female: 1. emotions of 'competitiveness', the tendency—the impulse—for attainment and dominance (whether this tendency, this impulse, is termed a 'need' or a 'drive'); 2.

relative suppression of other emotions and needs and a sacrifice of rewards (health, family, relaxation, and so forth) that compete with the need for attainment and dominance; and 3. actions required for attainment of position, status, and dominance. The specific actions required by a given society are socially determined; it is the tendency towards attainment and dominance—the tendency to choose and to learn the actions leading to attainment and dominance, whatever they be in any given society—that is rooted in physiology.

The theory presented is a theory of *society* and it is from this level that any promising counter-example would have to be taken. On the level of individuals all psychophysiological factors are statistical. Thus, a society with women sharing equally the hierarchical positions of power would refute the theory, but the occasional female prime minister or senator would not.

The theory does not deny the role of socialization, but it does hold that socialization is a dependent variable that is given its limits and direction by the independent variable of the physiological difference between men and women. It sees social expectation and socialization as conforming to a population's observation of differences between male and female behavior, differences engendered by male and female physiology. This explains *why* socialization never acts as counterpoise to physiology (why no society sees females as more aggressive than males) where an explanation seeing socialization as the independent variable merely begs the question: Why is it always the *male* who is seen as dominant and is socialized to the specific ways dominance is attained and maintained in his society?

Non-physiological theories of the empirical universalities will be considered and found to be refutable with the empirical ethnographic evidence, demonstrably internally illogical, or implausible in the extreme. Moreover, all such environmental explanations of universality simply ignore a wealth of direct neuro-endocrinological evidence.

The Differentiation of Dominance Tendency

In the first edition of this book I referred to the male tendency to attain and dominate as "aggression". I had in mind the use of 'aggression' as in 'He's an aggressive businessman who will get to the top.' I think that this use of the word illustrates that the general population observes the importance of dominance tendency to attainment of position and status.

Unfortunately, many readers interpreted 'aggression' as necessarily implying physical aggression or, yet more confusing, as implying territoriality, male bonding, or killer instincts (concepts that, as we shall see, have nothing to do with the theory presented here). I now avoid this confusion by employing the term 'dominance tendency'; this chapter is devoted to defining the term and to describing some of the behaviour in which the tendency is manifested.

Physical aggression is not irrelevant to what we discuss here. Let us consider that in situations in which physical aggression can be invoked (whether by human beings or in other mammalian species) the important psychophysiological element is not the physical aggression *per se,* but the tendency, the 'motivation', that moves the individual to use physical aggression. Physical aggression is merely the *means* to an end, a means that will not be used if it can be avoided. This point is missed by those who acknowledge that male physiology is such that males are more easily moved to physical aggression, but who argue that this is irrelevant when physical aggression is prohibited. For even when the means is no longer permitted, the end is still attainable. In other words, if the male tendency towards dominance is greater, males will tend more strongly to invoke physical aggression in the pursuit of dominance if physical aggression is an option; if physical aggression is not an option, males will tend more strongly to behave in whatever ways are permitted that lead to dominance.

In this edition I substitute the term 'dominance tendency' for 'aggression' and discuss, to a greater extent than I did in the first edition, the actions in which dominance tendency is manifested. (In the first edition I relied on the correlation between male physiology and patriarchy and used 'aggression', meaning 'dominance tendency', as a more or less undefined nexus term.) In the rest of this section I discuss certain theoretical issues concerning the term.

The casual reader will miss little if he skips the rest of this section. If he thinks of 'dominance tendency' as 'competitiveness', he will be able to grasp all that is substantive in the theory while missing only a bit of conceptual discussion. If he thinks of the greater male competitiveness as being rooted in male physiology, cued by competitive situations, and manifested in the emotions and actions associated with competitiveness he will have no difficulty in following the rest of the book, and may now wish to turn to the beginning of the next section, on page 70.

I prefer the term 'dominance tendency' to describe the emotional-behavioral differentiation that results from physiological differentiation and is responsible for patriarchy, male attainment and male dominance. It avoids problems of tautologicality, vitalism, and teleologicality inherent in the terms 'motivation' and 'need', and a host of other problems that will probably occur to the philosopher, but that can be avoided with only stylistic difficulty by speaking of the male's 'greater tendency for hierarchical and dyadic dominance'. The reader will note that I occasionally use the term 'motivation' to avoid stylistic infelicity; those bothered by this term should note that the unobjectionable paradigms of 'tendency' or 'threshold' can always be substituted. One may substitute other terms and may conceptualize the emotional-behavioral differentiation in terms of another paradigm without affecting the argument being presented here. There are theoretical differences between the paradigms listed below, and certain logical difficulties with some of them, but these are irrelevant for our purposes.

One can conceptualize the 'male's greater dominance tendency' as: a. a lower male *threshold* for the release of dominance behaviour; b. a greater male *need* for dominance (or a male *hierarchy of needs* in which the need for dominance ranks higher than the need for dominance ranks in the female hierarchy of needs); c. a greater male *drive* towards dominance; d. a greater male *readiness to learn* (or propensity for learning) dominance behaviour; e. a stronger (or more easily released) male *status need* (or status drive); f. a *weaker* male *ego* (which needs shoring up through dominance more than does the stronger female ego); g. a stronger male *tendency for responding* to dominance-eliciting *environmental stimuli;* h. a greater male *aggression;* i. a male *aggression* that is more *active* than the female's quantitatively equal, but *passive aggression;* j. a stronger male *competitiveness* (this is probably the most suitable everyday word for the tendency that is differentiated); k. a stronger male *motivation* for dominance.

All that matters for our purposes is that whichever paradigm one favors will recognize that a male-female differentiation of tendency exists (it cannot fail to do so because this is the empirical reality which it is there to explain) *and that this differentiation of tendency is rooted in neuro-endocrinological differentiation.* Perhaps the reader will see the point being made here most clearly if he considers the analogy of the tendency that we loosely describe as the 'sex drive'. Is this a 'drive' or a 'need'? While the word chosen may well affect our *attitude* ('drive' seems more powerful, 'need' more vulnerable) they are simply different ways of saying precisely the same thing.

Devra Davis and a number of other critics[2] mistakenly believe that the fact that we can view the psychophysiological differences between males and females as a difference in 'drive', 'need', 'tendency', 'aggression', 'dominance', 'ego strength', 'threshold', and so forth renders the formulation somehow

2. *Dissent,* Summer, 1975.

unscientific. Their error is a confusion between a ubiquity of predictiveness (which *would* render a hypothesis unscientific by virtue of untestability-in-principle) and a ubiquity of terminology that can be employed in testing the hypothesis. We have discussed the ways in which the theory can be shown to be incorrect if it is incorrect. If the theory I present is incorrect, then it can be shown to be incorrect in any of the terms mentioned. If it is not incorrect, then it cannot be shown to be incorrect in any of the terms mentioned. All that matters for purposes of testability of the theory presented here is a male-female difference; whether one wishes to call this a difference in 'drive', 'need', 'aggression', or anything else is, for our purposes, irrelevant. (The choice of model and terminology may matter in other contexts, but that need not concern us here—especially since we are willing to let the *critic* select any of these terms and then to demonstrate the sex difference in the terms selected.)

Whatever the terminology used, the important point, and the central argument presented in this book, is that differences in the male and female neuro-endocrinological systems are such that the environmental stimulus of hierarchy, status, or a member of the other sex elicits from the male a stronger tendency to give up whatever must be given up—time, pleasure, health, physical safety, affection, relaxation—for the attainment of a higher hierarchical position, for a social role which is rewarded by greater status, and for dominance in male-female relationships. This differentiation of tendency, and a population's observation of the behavioral differentiation through which it is manifested, is the 'causal' connection between physiological differentiation on the one hand, and differentiation in the social values, socialization, and institutions we wish to explain on the other. (We shall discuss the role of 'feedback' and the role of socialization in increasing the differentiation of dominance tendency later; here my point is merely that the differentiation of tendency is primarily a result of neuro-endocrinological differentiation, and that, together with a population's observation of the behavioral differentiation through which it is manifested, it is the primary 'cause' of the differentiation in social values, socialization, and institutions.)

Feminists do not deny that dominance tendency determines attainment and dominance, or that males exhibit it far more strongly and more often. Feminist writings document extensively the greater male dominance tendency, sometimes incorrectly explaining it in terms of socialization. We shall discuss the difficulties they run into later; here we need merely note that there is no disagreement over its existence but only over the explanation for it.

When I say that differences between male and female physiology are such that the presence of hierarchy, status, or a member of the other sex tends to elicit dominance behaviour more strongly from the male than from the female, I am saying that—to use a less accurate but more common terminology— males are more strongly 'motivated' to exhibit whatever behaviour is necessary to achieve position, status, or dominance. I am not saying that the specific action is determined by physiology, only that the 'motivation' is. The voice of our hormones is expressed in feeling, and such emotions are not primarily learned. But the language in which the voice speaks—the actions that satisfy the feelings—must be learned. Thus, if fighting ability is a necessary condition for hierarchical attainment, males will be more strongly 'motivated' to develop their fighting ability; if it is looked down upon, but co-operation is given high value, then they will be more strongly 'motivated' to at least *seem* more co-operative. There is tremendous cross-cultural and historical variation in the qualities and behaviors which societies expect from their leaders, but whatever they may be they will be more often exhibited by males, since males are more strongly 'motivated' towards the dominance that perfection of that quality makes possible. Males feel more strongly the 'need' for dominance—and will more often give up other day-to-day sources of satisfaction in order to attain it—because, as we shall see in the next chapter, they are built that way. Modern males do not manifest the behavior necessary for becoming leading politicians any less strongly or less often than the males of primitive societies manifest that which is necessary for becoming members of the tribal council; the specific behavior changes, but male physiology and male 'need' do not.

The theory I present here predicts that in every society it will be males who, far more strongly and more often than females, exhibit whatever behaviour— fighting, kissing babies for votes, or whatever—is necessary for hierarchical attainment; it could be falsified by the discovery or development of a single hierarchical society in which the upper positions in the hierarchy are not overwhelmingly occupied by males. It is not possible to predict what the necessary behavior will be in any given society, because this will be determined by social factors: but whatever it may be, it will be manifested by males.

However, I do not think that, in practice, we need remain so general. We can go a long way towards specifying the behavior by noticing, as have virtually all observers of political behaviour, that the most important element in hierarchical success is dominance tendency, and that there are certain actions that always represent the tendency and that virtually always facilitate hierarchical attainment, *whether the actions are in themselves positively sanctioned by the society or not.* Thus, long hours devoted to developing political skills, 'staying late at the office', attaching greater importance to success than to virtue, and similar manifestations of hierarchical dominance tendency will nearly always facilitate hierarchical attainment, even if the society finds such behavior too 'aggressive' in the abstract—which merely leads the individual with a strong dominance tendency to camouflage his behavior and appear to exhibit whatever behavior is considered desirable and virtuous. 'Dominance tendency' *means* the willingness to give up the objectives of other tendencies, to endure pain, frustration, tension, and defeat to satisfy a strong 'need' to attain position. The upper hierarchical positions (and here I do not just mean politicians, but executives of even small companies) are relatively few in number and are occupied by those most willing to give up other satisfactions in order to attain them. Attainment of such positions demands a 'motivation' possessed only by the small minority of people who have the strongest dominance tendency. This minority, like the minority of people who are six feet tall, will be composed primarily of men.

What is important here—and is a function of physiological differentiation —is not just the behavior, but also the environment that is capable of eliciting it, of 'motivating' the individual. One might well argue that a woman whose child is endangered will be as strongly 'motivated' to do whatever is necessary to protect her child as the male is to attain hierarchical position; as we shall see in the 'analogy' below, environment is intimately involved with physiology in generating the tendency. However, it should be clear that 'environment' does not mean mere socialization. The presence of *any* hierarchy is sufficient to elicit dominance 'motivation' and the resulting behavior (whatever the social values relevant to hierarchical dominance), just as any threat to the child is sufficient to elicit protective 'motivation' and its resulting behavior (whatever the social values relevant to protective behavior). That males are more strongly 'motivated' than females by hierarchy and females are (I assume, but do not argue here; see 6 below) more strongly motivated than males by a threat to the child results from differences in male and female physiology.

Seven Claims That Are Neither Assumed Nor Implied

The theory of the differentiation of dominance tendency does not imply the correctness of any of the following hypotheses. Some of these may well be correct, but it is irrelevant for the theory whether they are or not.

1. The theory does not imply that males *perform* better than females in the positions and roles they attain. It is argued that male physiology is such that males are more strongly 'motivated' to become, say, politicians, and are

therefore more likely to make the necessary sacrifices; it is not implied that males make better politicians than females (though, of course, one cannot be a good or a bad politician until one has become one). One might argue that the dominance tendency relevant to attainment is valuable in performing a leadership role, but that argument is not made here; one might, on the other hand, argue that the weakness of dominance tendency which precludes large numbers of women from attaining upper hierarchical positions would make women better leaders, but that argument is not made here either. (I will suggest, in an argument which is separate from the theory of patriarchy proper, that certain cognitive differences between males and females are rooted in physiological differences, and that this implies that—statistically speaking— each sex may be expected to perform certain roles better than the other, but this need not concern us here.)

2. The theory does not imply that women who *do* attain hierarchical position have a weaker dominance motivation than men who attain equivalent positions. The female politician is just as strongly motivated as her male equivalent, just as the six-foot-tall woman is as tall as the six-foot-tall man. The statistical theory presented here argues only that male physiology makes it more often males who are 'motivated' sufficiently to attain the position, just as male physiology is responsible for the fact that most six-footers are male. Thus, there is no implication that Golda Meir differed in any relevant way from any male leader.

3. Nor, as we shall see in the section on exceptions, is there any implication that Golda Meir differed physiologically from other women[3] (there are many non-physiological factors that increase dominance motivation in exceptional cases). It is implied only that Golda Meir is, like the woman who is six feet tall, much more of an exception for her sex than the male leader is for his, and that this is based on physiological differences between the sexes.

4. The theory does not imply that a strong dominance 'motivation' is *sufficient* for hierarchical attainment, only that it is *necessary* (or, more precisely, that it is a strong facilitator). Clearly, there are always other necessary

---

3. However, neither is it implied that female leaders do *not* differ physiologically from most women. I happen to believe that CNS-hormonal differences between men are important to differences in dominance tendency between men and that CNS-hormonal differences between women are important to differences in dominance tendency between women. However, nothing in the theory presented here requires that this be the case. Only *between-sex* physiological differences are relevant to the *between-sex* differences in dominance tendency. One may, for our purposes, assume that the small, *within*-sex variation in neuro-endocrinology is unimportant in people not suffering neuro-endocrinological pathologies.

conditions. No black man, in the days of *apartheid,* could become prime minister of South Africa. No illiterate is likely to become president of General Motors. But someone who lacks motivation for attaining hierarchical positions is as unlikely to occupy them as a five-footer is to make a professional basketball team (whatever his other qualities). Thus, there are many societies in which only four or five percent of the population meet the various hereditary, economic, or social necessary conditions, but within this group strong dominance motivation is necessary for hierarchical attainment.

5. The theory does not imply that there are tendencies which are found only in the members of one sex, or that there is any quality which is more represented in the member of one sex who exhibits it the least than in the member of the other sex who exhibits it the most. Clearly, just as there are many women who are taller than many men, there are many women for whom hierarchy elicits a stronger dominance tendency than it does from many men, and many men from whom the child in distress elicits a stronger protective tendency than it does from many women. We shall discuss this at length in the section on exceptions; here I wish merely to emphasize that throughout we are discussing the *statistical* differences between men and women, manifested in the social realities whose explanation is the purpose of this book.

6. The theory does not imply that women have a stronger, physiologically-rooted nurturant tendency than men, though I cannot imagine that anyone now seriously doubts that this is the case. I refrain from implying this because it need not be so for the theory presented here to be correct (the male's greater dominance tendency is sufficient to explain patriarchy, male attainment, and male dominance). Clearly, however, the presence of such a female tendency complements the male dominance tendency and increases the hierarchical discrepancy: if a woman is more strongly 'motivated' to respond to her infant, she is that much less 'motivated' to satisfy her 'need for dominance'.

7. Similarly, the theory does not imply that there is any physiologically-rooted female tendency to prefer male dominance, though observation (rather than ideological claims) would lead one to believe that this may be the case. There is, after all, a general belief that women prefer 'dominant' men, which some feminists decry and try to explain in terms of socialization. Again one can accept this feminist observation without accepting its 'explanation', and again I would emphasize that I need not assume a female tendency of this sort; its presence would complement male dominance and increase the differentiation of the sexes, but it is irrelevant whether or not such a factor exists (either with

reference to dyadic relationships, which seems likely, or male hierarchical attainment, which seems less likely).

The Iron and Magnet Analogy

There is a tendency for contemporary readers to picture physiologically-rooted psychological tendencies (be they the dominance tendency that interests us, the 'sex drive', or whatever) in terms of a hydraulic analogy. This analogy, which depicts an internal reservoir of anger, or aggression, or sexuality 'pouring out', with various factors affecting the size of the reservoir and the strength of the flow, is satisfactory for many purposes—often because memory 'internalizes environment' (as when fantasy generates sexual arousal), so that one may proceed as if environment played no initiative role—but is less than accurate when considering the differentiation of dominance tendency. I suggest that the reader would do better to think of the inherent attraction of iron to a magnet. Iron does not have an inherent 'need' or 'drive' to find a magnet, but the tendency to respond to a magnet is inherent in its physical make-up. The analogy is an appropriate one, at least as far as tendencies towards hierarchical dominance and high-status roles are concerned. The analogy accepts the crucial role of environment (the magnet in the analogy and the hierarchy or high-status role in the reality we wish to explain) without confusing the necessary environmental stimulus-cue with mere socialization (*any* hierarchy or high-status role is sufficient 'environment' to cue the physiologically-rooted tendency and give it play) and without implying that the tendency devolves from environment—the dominance tendency needs a stimulus, but it is physiology that determines that one reacts with dominance tendency rather than, say, thirst.[4]

---

4. This analogy is helpful in many other contexts. For example, one might depict the decreasing age of menarche in American girls in these terms and see the earlier sexual environment encountered by contemporary girls as cueing the earlier onset of menstruation. The psychoanalyst may object that this analogy does not represent the situation—often encountered by him—in which a neurosis-producing environment produces an individual for whom an environmental stimulus cues an inappropriate tendency (for example, the individual who responds with fear when most would respond with sexual arousal). These statistically unusual cases are not crucial here. By depicting the male as iron and the female as nickel, a substance that is usually less magnetic than iron, but which can be made more magnetic under certain conditions, we have a good, though not perfect, analogy for the differentiation of dominance behavior, a differentiation that is statistical, rather than absolute—in other words, the tendency is stronger in most males than in most females, but there are some females with a stronger dominance tendency than some males.

First Digression: The 'Non-Patriarchal Society' as Refutation

The reader may remember that I described my statement that the theory could be refuted by the discovery or development of a single non-patriarchal society as 'an oversimplification, but one which the universality of patriarchy permits'. It should now be clear why the qualification was necessary. The analogy we have just examined makes it clear that every physiologically-rooted psychological tendency, every 'motivation' of the type we discuss, *requires an environmental cue and an environment in which the cued behaviour can be manifested.*[5]

One might argue for the possibility of a society that lacked hierarchies altogether and therefore lacked the environmental cue and the environmental arena necessary for patriarchy. I have tried to show that no such society has ever existed and I shall argue that—because every society must have a value system of some sort, and because any value system entails some sort of hierarchy, some individuals exhibiting the valued qualities and behaviour more than others—no such society could exist. However, it is necessary to make the point that, while any society in which there *was* a significant amount of hierarchy and in which males did not attain the overwhelming number of upper positions in that hierarchy *would* refute the theory presented here, a non-hierarchical society would not be sufficient for refutation. (As explained earlier, it *would* refute the claim of universality. The point here is that it *would not* refute the theory of differentiation of dominance tendency.) This is because the non-hierarchical society, the society that lacked the necessary environmental cue and arena, would not be sufficient to demonstrate the possibility of a society that did have hierarchy, but whose hierarchy was not patriarchal. *Once there is hierarchy, the hierarchy will cue dominance tendencies more strongly in the male.* But, again, there has never been any non-hierarchical society and there is, as we shall see, strong theoretical reason to believe that there never could be one. (If we think of the hierarchical dominance tendency as 'competitiveness', we see that this is recognized even in everyday language. When we refer to a person as 'competitive' we do not necessarily mean that he searches out competitive situations or attempts to create them where they do not exist, but that a competitive environmental situation cues this individual's 'motivation' to attain or to win more strongly than that of a less competitive individual.)

Moreover, the modern societies in which virtually all human beings will live

---

5. Remembering that, as in the case of sexual arousal, memory, and fantasy based on memory, can serve as 'internalized environment' and cue the tendency.

for the foreseeable future are virtually *defined* by the extensiveness of their hierarchies. One might well argue that modern societies—with their extensive hierarchies, extensive specialization, extensive division of labor, and status that is achieved rather than ascribed—must be more 'masculine' than some primitive societies which limit hierarchy—and the environmental stimulus it represents—to an extent that is not possible in modern society.[6] This argument is difficult to carry further in the context of this book, since every primitive society has sufficient hierarchy to cue the male tendency and result in patriarchy. We shall consider this somewhat further in our discussion of the Mbuti; here I will end by emphasizing that the 'environment' of which we speak is not mere social values or socialization, but the very presence of hierarchy (*any* hierarchy). *The environment that is necessary for patriarchy is inherent in society itself.*

---

6. As we shall see in the Chapter 5 section entitled 'The Limits of Possibility', I am not suggesting that no primitive or non-modern society has extensive hierarchy, only that it is possible for a primitive society to have far less hierarchy than a modern society, whose social and economic system requires extensive hierarchy.

Chapter *IV*

Physiological Differentiation

Introductory Note

This chapter is not, by any stretch of the imagination, meant to be a definitive discussion of the physiology of sexual differentiation of dominance behavior. Even were I qualified to undertake such a task, the volume of evidence which demonstrates how sexual neuro-endocrinological differentiation determines the sexual differentiation of dominance tendency would preclude the possibility of full discussion here. The purpose of this chapter is merely to show that there is overwhelming evidence for the physiological basis of the differentiation of dominance tendency that the anthropological evidence would force us to postulate even if there were no direct physiological evidence. While I have made every effort to make this chapter completely accurate, there is little that is original in it; if this book makes an original contribution, it is in its discussion of the logical and theoretical aspects of the role of physiology in setting limits on social life, and not in its discussion of physiology *per se*.

Two semantic points are worth stressing. 1. Throughout this chapter and this book, the word 'physiology', as well as the occasionally-used 'biology', refers to the neuro-endocrinological differentiation relevant to dominance tendency, and not to anatomy, physical size, or reproductive system. 2. The word 'environment' refers to social and economic environment and to socialization; it does not refer to unusual fetal environments that affect physiology in gross and direct ways. These kinds of 'environment' are important in rare cases, and they are often most helpful in increasing our understanding of physiological differentiation, but they are unimportant to an explanation of a sexual differentiation that is found in every society. Thus, it has been shown that an exceptionally fraught environment can affect a pregnant rat in such a way that her female offspring are physiologically masculinized and exhibit the dominance behavior of a male. But, clearly, no one would suggest that the male's greater dominance tendency is attributable primarily to maternal shock.

Needless to say, I could not possibly have prepared this chapter without the advice of biochemists, biologists, endocrinologists, and psychologists who are too numerous to mention. I am particularly grateful, however, to Drs Frank Beach and David Edwards of the University of California, Bruce McEwen and David Blizard of Rockefeller University, John Money of Johns Hopkins University, and Geoffrey Raisman of Oxford University. If there are any errors in this chapter, they are, of course, mine.

The Meaning of the Physiological Evidence

I have suggested that the anthropological evidence forces us to claim that the sexual differentiation of dominance tendency is of central importance to an explanation of the universality of patriarchy, male attainment, and male dominance; and that both logic and anthropological evidence would seem to suggest very strongly indeed that sexual neuro-endocrinological differentiation is of central importance to the differentiation of dominance tendency itself *even if we had no direct neuro-endocrinological evidence whatsoever*. In this chapter I will suggest that we need not posit the importance of neuro-endocrinological evidence on hypothetical grounds alone. There is an enormous amount of evidence which demonstrates beyond doubt that the testicularly-generated fetal hormonalization of the male central nervous system promotes earlier and more extensive maturation of the brain structures that mediate between male hormones and dominance behavior; this makes the male hypersensitive to the presence later on of the hormones which energize dominance emotions and behavior, and result in his stronger tendency to respond to the environment with dominance behavior. *This is the only physiological difference between the sexes the existence of which is necessary in order for the theory presented in this book to be correct.*[1] (Once again, those who object to such terms as 'energize' and 'emotions' can easily translate what is being said here into the terms of the paradigm they prefer.)

---

1. Because I am looking for a *sufficient* explanation of the universality of patriarchy, male attainment, and male dominance (see the first section of Chapter 3), I ignore the role of female physiology—both that which leads the female to favor other tendencies over dominance tendency and that which, if such exists, leads the female to favor and select dominant males. The male physiological tendency towards dominance would be sufficient to explain the universality even if women differed physiologically from men *only* in the physiological underpinnings of dominance tendency. To the extent that the many unique aspects of female physiology do, in fact, complement male physiology and contribute to the institutions discussed here, the argument presented here is that much stronger. But a sufficient explanation can assume that there is no such female physiological contribution.

Before we discuss the physiological evidence, it is necessary to make clear what we are *not* discussing. We are not discussing any sort of 'territoriality' or 'male bonding'. We will examine these concepts in the second 'digression'; here I merely want to emphasize that it would not matter to the theory presented here if there were no reality corresponding to these terms. Likewise, there is no implication that there are any human 'instincts' (a term that is inadequate for a number of reasons), let alone an 'aggressive instinct' or 'killer instinct'; we are only discussing the hierarchical and dyadic dominance tendency.

I am not making an evolutionary or functional argument nor am I trying to explain *why* men and women have evolved the way they have, or what functions the mammalian differentiation of dominance tendency has served. Such evolutionary analyses are fascinating and important, but they are, by their nature, far more speculative than is necessary here. Nor am I presenting one of the equally interesting analyses—usually referred to as sociobiology—that *postulate* exceedingly complex and as yet undiscovered genetic and physiological underpinnings of behavior. Here I am discussing only the directly specifiable, observable, and describable neuro-endocrinological differences between the sexes and the behavioral tendencies (the emotions and 'motivations') which these neuro-endocrinological differences can be shown to engender. I am in no way implying that there is some law of nature which requires that the males of a species should dominate. Each species' physiology develops in concordance with its environment. The association of dominance tendencies with the male serves obvious survival functions for mammalian species; one male can impregnate a thousand females, so males are far more expendable (each female lost means a loss of offspring). But while it is true in all primates which even vaguely resemble man, probably in all other primates, and in virtually all other mammalian species that male behavior is analogous to that found in man (we shall discuss possible exceptions below), it would make no difference to the line of reasoning used in this book if the females of all non-human species exhibited behavior analogous to dominance behaviour. There is no reason to dismiss the possibility that unusual evolutionary environmental conditions could engender in even a mammalian species a physiological differentiation which led to the female having a stronger dominance tendency. Certainly there are a number of non-mammalian species in which females exhibit what would be male behavior in mammalian species, and *vice versa*. We should no more expect this to have any bearing on the effects of human physiology on human tendency and behavior than we would expect men to fly because birds have wings. Human physiology is what is relevant to patriarchy. When I invoke non-human evidence it always (with the one exception noted below) concerns *direct* neuro-endocrinological alteration of mammals whose neuro-endocrinological systems are similar to ours.

I do not, therefore, use any ethological evidence (evidence derived from the study of non-human animals in their natural environments); although it strongly supports my theory, such evidence is not necessary for it and—since it invariably elicits the objection that it represents unwarranted anthropomorphism—is ignored here. Similarly, I ignore both the powerful evidence of controlled, non-neuro-endocrinological studies of primates[2] and well-documented studies which demonstrate the feminizing effects of castration on human and non-human primates and other mammals.

It is understandable that many sociologists should abhor any explanation of behavior which invokes physiology. This is not merely because some sociologists feel that they have a vested interest in purely social explanations, but is attributable to the host of inadequate and teleological evolutionary analogies with which the history of sociological theory is replete, and even more so to the horrors of slavery and Naziism, both of which made use of bogus biological evidence in the service of fallacious arguments. To these sociologists I would repeat that: 1. Such arguments are almost always of the 'evolutionary analogy' rather than 'direct physiological' type; 2. No scientific analysis of empirical relationships can ever entail a social policy (what *is* cannot entail what *should* be); 3. No scientific argument can be refuted on the basis of the uses to which it is put, but only on logical and empirical grounds. The biological arguments of Nazis and slave-owners were not *incorrect* because they were put to horrendous uses, but because they failed on logical and empirical grounds; moreover, the argument that slavery is inevitable for some physiological reason is easily refuted by demonstrating that most societies do not have slavery; 4. To deny the correctness of one physiologically-rooted theory because another is faulty is as silly as denying the validity of a scientific argument on social or moral grounds. Some physiologically-rooted theories are correct and others are not. To reject them all because some have been incorrect is to put oneself in the position of

---

2. For example, Harry F. Harlow and Stephen J. Suomi have demonstrated that monkeys reared in isolation will, when brought together, exhibit the play behavior expected of normal monkeys; male play behavior is far more aggressive than female play behavior (as is the case with human children). Since the monkeys were reared in isolation they could not have learned this mode of behavior from other monkeys. The indication is very strong that the aggressive play is a behavioral manifestation of innate male aggression. See Harry Harlow and Stephen J. Suomi, 'Social Recovery by Isolation-Reared Monkeys', *Proceedings of the National Academy of Science*, 68 (July 1971), 1534–38.

denying that infant physiology has something to do with the fact that no society expects leadership from its one-year-olds. It is as absurd to dismiss all physiologically-rooted social theories because some have been false and misused as it would be absurd to dismiss all environmental theories because Stalin's theories were false and misused.

Human Hermaphrodites

It should not be necessary to say that there have not been planned experiments in which hormones of the other sex have been introduced into normal human embryos or fetuses; such experimentation would not be ethical. However, accident has provided the researcher in this area with the hermaphrodite. Ironically, until a very few years ago hermaphrodites provided the strongest argument for the totally environmental theory of sex-role development; for there is a type of hermaphrodite who is genetically male, but who is born without external male genitalia. Such hermaphrodites are often raised as girls and develop into normal, though infertile, women. This seemed strong evidence indeed that physiology is unimportant to the development of sexual temperament and behavior. However, research in the past few years, particularly that of Dr John Money of Johns Hopkins University, has demonstrated beyond question that such hermaphrodites do not merely lack male genitals; they also never received the hormonal stimulation of the brain by the male hormone, which all normal males receive fetally and again in puberty. The masculinization of the fetal brain is programmed by the testes (which develop on instruction from an XY chromosomal program). If a mistake causes a break in the chain so that fetal testes do not develop, as is the case with the genetic male hermaphrodites who lack external male genitals, there will be no masculinization of the brain (no generation of testosterone, the 'male' hormone) and it will be possible to raise the genetic male as a female. However, when the 'break in the chain' comes after fetal hormonal masculinization, but before the period when the external genitals should develop, the individual becomes one who tends to exhibit the male behavior we discuss in this book. This indicates the determiniveness of the fetal hormonal masculinization even when anatomy and socialization are female.

So many authors have misunderstood this aspect of Dr Money's work, and have misrepresented it as demonstrating the entirely social etiology of dominance tendency, that it is necessary to demonstrate at some length that Dr Money's work cannot be legitimately interpreted as demonstrating this, and that to the extent that Dr Money's work casts light on dominance tendency, it indicates that the male-female differentiation of dominance tendency is rooted in neuro-endocrinological differentiation.

The crucial empirical relationship that is at the heart of the theory advanced in this book is the relationship between male hormonalization and the stronger and more easily released male dominance tendency. For the vast majority of people, of course, hormonalization is mirrored by anatomy, gender self-conception, and gender social identification. But it is the male hormonalization that is primarily responsible for the greater male dominance tendency. Even if it were possible (and ethical) to get an experimental group of normal males, ignore their anatomy and raise them as females, those males, who, unlike the hermaphrodites, have had a normal hormonal development, would exhibit male behaviour (at least with reference to the dominance behaviour that concerns us). This is because—as the evidence we shall discuss demonstrates conclusively—dominance tendency is primarily a result of hormonal development and not primarily of anatomy, gender identity, or the socialization that reflects anatomy and gender identity. The experimental individuals might well perceive themselves as *females* who had dominance tendencies that were unusually strong for females, but this need not concern us here; it is the dominance tendency that is relevant here.

We are not concerned with *gender identity*—the conception of oneself as male or female. It is the confusion of gender identity with dominance tendency that has led to misunderstanding. *For the theory presented here it would not matter if gender identity had a purely social cause.* An analogy should make this clear: if one argues that male hormonalization plays a crucial role in muscular development—as I argue that male hormonalization plays a crucial role in the development of dominance tendency—one makes no claim about gender identity; whether or not the chromosomal female who undergoes fetal and pubertal hormonal masculinization sees herself as a male or as a muscular female is irrelevant to the argument. It is the muscular development that is relevant to that analysis, just as it is dominance tendency that is relevant to ours. As we shall see, gender identification does play an important secondary role in that it increases sexual differentiation; male identification makes it more likely that an individual will lift weights, and less likely that he will suppress dominance tendency. But the association of greater muscular strength and greater dominance tendency with males, and the direction of male and female socialization, are determined by physiological differentiation.

If one *includes* dominance tendency in gender role/gender identity, then one *cannot*—and Dr Money *does not*—conclude that gender role/gender identity has purely social causes. At least with respect to the sexual differentiation of dominance tendency and the behaviour that reflects it—which is all that concerns us in this book—one must conclude that neuro-endocrinological differentiation plays a crucial role. Dr Money writes:

Gender identity in adulthood is the end product not of an either-or determinism of heredity versus environment, but of the genetic code in serial interaction with environment. From the time of conception, the genetic code unfolds itself in interaction, first with the intra-uterine environment, then the perinatal environment, the family environment, and eventually the more extended social, biological, and inanimate ecological environment. Interactionism is a key principle, but an even more basic key is the principle of serial sequence of interaction.

Serial interactionism means that interaction between the genetic code and its environment, at a critical or sensitive developmental period in an individual's existence, from conception to death, may leave a permanent, ineradicable residue upon which all else is subsequently built. This residue may be so indelible or insistent in its influence as to resemble the potency of the genetic code itself. Moreover, such indelibility or insistence may be residual to what has traditionally been referred to as learning—in which case learning should be referred to as imprinting, in recognition of the persistence and durability of its influence.[3]

The sequence begins with the dimorphism of the genetic code as manifested in the XX and XY chromosomal dimorphism. From the genetic-code, sexual dimorphism is translated into the dimorphism of embryonic differentiation of the gonads, which, through their hormonal secretion, in turn differentially regulate the dimorphism of first the internal reproductive structures and then the external genitalia. At the same time in embryonic life, gonadal secretion dimorphically regulates the differentiation of structures in the brain, specifically the hypothalamus, that in turn will regulate the sex-related functioning of the pituitary. In all probability gonadal secretion at this same time also dimorphically regulates other structures of the brain that will eventually be involved in the regulation of certain aspects of sexually dimorphic behaviour, namely, those aspects that are phyletically widely distributed (like motherly attentiveness to the new-born or coital postures and movement)[4]

The prenatal determinants of gender identity can be perhaps not entirely over-

---

3. John Money, 'Matched Pairs of Hermaphrodites: Behavioural Biology of Sexual Differentiation from Chromosomes to Gender Identity', *Engineering and Science* (California Institute of Technology), 33:34, 1970. Special Issue: *Biological Bases of Human Behavior.*

4. John Money, 'Sexually Dimorphic Behaviour, Normal and Abnormal', *Environmental Influences on Genetic Expression: Biological and Behavioural Aspects of Sexual Differentiation* (Fogerty International Center Proceedings No. 2, US Government Printing Office), 1971, 209.

ridden, but they can be and are incorporated into the postnatal program of differentiation . . . [5]

The evidence . . . shows rather conclusively that there are in human beings some gender dimorphic behaviour differences based on antenatal hormonal history, but that these differences do not automatically dictate or totally preordain the course of postnatal dimorphism of behavioral differentiation.[6]

This is all that the theory presented in this book assumes about physiological differentiation as far as the sexual differentiation of dominance tendency is concerned. The only neuro-endocrinological differentiation posited by the theory presented here is that which is responsible for, first, the male's stronger tendency to react to the environmental presence of a hierarchy, status role, or member of the other sex with dominance behaviour, and second, the differentiation of social values, socialization, and institutions (the 'postnatal program of differentiation') that reflects, and increases, the differentiation of dominance tendency. It would not matter for the theory presented here if every other aspect of sexual differentiation had purely social causes. The fact that a certain exposure to nurturance is a necessary condition for the development of the ability to nurture no more demonstrates that nurturant behavior is 'learned' (in the usual sense) than does the fact that an infant kept in a dark closet for a year will never develop sight indicate that the ability to see is 'learned'.[7]

I do not deny the importance of social reality and socialization, of the 'postnatal program of differentiation'; indeed, the purpose of this book is to explain why this 'program' always associates dominance with the male. The point is not that the social reality is unimportant, but that it is not, in any important respect, the independent variable; social values, socialization, and institutions (and the other elements that constitute the 'postnatal program') are

---

5. John Money, and Anke Ehrhardt, *Man and Woman, Boy and Girl* (Baltimore: Johns Hopkins University Press, 1972), 114.

6. *Ibid.*, 117.

7. In addition to the cue-stimulus role discussed in the previous chapter, environment may also play a crucial role in an imprinting process that is a necessary condition for the development of dominance tendency. This seems to be the case with the development of female nurturant tendencies. This does not, as some have inferred, imply that the tendencies are 'learned' in the usual sense of the word, but only that extreme enough environmental deprivation during the critical imprinting period will preclude the development of the tendency. Thus the female primate who receives no maternal nurturing at all will be incapable of nurturing her offspring. However, among normal primates who do not suffer this deprivation, females will exhibit stronger nurturant tendencies than males and the differentiation will be owed primarily to physiological differentiation. Such cases of extreme environmental deprivation are clearly irrelevant to behaviour that is exhibited by the vast majority of people in every society.

given their limits and direction by people's observation of the differentiated behavior of men and women generated by neuro-endocrinological differentiation. We shall discuss the senses in which environment is the independent variable. These are either irrelevant for our purposes (the long-term evolutionary conformation of physiology to environment) or unimportant ('feedback'). Socialization increases the differentiation of tendency and behavior by making qualitative, separate, and absolute ('men are aggressive', 'women are passive') a psychophysiological reality that is quantitative, continuous, and statistical (the statistical difference in dominance tendency). But socialization gets its direction and limits from the physiological differentiation and observation of its behavioral manifestations. There is no outside experimenter in society.[8]

Tomboyism

The aspect of Dr Money's work that most interests us concerns 'tomboyism', a rare situation in which genetic females experience a hormonal masculinization of the CNS (central nervous system) during the fetal stage. We are particularly interested in those individuals whose fetal masculinization was such that the CNS was altered, but not the anatomy—in other words, individuals who were identified and socialized as females. Such individuals lacked the enthusiasm for motherhood that marked the control group with which they were compared; demonstrated a greater interest in a career and a lesser interest in marriage; and showed a preference for 'male' toys like guns and little interest in 'female' toys like dolls. In short, they manifested an interest

---

8. In an attempt to demonstrate that fetal hormonalization is not crucial to gender identity (a point that is not central to our discussion) Jessie Bernard (*Women and the Public Interest* [Chicago: Aldine-Atherton, 1971], 17–18) has prepared a matrix based on the published case studies of Robert Stoller (*Sex and Gender*. New York: Science House, 1968). After examining Stoller's cases in terms of genetic sex, internal anatomy, external anatomy, gender assignment, and gender identity, Dr Bernard concludes that there is an ". . . independence of gender identity from either heredity or anatomy". The conclusion that flows from her material is just the opposite of this; excluding the category of individuals for whom all variables save gender identity were female, we see that a male gender identity never developed in the absence of fetal male hormonalization, but that it did develop even when a fetally masculinized male was socialized as a female. (Technically, of course, accidental fetal hormonalization of a female is not 'heredity', but the implication for the development of gender identity in normal humans is that hereditary male hormonalization is determinative to male gender identity.) The one excluded category *must* contain an error, for the claim that a male gender identity develops when a normal female is socialized as a female implies that the male gender identity in this case has no cause at all; this is not possible. What this category most strongly indicates is that *socialization* is not determinative to gender identity. It is possible that some rare psychological factors proved capable of over-riding both heredity and socialization for this category, but it would seem more likely that there was an undetected fetal hormonalization.

in the objects and goals associated with masculinization rather than feminization. This cannot be explained in terms of socialization, because these individuals were identified and socialized as females. Dr Money writes: "The most likely hypothesis to explain the various features of tomboyism in fetally masculinized genetic females is that their tomboyism is a sequel to the masculinizing effect on the fetal brain."

Dr Money mentions that these individuals were no more 'aggressive' than normal females. A number of critics invoked this as demonstrating that the masculinization does not produce dominance tendencies, yet none of them felt it necessary to point out that Dr Money was referring here to fighting behavior and that his very point was that the correct term for the differentiated behavior is dominance assertion, striving for position in the dominance hierarchy— precisely the variable that is relevant here. Fighting behavior *per se* is irrelevant.[9]

While there is nothing in Dr Money's work that deals directly with the question of the development of the system of social values and socialization that determines the nature of the postnatal program by which a society's males and females will be socialized (he merely states that it incorporates the prenatal determinants), it is worth noting that, as the above quotation indicates, he stops short of saying that socialization can ever completely override prenatal determinants *even in individual cases* (to say nothing of its doing so in so many cases in a given society that there were no longer the observable differences in the behavior of males and females which determine the limits and direction of the socialization system). It is also worth noting, for those who are interested in individual cases rather than the statistical realities that are relevant to patriarchy, that there is only one type of case out of all those mentioned by Dr Money that *could* imply that the *socialization* might be capable of over-riding the prenatal determinants in a *normal* individual; this is the case of the hormonally normal male who lost his penis in a circumcision accident and who was not subsequently given hormonal treatment. In all other cases of all types, prenatal hormonal development was ambivalent and it is certainly possible that such individuals can be successfully socialized to the behavior of the other genetic sex where normal, physiologically unambivalent individuals cannot be; successful socialization of such individuals no more necessarily implies that socialization has this power in normal individuals than the fact that a female hermaphrodite can be successfully socialized (told) to grow facial hair implies

---

9. Money and Ehrhardt. *op. cit.,* 98–103.

that a normal woman could grow facial hair if that were the way she were socialized. (That normal women can be *hormonalized* to grow facial hair, or to manifest male behavior, demonstrates the importance of male hormonalization to growing facial hair and to manifesting male behavior, and supports our assumption of the importance of male hormonal development to male behavior.)

Dr Money presents only one example of the only type of case (the circumcision accident victim) that *could* imply that *socialization* is capable, in individual cases of *normal* human beings, of completely over-riding the prenatal determinants. This individual has been surgically, but not hormonally, feminized and has been raised as a *girl*. (Hormonal feminization will be introduced at puberty.) Dr Money reports that this girl "was often the dominant one in a girl's group" and exhibited tomboy behavior. Obviously this one case does not constitute a large enough sample to allow any generalizations to be drawn, but I think it worth noting that this individual, who was socialized so successfully that she manifested the behavior and characteristics of a normal girl in almost every respect, also manifested the dominance behavior that is associated with male hormonalization. I mention this not as demonstration of the importance of hormonal differentiation to sexually differentiated hierarchical and dyadic dominance behavior, but merely to show that one may disregard this particular case or one may see it as tentative evidence for the impossibility of socialization completely over-riding the hormonal factor. However, one cannot invoke it as evidence that socialization *is* capable of completely over-riding the hormonal factor.

In any case, I do not argue that environmental factors can never over-ride hormonally-rooted tendencies. We shall see that environmental factors, certain familial situations, for example, are capable of engendering in some women hierarchical and dyadic dominance behavior greater than that which hormones engender in some males—though they engender in some men hierarchical and dyadic dominance behavior greater than that which is manifested in any women. The argument advanced in this book is that the quantitative and continuous statistical reality of differentiation of hormonally generated behavior is made qualitative and discrete by the social values and socialization that are given their direction by the observed (hormonally directed) behavioral differentiation. Note that the environmental factors that are capable of over-riding the hormonal factor in some women do not include socialization; no group socializes its women (relative to its men) towards hierarchical and dyadic dominance.

This hierarchical and dyadic dominance behaviour is the only type of behavior that is relevant to the theory I present; that the individual under discussion socialized as an average female in any or all other respects is irrelevant to the theory. If there were a large enough sample of such individuals to allow experimentation, and if such experimentation were ethical, we might hypothesize that in a group comprising ten such individuals and ten normal females, the former would tend to dominate the group. There is nothing surprising about this: we already know from Dr Money's studies of 'tomboyism' that even when the hormonal masculinization is partial, male behavior is exhibited. We should certainly expect it when the individuals have—like the circumcision victim—experienced a normal fetal masculinization.

Testosterone and Dominance Tendency

My primary purpose for invoking Dr Money's work is not to demonstrate the neuro-endocrinological origins of the differentiation of dominance tendency *per se,* but to present a general description of the role of physiology in the sexual differentiation of tendencies in general, and to show that his findings are completely compatible with everything that I say in this book. As we have seen, where Dr Money's work touches on the subject of dominance tendency, or on those tendencies which seem to be closely related to it, it indicates that neuro-endocrinological differentiation plays a crucial role. But the differentiation of dominance tendency is not his primary concern, and if his work were the only evidence we had on the subject one would be correct in assuming that the role of physiology in the differentiation of dominance tendency remained an open question, provided one ignored the anthropological evidence already discussed.

However, there is another line of evidence with a bearing on the subject, namely the direct psychophysiological study of mammals which resemble human beings in the physiology of the system being studied.[10]

Such studies minimize the influence of unwarranted anthropomorphism, always a danger in ethological studies. Readers who categorically dismiss even the direct study of non-human mammals as irrelevant should ignore this section; I trust that the anthropological evidence and that provided by human

---

10. 'Resemblance' here means that the physiological system being studied resembles its human equivalent both physically and in the ways it responds to a *wide range* of chemical substances and environmental stimuli.

hermaphrodites will convince them of at least the strong possibility of the determinativeness of physiological differentiation. But I would remind such readers that nearly all medical research supports the validity, and the relevance to human beings, of studies of the type presented here, and that such readers acknowledge their validity and relevance every time they take pills.

The role of hormones in the etiology of dominance tendency is exceedingly complex. It is a gross oversimplification, at best, to speak merely of hormone levels. Dominance tendency results from the interaction between a fetally-prepared central nervous system and the presence of endogenous testosterone. This explains the possibility of the rare species in which the effect of testosterone on the male is the reverse of that in humans, with the result that dominance behavior is associated with the female. It is by no means clear that there are any such exceptions among mammals; certainly there are none among the species most closely related to man. It has been suggested that the golden hamster is the single experimental exception to the development of sexual differences in aggression outlined here[11] but this has been brought into question.[12] Even if the female hamster is an exception, this does not indicate an unwarranted selectivity on our part when we consider the mouse, the rat, and all the other animals for which dominance is associated primarily with the male, as analogues of the human male, and exclude the hamster. For, unlike the mouse, rat, and other experimental animals, the hamster female is also larger than the male. This would seem a good indication that the entire CNS (Central Nervous System) hormonal development of the hamster is the reverse of that in the other experimental animals so that, if one wants to consider the hamster rather than the other animals, as analogous in its development to humans, one must not only show that the human female is more aggressive than the human male, but also that she is larger.

Not coincidentally, this is exactly the situation one finds if one looks for an exception among the primates. While none of the three primate species for which it has been suggested that the males do not exhibit dominance are even vaguely homologous, species *Saguinus, Aotus,* and *Callicebus* have been suggested as exceptions to the association of dominance with the male in all primates. As with the hamster, it may well be incorrect to assume that because

---

11. C.H. Phoenix, *et al.*, 'Sexual Differentiation as a Function of Androgenic Stimulation,' in *Perspectives in Reproduction and Sexual Behavior*, M. Diamond, ed. (Bloomington: Indiana University Press, 1969), 33–49.

12. Leonore Tiefer, 'Gonadal Hormones and Mating Behavior in the Adult Golden Hamster', *Hormones and Behavior*, 1 (1970), 189–202.

the male of these species behaves in a 'female' way in some *other* areas he is not dominant. In these three species alone, the male cares for the young (though the female, of course, suckles them). This does not necessarily imply that even for these species fighting is not primarily male behavior (see Adolph Schultz, *The Life of Primates,* London: Weidenfeld and Nicolson, 1974). But, for argument's sake, let us assume that these species do represent exceptions. If they have taken evolutionary paths somewhat divergent from those taken by all other primates, if they differ from the other primates as the hamster differs from the other experimental animals, if the etiology of CNS-generated dominance for these species differs from that in all other primates as that of the hamster differs from that of the other experimental animals, in short, if we have a right to consider these three species as not homologous with respect to dominance as we consider all the other primates as homologous (as we consider the hamster as not homologous while the other experimental animals are accepted as homologous), then we might expect that, as was the case with the hamster, for these three species, but for none of the others, the female would be larger than the male. *This is precisely the case.* Of the 32 species of primates listed by Napier, only for *Saguinus* and *Aotus* is the female larger than the male. No *Callicebus* female has been measured, but because *Callicebus* is so closely related to *Saguinus* and *Aotus,* it is fair to assume that this holds for *Callicebus* also. Even though I am not including primate evidence in the line of reasoning I use in this book, this point is worth making. Those who would deny the relevance of primate studies to an understanding of human dominance often imply that those who advance primate evidence pick and choose their subject species in order to support their case. I have tried to show that this criticism is without merit. Even if we assume that the females of the three primate species mentioned *are* dominant, even if we do not consider them so little homologous as to be irrelevant, even then we see that there is complete justification for considering the sexual differentiation in dominance for these species as not analogous to that of man while we consider the differentiation found in all other primates as analogous to that found in man. (See J.R. Napier, *A Handbook of Living Primates* [New York: Academic Press, 1967]).

With all this in mind, I refer the reader to a number of experiments that indicate clearly that, at least among rats, mice, and many other mammals, testosterone is related not only to sexual differentiation but to dominance tendency itself. In paired tests, females treated with exogenous testosterone during the crucial period just after birth will develop a dominance tendency as adults, if appropriately hormonally treated as adults, equal to that of the male who receives neonatal testosterone stimulation of the CNS endogenously from his own testes. Females treated with androgen on the tenth day following birth will, as adults, demonstrate a dominance greater than that of the normal female, but less than that of neonatally treated females or normal males. Neonatal experiments, particularly a series by David Edwards, demonstrate that testosterone does not *create* the neural mechanisms for aggression (if it did, the female would be totally incapable of dominance behavior and would be passive) but that such fetal or neonatal stimulation affects the ultimate sensitivity of the CNS to androgenic stimulation later in life, thereby rendering the postpubertal male more likely to react to the environment with dominance behavior than the female. Dr Edwards concludes that:

> the commonly observed male-female dimorphism, with respect to fighting in mice, has as its basis, the fact that males develop with testes and females do not. In the male, early testicular secretions probably effect some change in brain mechanisms for aggression such that most adult male pairs will fight in the presence of endogenous or exogenous testosterone. In females this change is not effected due to the absence of testes and correlated testicular secretions.
>
> In addition, there appears to be a critical period for the androgen-influenced organization of a neural substrate for aggression. This period may be tentatively characterized as a period of time, in the development of the mouse, during which endogenous or exogenous androgen stimulation will enhance adult sensitivity to androgens with respect to the arousal of the tendency to display aggression. Furthermore, the data indicate that the period of development during which androgen stimulation will produce maximal sensitivity in the adult occurs in the first few postnatal days of development. Androgen stimulation before or after this optimal period will enhance adult sensitivity to androgens but to a lesser extent.[13]

Dr Edwards's findings and those of other behavioral biologists, endocrinologists, developmental psychologists, and researchers in related fields showed with

---

13. David A. Edwards, 'Early Androgen Stimulation and Aggressive Behaviour in Male and Female Mice,' *Physiology and Behaviour*, 4 (1969) 338. There is such an abundance of evidence leading to the conclusion that sexual hormonalization determines CNS development and aggressive behavior that it is possible here to give merely a sampling; these will lead the interested reader to hundreds of similar studies. General discussions of the relevant research can be found in: Richard E. Whalen, 'Differentiation of the Neural Mechanisms Which Control Gonadotropin Secretion and Sexual Behaviour', in Diamond, *op. cit.*, 303–340, and the contribution of C.H. Phoenix, R.W. Goy, and W. Young to *Neuroendocrinology: Volume II*, L. Martini and W.F. Ganong, eds. (New York: Academic Press, 1967), 163–96. Somewhat dated, but more accessible to the general reader are Seymour Levine's 'Sex Differences in the Brain' and Alan Fisher's 'Chemical Stimulation of the Brain,' both in *Psychobiology* (San Francisco: Freeman, 1967). The journal *Hormones and Behaviour* provides the ambitious reader with over a hundred similar studies.

a high degree of certainty that sexual differences in dominance are a function of testosterone and the hormonalization of the fetal brain. The specific morphological changes in the CNS engendered by this hormonalization, however, had never been seen and could be only inferred ('some change in brain mechanisms'). In 1971, however, Dr Geoffrey Raisman and Dr Pauline M. Field, of Oxford's Department of Human Anatomy, photographed the preoptic area of the male and female central nervous systems and demonstrated that in this area, which is known to be crucial to sexual behavior, there is an extensive sexual dimorphism; the sexes differ in the distribution of synapses on the dendritic spines. Having seen that testosterone was directly related to dominance, and that the central nervous systems of the sexes differ morphologically in an area of the brain necessary for male behavior, all that was needed was a direct demonstration that it was testosterone that effected the morphological changes. That testosterone is the determining factor here has been inferentially demonstrated many times in the past dozen years, as we have seen. Direct evidence was provided only as recently as the 1970s—at the conference on the Neurobiology of the Amygdala in Bar Harbor—at which Dr Raisman delivered his findings that testosterone does generate specifiable morphological sexual dimorphism in the brain.[14]

To be sure, the Raisman-Field photographs were not of human beings and, certainly, there is much that science has yet to learn about the exact manner in which sexual differences in the arrangement of the central nervous system are manifested in differences in dominance. None the less, it is simply preposterous to attempt to portray the overwhelming evidence that testosterone is crucial to dominance tendency as mere isolated findings that have no apparent significance for sexual differences in behavior. Only the most fanatic purist or the behaviorist for whom such a conclusion would be intolerable would deny us the right to strongly suspect that, within ten years, the same central nervous system differences found in experimental animals will be found to exist in the brains of men and women. Those who now refuse to admit the persuasiveness of the considerable evidence provided by the hermaphrodite and the voluminous amounts of evidence provided by the studies of experimental animals will continue to do so when our knowledge of hormones has doubled or tripled. None the less, even at this point the tightening web of evidence allows no escape from the conclusion that human sexual differences in 'aggression' are

14. Geoffrey Raisman and Pauline M. Field, 'Sexual Dimorphism in the Preoptic Area of the Rat', *Science* (20th August 1971), 731–33.

strongly related to irreversible differences in the central nervous systems of men and women that are generated before birth.[15]

The Irrelevance of Exceptions

When we speak of men and women we speak in virtually absolute terms; with the exception of the hermaphrodite, everyone is unambiguously a male or a female. When we speak of masculine and feminine characteristics we speak in statistical terms, with the result that we expect to find many 'exceptions.'[16] This would all seem too obvious to mention, but so many authors have invoked exceptions in attempts to deny the neuro-endocrinological basis of the sexual differentiation of dominance behavior that it is worth emphasizing the point here.

It does not matter whether the exception is invoked on the behavioral level (women who exhibit greater dominance tendency and behavior than some men) or on the physiological level (women who have higher testosterone levels than some men).[17] Even when we speak of a characteristic whose etiology is virtually purely hereditary, such as height, we expect to find many exceptions.[18]

It would hardly be persuasive to argue that, because some women are taller than some men, the general male height advantage must result from environmental factors. It is similarly unconvincing to argue—as have many critics— that the fact that the range within a sex in a given characteristic is greater than

---

15. While the evidence is not as extensive as that demonstrating the effects of testosterone on aggression, there is considerable evidence that estrogen ('the female hormone') increases submission behaviour. See: Murray S. Work and Hilliard Rogers, 'Effect of Estrogen Level on Food-Seeking Dominance Among Male Rats,' *Journal of Comparative and Physiological Psychology*, 79 (1972), 3.

16. Two points: 1. This assumes, of course, that there are not so many exceptions that the 'rule', the statistical hypothesis, can no longer be maintained. 2. The word 'exception' is used loosely here. A statistical hypothesis includes the 'exceptions'. If we predict that it will rain one day out of every four and it does, the days that it rains are not exceptions, but are predicted by the hypothesis.

17. Two futher points: 1. A woman whose testosterone level is even half that of a normal male displays obvious signs of hirsuteness and general virilization. The concentration of plasma testosterone in young adult males ranges from 0.44 to 0.96 mcg. per 100 ml. (mean 0.65 mcg. per 100 ml.) and the concentration in women varies from 0.034 to 0.101 mcg. per 100 ml. (mean 0.054 mcg. per 100 ml.) *Textbook of Medicine*, Paul B. Beeson and Walsh McDermott, eds. (Philadelphia: Saunders, 1971), 1805. 2. It will be remembered that fetal preparation of the CNS is as important as the later level of testosterone acting on that CNS; thus, even a (previously normal) female with a male-level CNS is not male with respect to the neuro-endocrinology of dominance tendency.

18. There are nutritional elements in the etiology of height, and other environmental factors play a role, but these are insignificant when compared to the role of heredity.

the difference between the means of the two sexes somehow demonstrates the irrelevance or unimportance of physiology. The range of height (the difference between the shortest and tallest) is much greater within the group of males (or females) than is the difference between the male and female means; but the sexual difference is maintained at each level, and one should not expect the best basketball teams to contain any women or the best high school basketball teams to contain more than one woman. I would guess that a good third of the objections raised to earlier editions of this book could have been avoided if the critic had simply asked himself whether his point could as well have been made with respect to height and if, when finding that it could and that it would not lead him to deny the role of physiology in the sexual differentiation in height, he had refrained from raising his objection.

If we expect exceptions even when the characteristic in question is almost purely hereditary, we can certainly expect them for a characteristic, like dominance tendency, which is determined not only by physiological factors, but by non-physiological ones (like early familial experiences) as well. Such non-physiological factors engender in some women a dominance tendency stronger than that found in most men. Similar factors combine with the male's physiologically-rooted stronger dominance tendency to give some males a stronger dominance tendency than all other males and all females. Because dominance tendency is the result of both physiological and non-physiological factors, every society will have a minority of women who exhibit a greater dominance tendency than some men and a minority of men who exhibit a weaker dominance tendency than some women. This would be the case even if there were no overlap on the physiological level.

In reality, of course, the 'physiological' and 'non-physiological' etiological components of dominance tendency are not causally independent. The non-physiological elements, which can produce the exceptions, far more often increase the differentiation. Consider the analogy of muscular strength. Male physiology is such that most males are physically stronger than most females, though there are many exceptions. This is recognized by the members of every society, and physical strength is associated with males (though, as we shall see, males will not necessarily do work requiring greater strength). Social values and socialization reflect this general rule, so that, for example, males are encouraged to lift weights far more than females. This increases the differentiation of physical strength. Logically it would be possible for women to do five hours of calisthenics while the men remained sedentary, and this would greatly reduce the sexual difference in physical strength. However, this is not possible in reality because the non-physiological is in general given its direction by the physiological.

As a general rule, statistical realities tend to be reinforced by marital selection; women tend to choose men who are taller and exhibit a greater dominance tendency than themselves. As I have mentioned, it would make sense, and would be compatible with the evidence, to suggest that female neuro-endocrinology plays a role in this female choice, but this need not concern us here.

Feedback and Suggestion

The example of physical strength and calisthenics demonstrates the possibility that environment can alter physiology ('feedback'). Environmental stimuli and situations can, similarly, alter testosterone levels. Dr Irwin Bernstein and associates have demonstrated that, to oversimplify somewhat, testosterone levels result not only from internal mechanisms, but from environmental situations as well; specifically, they have shown that a new hierarchical setting can influence testosterone level.[19] They provided each of four rhesus monkeys with a group of receptive females and found that each of the four assumed dominance of his respective group. The plasma testosterone levels of each of these males increased two to threefold in the new environment. These males were then placed in male groups in which they were subjected to sudden and decisive defeat. This resulted in a drop in these males' plasma testosterone levels. Two of the males were later reintroduced to the female groups and their testosterone levels returned to their previous high levels.

Now some readers misinterpreted this research and inferred that it demonstrates that the relationship of testosterone level and dominance behavior/position represents nothing more than the conformation of hormone level to environment. It is not clear that the research demonstrates this even for males; the males in the research were introduced into already formed groups which presented the newly introduced males with the resistance of the entire group—a stimulus that is, as the researchers demonstrate, capable of defeating the new males and driving down their testosterone levels. However, this still does not tell us what it is that generates the behavior that enables males in

---

19. Irwin Bernstein, *et al.*, 'Plasma Testosterone Levels in the Male Rhesus: Influences of Sexual and Social Stimuli', in *Science* 178 (10th November 1972), 643–45.

relatively stable groups to attain dominance positions (and high testosterone levels). More importantly for our purposes, the research does not imply that environmental stimuli are capable of lowering a male's testosterone level to that of the female, or raising the female's level to a male level; indeed it shows that when males are reintroduced to female groups their dominance returns and their testosterone levels return to the old level. Why does no environmental stimulus result in either female dominance or female levels of testosterone equal to the levels of even the lowest-level males? This research indicates that it is not a question of strength, size, or pugnacity. The most reasonable answer is that the fetal masculinization renders males more sensitive to the testosterone-affecting environmental stimuli. Thus, environment does affect male testosterone levels and dominance, but environment is not, in these studies, capable of engendering a lowering of male testosterone levels to anything approaching the female level. And even if this were not the case, we would ask anyone who argues that feedback somehow demonstrates the unimportance of fetal sexual physiological sexual differentiation to dominance tendency, the usual question: *why does the environment,* which he sees as the independent variable, *always initiate a male rise in testosterone?* Attempts to answer this question will encounter the same insurmountable problems which face all non-neuro-endocrinological explanations of the universality of patriarchy (we shall discuss these at length later).

We might ask the same question of those who invoke Schachter and Singer's well-known demonstration that the behavioral effects of epinephrine tend to reflect suggestion (individuals given adrenalin will be fearful or exhilarated, depending on the behaviour of those around them). Even if we ignore such obvious dissimilarities between testosterone and epinephrine as the fact that a fetal differentiation of CNS structures plays a crucial role in determining the effects of the former (but not the latter), and even if we ignore the fact that it is absurd to assume the malleability of the effects of one substance on the basis of another (would anyone argue that the effects of insulin are as varied as epinephrine?), we still find that to invoke suggestion as an explanation of male dominance is begging the question: *why* does every environment suggest *male* dominance?

Physiology and Within-Sex Differences

The theory advanced here does not imply that physiology is at all involved in differences in dominance tendency and behavior within the group. While I happen to think it quite likely that the small differences between different males' central nervous systems and testosterone levels do contribute to differences in the strength of their dominance tendency (and that the same is true of females), it would be irrelevant to the theory advanced here if differences within the sexes were caused by non-physiological factors alone. All this would indicate is that once the physiological differentiation is removed as a variable (once the physiological 'necessary condition' is met), then physiology is no longer relevant. If the reader can stand one more physical analogy: the fact that weight is irrelevant to differences in boxing ability among men who weigh over 200 pounds hardly demonstrates that weight is not crucial to becoming a heavy-weight boxer, or to the fact that all such boxers are men. Moreover, even if physiological factors *are* relevant to differing males' differing dominance propensity, such differences are not anatomically observable by the population and, therefore, cannot be associated with categories of people or manifested in the socialization system. *If* the difference in dominance behavior between brown-haired men and blond-haired men were like the difference in dominance behavior between men and women, this would be reflected in the socialization system.[20]

Dominance Behavior in Boys and Girls

Socialization is the process by which society prepares children for adult-hood; that it conforms to the reality of physiology can be seen quite clearly when we consider boys and girls, rather than men and women. Boys and girls have roughly equal testosterone levels, yet boys clearly demonstrate a stronger dominance tendency, as well as a greater tendency for rough and tumble play, fighting, and other male behavior. This fact is often invoked by those who deny the importance of physiological differentiation to the differentiation of domi-nance behavior. Now, in fact the boys' greater dominance tendency results primarily from their physiology. We have seen that it is a gross oversimplifica-tion to speak only of hormone levels; it is the fetal masculinization of the CNS (and the increased sensitivity to the dominance-related properties of

---

20. Those who argue that the fact that within-group differences exceed between-group differences somehow demonstrates the unimportance of between-group differences, seem to invoke this fallacious argument only when the causation is primarily physiological. They do not (and should not) argue that the fact that income differences within the group of males or within the group of females is greater than the difference between the average income of men and the average income of women demonstrates the unimportance of the difference between the average incomes.

whatever testosterone is present that the masculinization generates) that is of primary importance.

But let us for the moment pretend that the only physiological factor relevant to dominance tendency is testosterone *level*. The boy's greater dominance tendency would then result only from socialization. But this does not demonstrate that socialization is not conforming to physiological reality (i.e. the adult male's higher testosterone level). Socialization reflects adult realities, and the reality is that after puberty the male has a much higher testosterone level. We shall speak about socialization later, so I shall make only two basic points here. 1. By 'socialization' I do not mean simply the consciously recognized values transmitted by parents to children (like 'stealing is bad'), but the constant recognition of adult realities that is transmitted simply as a result of the parents' observation and experience. When parents tell the little girl that 'boys are more "aggressive"' they are socializing the girl more strongly away from 'aggressive' behavior, but they are also transmitting their observation of reality; men *are* more 'aggressive' than women. 2. My point is *not* that parents *should* do this. While I do think that with many types of behavior it is necessary (the girl who comes to depend on fighting is going to be in serious trouble after pubertal male growth has left her at a great disadvantage), my point is here that there will always be at least a loose concordance between reality and what parents tell their children about the world. To what extent they *should* do this and to what extent they could get away with misrepresenting the world to children (who are not blind) is a question the reader is as well prepared to answer as I am.

A Crucial Question This Book Leaves Unanswered

The view of the universe which is fundamental to my approach in this book (and, I would argue, to all empirical science) is that of the physicalist or materialist. I start from the premiss that all reality is, in theory, reducible to physical components, and that all reality is, in theory, predictable, at least in the statistical terms of the physicist, from the actions of sub-atomic particles. This view is, of course, merely a philosophical position. No one expects the historian to write the history of England in terms of the interplay of atoms, or to describe the positions of the atomic constituents of Romeo and Juliet; no one denies that, given the nature and limits of the human central nervous system, Macaulay and Shakespeare give us a far deeper understanding than would some kind of atomic description. Nor does the physicalist view deny the necessity of incorporating physical realities into non-physical constructs like 'government' and 'class', or the necessity of terms that represent neurochemical-electrical activity ('love', 'fear'). What the physicalist abhors are non-physical constructs that are claimed to exist in reality ('soul') and non-explanations ('miracle'). I realize that many find this view life-denying or godless. Here I can merely suggest that they fail to see the dance of matter, which has a far greater beauty than any man-made 'spirit' could possess. I bring up the controversial philosophical issue of physicalism here merely to introduce a question which this book raises, but does not solve. (I should add that a number of philosophers with whom I have discussed the question find no problem and accept the first 'solution' offered below. I cannot, however, shake off a feeling of dissatisfaction with it.)

The question is simply this: how can a hierarchy, an abstraction, affect an individual's central nervous system? There is no problem when we speak of male dominance or sexual arousal; perception of another individual and an alteration of the CNS is easily seen in purely sense-data and physical terms. But how does a hierarchy bring about an alteration of the CNS? I can think of only two responses: 1. a 'hierarchy' is simply our abstractive term to describe the resolution of a sort of 'vertical tournament' fought between pairs of men; the human capacity for memory and abstraction enables one to generalize about these 'battles', but the basic environmental stimulus is another human being; or 2. we, and many other species, have some CNS programming which enables us to recognize the abstraction we term a 'hierarchy'; however, this 'answer' is so unsatisfying to the physicalist that it is perhaps worse than no answer at all.

Physiological Evolution

While acknowledging the role of feedback, I have argued throughout this chapter that physiological differentiation is basically an independent variable that sets limits on, and gives direction to, environmental factors. It is of course true that in the evolutionary long run environment is basically the independent and physiology the dependent variable. Should physiological evolution erase the neuro-endocrinological differences responsible for patriarchy, then, of course, males would not attain the overwhelming number of hierarchical positions. I would argue that such males and females would be so different on a neuro-endocrinological level from men and women as we know them that they would not be 'men' and 'women' in any meaningful sense, and that 'patriarchy' refers to hierarchies in societies composed of men and women. I realize that some will see this defense as tautological; to them I can merely point out that every scientific theory is tautological in the sense that it must, at some empirical perimeter, invoke a *ceteris paribus* clause. Given the fact that a genetic male or female who undergoes other-sex hormonalization is (if untreated) hermaphroditic and sterile, I do not think I invoke the *ceteris paribus* clause at an unreasonable point. More important, however, is the fact that those who blithely speak of evolutionary or pharmacological eradication of CNS differences grossly underestimate the depth and extent of the differences. We are not speaking here of such superficialities as skin or eye color, or even of (perhaps mutable) differences in capacity; we are speaking of the basic 'motivational' properties of the male and female brains and central nervous systems. This differentiation developed long before our species walked the earth and there is, as we have seen, no evidence that it is diminishing.

Second Digression: Race and IQ, Territoriality, and Male Bonding

We live in a time when many academics like to believe that the variations of human behaviour and social institutions are virtually unlimited. This explains the readiness to invoke cultural variation as evidence of human malleability whenever possible, while ignoring, and leaving unexplained, the universality of the institutions discussed here (a universality that seems all the more astonishing when one considers the extent of the cultural variations that such academics can draw upon). An analysis such as this, which concludes that our psychophysiological natures set immutable limits to human malleability and institutional possibilities, meets strong resistance from those who favor the prevailing view. One form of this resistance is the tendency to bracket together all analyses which stress the importance of physiology to behavior, and to treat them as if they all exhibited the weaknesses of the weakest among them. Thus, many have failed to differentiate between analyses of very differing degrees of persuasiveness. I have already considered both evolutionary and ethological analyses and have made the point that, suggestive as they often are, such analyses are by their nature far more speculative and far more open to logical and evidential criticisms than those which can invoke the types of precise evidence that are available for an explanation of patriarchy. It is necessary to make some crucial distinctions here in order to show that neither the validity of the reasoning nor the correctness of the conclusions of any of these sorts of investigations has any bearing on the correctness of the theory advanced in this book.

The most controversial of the investigations which emphasize the importance of physiology to social life, and the first to be lumped together with the analysis presented here by those opposed to all physiologically-rooted analyses, are those which claim that racial differentiation in IQ scores have a genetic basis. I am not qualified to assess the validity of these specialized and sophisticated statistical arguments, though the fact that I, too, do not like the idea that IQ depends primarily on heredity is hardly much of an argument against it. I would, however, mention some differences, which I am certain the authors of these works would acknowledge, between the kinds of evidence available to those attempting to explain racial differences in IQ and to those attempting to explain the universality of patriarchy.

The evidence concerning race and IQ is, by and large, based on one *minority* living under very special conditions in one society (blacks in the United States). For the basis of evidence of the IQ argument to be equivalent to the evidence relevant to sexual differentiation of dominance tendency, all societies that have ever existed—with all their varied social, economic, political, and religious systems—would have to be half white and half black, and in every one whites would have to surpass blacks on IQ tests.

And even if this were the case, the genetic argument could 'merely' (but most persuasively) be hypothetical; no one could specify the physiological factors relevant to the differentiation of IQ in the way that we can specify those relevant to the sexual differentiation of dominance behavior. And even if we could do *this*, we would still be speaking of capacities, which are probably more malleable and of less importance to social life than the behavioral tendencies that 'motivate' the members of a society.

The race and IQ arguments are limited by the available evidence and by our knowledge of genetics; whether ultimately correct or not, they are cogent and well argued. The same cannot be said of the various works positing a human 'territoriality'. The problem with such works is not that they have the audacity to suggest that our physiology has something to do with our behavior, or even that they suggest that the 'territoriality' that seems to be programmed into lower animals may be relevant to human beings, but that they fail to specify not merely the physiological elements, but also—with any precision—the behavioral and social manifestations allegedly resulting from them. It would not necessarily be illegitimate to postulate the existence of (as yet undiscovered) physiological factors *if* this made possible a more plausible explanation of an observed empirical reality; indeed, I have argued that the empirical anthropological evidence is such that we would be forced to posit the importance of differentiated physiological factors to patriarchy even if we did not have the direct CNS-hormonal evidence. However, while patriarchy (the ultimate manifestation of the differentiation of dominance tendency and the physiological differentiation that underlies it) is easily identified by merely counting the relative numbers of men and women in hierarchies, the alleged manifestations of territoriality are so loosely defined that it is never clear what is being explained or even if there is anything to explain that is not more plausibly explained in social terms. My theory specifies the characteristics of the empirical realities it explains (patriarchy, male attainment, and male dominance), the motivational nexus that links the physiological and the institutional (the differentiation of dominance tendency—behaviorists can ignore this step), and the physiological factors (the CNS-hormonal differentiation we have discussed). In short, theories of human 'territoriality', while they may be suggestive, are as unfalsifiable as the theory presented in this book is falsifiable. At best they demonstrate that human beings have the capacity for doing certain things that human beings do; this is true by definition and need not be demonstrated. What gives a physiologically-rooted social theory meaning is the demonstration that physiology engenders *tendency*.

While it seems to me that theories that posit a male tendency to 'bond' are more interesting and more likely to be productive than those concerned with 'territoriality', these too suffer (though less seriously) from an inability to specify with much precision either manifestations of the male bonding tendency or direct physiological evidence. (These theories invoke physiological evidence relevant to sexual differences in dominance, but not to male bonding itself; in other words, while there is a wealth of evidence demonstrating that other-sex hormonalization directly affects dominance behaviour, there is little such evidence on male bonding.) In any case, I wish here merely to stress that male bonding has nothing whatsoever to do with the theory advanced here, a point missed by many critics.

Chapter V

Social Conformation to Psychophysiological Reality

Socialization

Physiology deals in probabilities, and societies are composed of large numbers of individuals. Patriarchy, male attainment, and male dominance are manifestations of the statistical reality of the male's greater dominance tendency. The social values and socialization that mediate between the dominance tendency and social institutions are given their direction by observation of the differentiated behavior of men and women and the expectations which it generates. The argument that males exhibit dominance behavior because they are socialized to do so merely begs the question: why is it *males* in every society who are so socialized? Claiming socialization as a primary cause is equivalent to arguing that the best boxers are male *because* little girls are told that boxing is unladylike. Indeed, begging the question in this way—and assuming that social values and socialization are independent of, and can render irrelevant, the physiologically-rooted tendencies which give social values and socialization their limits—was the central error of those old-style feminists who tied their feminism to 100-percent environmentalism. The frequently-heard argument that we cannot know how important physiological differentiation is until we have a society that does not differentiate, that 'treats everyone as an individual', is unhelpful: if physiological differentiation is fundamental it will be observed and reflected in socialization and institutions, and a society without differentiation will not develop. One might as well argue that we cannot know whether physiology is responsible for the fact that women give birth until we no longer associate it with them.

On a theoretical level, patriarchy, male attainment, and male dominance are causally independent of each other. Male dominance is not merely a 'filtering down' of patriarchy and patriarchy is not merely a generalization of male dominance. It is true that if only one of these three institutions was a resolution of biopsychological differentiation, the other two would 'automatically' follow suit: even if, for example, only male dominance in male-female relationships was the resolution of biopsychological differentiation, it is likely that authority in the hierarchical area would reflect the dyadic-familial experience and expectation. However, each of these three is the resolution of the differentiation of motivation and *each would develop in the absence of the other.* The implications of the experimental evidence are quite clear on this: males who have never been in male-female encounters will exhibit hierarchical dominance behavior, and males who have never been exposed to other males will exhibit dominance behavior in encounters with females. In reality, of course, the three institutions tend to reinforce one another.

We have discussed all this already. In this section I wish to consider, so far as is necessary for our purposes, the role of socialization. I am limiting myself here to the socialization of children because it is most important to conceptions of masculinity and femininity. 'Socialization' in general refers to the process by which adults, as well as children, internalize social values and social roles; it should be clear that here it does not merely refer to the transmission of fully verbalized rules, but, more importantly, also the cues and conceptions of the world which determine one's view of reality. There are at least three determinants of the nature of socialization, the first of which is all that really need be mentioned in a *sufficient* explanation of the universality of patriarchy.

1. Socialization is limited by the observation of physical or behavioral manifestations of psychophysiological factors, and it is these limits which concern us. Even if it were possible for socialization to ignore the psychophysiological reality—and for children to be socialized to believe that fathers were not dominant and tall, mothers not nurturant and short—the physiological factors responsible for these realities would still be at work and fathers would still be dominant and tall, mothers nurturant and short. Socialization is simply not that important a causal factor as far as the realities under discussion are concerned, and even if it were not given its direction by observation of psychophysiologically-differentiated behaviour, it would not eradicate or even considerably reduce the sexual differentiation of dominance behavior.

2. While the sociologist is quite correct in seeing parents as the agents who transmit society's values to children, the mother who tells her eight-year-old daughter that 'fighting is unladylike' is not primarily concerned with transmitting society's values, but with preparing her daughter for a world in which fighting *is* unladylike (fighting is usually done by men), and in which her daughter, who might do quite well in fights against boys of her own age, will be

at a big disadvantage if fighting ranks high among the methods with which she hopes to cope with adult life. In real life most parents want to prepare their children for the real world, and are unwilling to sacrifice them to the demands of ideology—which is what they do when they grossly misrepresent the world and leave their children unprepared for life—even if such a sacrifice were not, for the reasons mentioned above, doomed to failure.

3. While every society follows many imperatives that are not efficient by rationalistic standards, there is, in the very nature of human experience, a tendency, *ceteris paribus,* towards efficiency. If, for example, women do have a greater nurturance tendency (if they react to a child in distress more strongly and more quickly than males), it is difficult to imagine a society associating child care with males. If human beings were totally instinctual animals there would be no socialization. But we are not instinctual and males do not instinctively know how to fire a rifle or women how to prepare baby food. Socialization does not consist primarily of parents telling little boys to be 'aggressive' and little girls to be nurturant—these tendencies exist without socialization—but of developing the skills and attitudes that make best use of such tendencies as already exist. Socialization is the process by which society utilizes the reality of differentiated tendencies. Note that 'society' here is not some outside experimenter, but the members themselves. If males have a dominance tendency that is stronger than their nurturance tendency and females a nurturance tendency that is stronger than their dominance tendency, they will be drawn to hierarchical pursuit and nurturance activity respectively even without the spur of socialization.

The role of observation is seen clearly when we consider, as we shall in the chapter on cognition, the stereotype. Like socialization, the stereotype is rooted in some reality; it is not arbitrary. There is not, and could not at present be, a stereotype of the American Jew as a great soldier. Stereotypes are pictures abstracted from reality; they are quintessential versions of reality and they must represent it. This is not to say that stereotypes cannot change; they can change as much as the realities they represent. A stereotype is invariably accurate as *observation;* it may be woefully inaccurate as causal explanation. A change in social values and social conditions could, as in Israel, lead to American Jews placing a value on, and developing an ability at, soldiering; eventually a stereotype associating fighting ability with American Jews would emerge. But the stereotype cannot change until the reality changes and, while it can reinforce the reality, is never its primary cause. This is not to deny that stereotypes can be unjustly invoked when applied to members of the stereotyped group who do not display the necessary characteristics, nor that the 'exceptions' to a stereotype may outnumber those whose behavior generates it. (For example, violent crime is associated with American blacks despite the fact that the vast majority of American blacks have never committed any crime; the stereotype is correct in that a greatly disproportionate amount of violent crime is committed by blacks, but it is incorrect in its association of crime with blacks in general, and it would be incorrect if it explained the difference in criminal behavior in hereditary terms.) I make this point because there is a contemporary penchant for dismissing stereotypes out-of-hand as being incorrect or for *assuming* that the causes of the reality observed by a stereotype are purely social. In doing this one is proceeding in precisely the opposite direction from that which science demands, whereby we make observations and then explain the reality that is observed.

In short, stereotypes and socialization can be altered, but only to the extent that the reality behind them can be altered. To the extent that the psychophysiological differentiation we have discussed is responsible for sexual differences in behavior that are observed and incorporated in stereotypes and socialization, the stereotype and socialization must represent the psychophysiological differentiation.

But all of this is, I repeat, irrelevant to our purpose of discovering why all societies are patriarchal or why, to put it another way, socialization always associates dominance behavior with males. For our *sufficient* explanation we need merely make the point that socialization conforms to the limits and directions set by observation of the differentiated dominance behavior resulting from the sexual differentiation of dominance tendency. This is sufficient to explain the universality of patriarchy.

Two Additional Aspects of Socialization

I suspect that I shall be criticized for paying insufficient attention to socialization, and I would emphasize that nothing I have written so far is meant to deny the role of socialization or the extent to which social values and socialization vary. At the very least these make qualitative, discrete, and absolute a sexual difference that is, on a psychophysiological level, quantitative, continuous, and statistical. Thus, the psychophysiological reality (that most men usually exhibit a stronger dominance tendency than most women) becomes the stereotype that 'men are "aggressive"' and 'women are passive'. This works to the detriment of those men and women who are exceptions. But, as we saw in the section entitled 'The Irrelevance of Exceptions', this no more demonstrates the primarily social basis of dominance behavior than the fact that a strong female weightlifter is ridiculed, while a male is not, demonstrates the primarily social basis of strength. In any case, socialization is important within the limits set by psychophysiological differentiation, while it is only the limits and their manifestations that need concern us.

I suspect that I shall also be criticized as having suggested that society *should* emphasize sex differences in its socialization. What society *should* do is a question that cannot be answered on scientific grounds and it is one that I do not concern myself with here. Whether it is better to minimize as far as possible the emphasis placed on sex differences in order to 'maximize individual potential', or whether it is better to present boys and girls with well-defined models of masculinity and feminity in order to enable them to develop the strongest possible sense of themselves as individuals following physiological as well as social imperatives, is a question each reader must decide for himself. The evidence provided in this book is only relevant to such a decision if the reader wishes to eradicate sex-role differentiation in a way that the evidence indicates to be impossible. To believe that males should not have a stronger dominance tendency or that members of society and the socialization system should pay no attention to it, is to hope for the impossible.

The Mbuti Pygmies

We have seen that the extent to which the differentiation of dominance tendency manifests itself depends on the extent to which the social system acts as the necessary environmental cue and provides a 'playing field' in which the cued behavior can be manifested. It will be remembered that 'environment' here does not refer to socialization, but to the presence of hierarchies, *any* hierarchies. The point being made was that, while there has never been a society without hierarchies and while there is, as we shall see, good reason to doubt whether there could be such a society, the existence of a primitive society that lacked hierarchies (and, of course, patriarchy) would not indicate that a society could exist which had hierarchies, but not patriarchal ones. Perhaps it would be helpful to examine a society in which sex-role differentiation is as minimally manifested as possible.

Some authors, having misconstrued Colin Turnbull's more popular works on the Mbuti Pygmies, have claimed that the Pygmies fail to demonstrate male dominance or even sex-role differentiation. Reference to Dr. Turnbull's scholarly work on the subject leaves no doubt that the Mbuti are not an exception: *"Emma* (mother) is associated with love; *eba* (father) is associated with authority *(mota)."* Authority is in the hands of the best male hunter or an elder male. Disputes are settled by discussions among groups of men, though women do play an advisory role. Status is related to hunting skill. The *molimo,* the ritual performed in times of great crisis, is exclusively male.[1]

Nonetheless, it may conceivably be true that sex-role differentiation in superfamilial areas is less pronounced among the pygmies than it is in any other society, and may well be not far above the minimal threshold necessitated by the hormonal differences between men and women. Before concluding that the degree of sex-role differentiation demonstrated by the Pygmies is all that is required by the differentiation of dominance tendency, however, we must examine the effect of the psychophysiological factor on behavior in the contexts of different social environmental realities.

The differentiation of dominance tendency is least important in a society, such as that of the Pygmies, where everyone, male and female, plays more or less the same economic role; the fact that the man holds the net will not result in a great deal of extra status. But now let us suppose that the society develops to the point where only half the population is needed for the hunt, and let us assume that women are as capable of hunting as men. If the theory presented here is correct, if what is true of all other societies proves to be true of this society, and if hunting is given high status, then we would expect men to develop the skills necessary for attainment of this high-status role, and that the hunters would be men. Indeed, among those Pygmies who are archers (as opposed to the net hunters we are discussing), this is precisely the case. We would expect that members of the society would soon come to associate the role with men and to see it as a 'male' role until—for whatever reason—it lost status, at which point men would pursue other roles that had higher status. Note that, as we have seen before, a 'male role' is not given high status merely because it is a male role (ditchdiggers have low status); it is a 'male' role because it has—for whatever reason—a high status to which men are drawn more strongly than are women.

---

1. It may be that in primitive societies with little hierarchy an unstructured extension of male dominance results in decision-making being as much controlled by males as when more formal structures exist. Feminists have often observed that even within groups claiming to support women's rights, in which women are equally or more than equally represented, males in fact tend to dominate. However, since no society lacks hierarchies, and since assessment of such unstructured authority would be more open to question, we need not concern ourselves with this here.

While in every society the male dominance tendency will manifest itself in dominance and authority, it can be least important in a society in which the existence of small, fluid bands results in a minimal degree of formal organization and authority being necessary. The importance of psychophysiological factors is a function of social realities, so that sex-role differentiation greater than that of the Pygmies is not necessarily artifically exaggerated, but is inevitable under conditions that enable such factors to manifest themselves more easily, or for which such factors have a positive value for survival and success.

The Limits of Possibility

I am not, of course, suggesting that primitive societies necessarily have such limited hierarchical systems; many have extensive hierarchical systems, and these are patriarchal. My point is merely that it is possible for a primitive society to have a far more limited hierarchical system than any modern society. A modern society cannot limit the cues and the opportunities (inherent in hierarchies) given to the male dominance tendency. In an industrial society members do not all play the same economic role, nor are the vast majority necessary for, or capable of, playing the highest status roles. Diversity of economic roles and bureaucratic organization are the very hallmarks of an industrial society. Whereas the Pygmies have minimal formal organization, industrial societies composed of millions of people must have economic-role differentiation and formal organization if they are to survive and function. In other words, where the Pygmy society minimizes the effect of the male dominance tendency, the very nature of modern, industrial society forces such a society to give it relatively free play. We cannot even say that industrial society *exaggerates* this aggression; given the nature of its economic and social realities, the minimal possible effects of the psychophysiological factor will be very great in determining the degree of sex-role differentiation. Nor will lovely, gentle societies, such as that of the Pygmy, survive when challenged by societies whose methods of organization and whose authority systems render them more efficient.

Similarly, I am not suggesting that modernization and an increase in hierarchy will necessarily increase the importance of the male dominance tendency or that there is an absolute correlation between a society's economic situation or degree of homogeneity and the extent to which it allows male dominance tendency to manifest itself in social institutions. As has been true throughout this book, I am speaking only of the *limits of possibility* within which a society must operate, and the psychophysiological forces that it must utilize or attempt to counteract. Within these limits, of course, there is an enormous range of possible alternatives, and this allows for the diversity of societies that the anthropologist encounters. The degree to which a society limits the manifestation of the male dominance tendency in its value system (how close it comes to the maximum possible reduction of sex differentiation) in any area depends not only on the limits set by physiology, but also on a complex of values, traditions, and environmental necessities that are more or less specific to that particular society. Therefore, we should not be surprised to learn that there are some primitive societies in which women have extremely few rights and little respect. I am saying only that the degree to which a society *could limit* the manifestation of male attainment and the degree to which it *could minimize* sex-role differentiation will be much greater if it is a primitive rather than a bureaucratic, industrial society. The United States, in other words, *could not* limit the social manifestations as much as a primitive society (such as the Pygmies).

Only a society which completely segregated males and females, had no values of any kind, and lacked hierarchies altogether could over-ride the 'advantage' given to males by their greater dominance tendency. Such a society would accomplish this by withholding the environmental stimuli which cue the male's propensity for dominance behavior, and could exist only in fantasy. A priest may be celibate for moral reasons, but—for the vast majority of the members of any society—intellect works in the service of emotion. As long as human psychophysiology determines that men and women are drawn to one another, complete sexual segregation seems unlikely. As long as societies equip their members with world-views of any kind, they will provide them with hierarchies of desired qualities (values); whatever a society values and whatever leads to status and position in that society—age, youth, appearance, social position, business aptitude, fighting ability, the ability to give birth and nurture the young, and so on—will result in some individuals being more highly valued by society than the rest. As long as societies need any kind of organization they will have relatively formal hierarchies of some sort.

Social Exaggeration of the Physiological

However, we *can* speak of a given society *exaggerating* the values relevant to male dominance tendency while acknowledging that the direction of those values is determined by the hormonal factor. Exaggeration could not be determined merely by comparing that particular society with another, for this would force one to conclude that all societies save that of the Pygmy exaggerate the tendency. To decide whether a society's values exaggerate the tendency, we must compare the degree to which they reflect the tendency with the minimum extent which would be possible for *that sort of society.* I think that all would agree that, in all areas except those which concern abortion, Japan's value system is more male-oriented than that of the United States. Because, very roughly speaking, both Japan and the United States are highly bureaucratized, democratic, industrial societies with the same threshold of minimal possible emphasis on the male dominance tendency, one might say that Japan exaggerates the tendency in that its values reflect a general male authority more than do those of the United States (and that this *exaggeration,* therefore, must result not from physiology and the general nature of industrial society, but from specific Japanese values). One could similarly say that the United States exaggerates the male dominance tendency (though not as much as Japan), but one must then measure the degree of exaggeration against a hypothetical minimum which is far greater than in a non-modern society such as that of the Pygmy. We could reduce the extent to which male dominance tendency is manifested in American society to the minimum possible for an industrial society, though this is unlikely to happen; we could, theoretically, reduce it to that found in Pygmy society if we were willing to give up science, industrialization, hospitals, and other advances for which extensive hierarchy is a necessary condition. But even if we did this, we would still find that there is a minimal threshold below which no society can limit the manifestations of male dominance tendency in its social system.

Discrimination of a Sort

It is not inconceivable that the dominance tendency of which we speak is relevant not only to the attainment of position, but to performance as well: when the executive is described as 'aggressive', his performance as well as his ambition is being praised. However, the relevance of male tendencies to *performance* need not be posited in an explanation of why males attain hierarchical positions, and it is not assumed here that men are, even in the statistical sense in which we are speaking, physiologically any better prepared for performance than women. If one defines as 'discrimination' a situation in which males occupy virtually all the upper hierarchical positions despite the fact that women would perform them equally well, one has to conclude that we do indeed have such 'discrimination', and that this is unavoidable.

Moreover, even if the male's greater dominance tendency were over-ridden and large numbers of women placed in positions of authority, it is unlikely that stability could be maintained. Even in our present male bureaucracies problems arise when a subordinate is more 'aggressive' than his superior and, if the more 'aggressive' executive is not allowed to rise in the bureaucracy, delicate psychological adjustments must be made. Such adjustments are also necessary when a male bureaucrat has a female superior. Very exceptionally, adjustments can be made without any great instability occurring, particularly if the woman in the superior position possesses sensitivity and femininity. It seems likely, however, that if women shared equally in power at each level of the bureaucracy, chaos would result for two reasons. Even if the bureaucracy were a closed system, male dominance tendency would soon manifest itself in men either moving quickly up the hierarchy or refusing to acknowledge female authority. But a bureaucracy is not a closed system, and the discrepancy between male dominance in private life and bureaucratic female dominance (from the point of view of the male whose superior is a woman) would soon engender chaos. The minute minority of women in positions of high authority at present expend enormous amounts of energy trying *not* to project the commanding authority that is seen as the mark of a good male executive. It is true that the manner in which authority is manifested will be affected by the values of the society in general and the nature of the field of competition in particular; authority in an academic environment is camouflaged far more than in an executive one. One might put forward the theoretical argument that women could attain positions of authority and leadership by countering the male's advantage with feminine abilities. Perhaps, but the equivalents of the executive positions in every area of suprafamilial life in every society have been occupied by men, and there seems no reason to believe that feminine means will be suddenly capable of neutralizing male authority in these areas. And, in any case, an emphasis on feminine abilities is hardly what the feminists desire. (It is interesting to speculate on what would happen if hierarchical leadership were given low status. Would males be drawn to the upper hierarchical positions (i.e. is it the *positions* that attract?) or would they devote their energies to whatever was given high status? It is inconceivable that any society would attach low status to its leadership roles, so this question is probably unanswerable.)

This is not, of course, to gainsay that there is much real discrimination against women. Many women have had the experience of seeing men with less talent *and* a weaker dominance tendency promoted over them. The fact that this injustice can be explained by expectations and attitudes that reflect real statistical realities offers little satisfaction to the woman who is being treated unjustly even by the criterion that accepts the justice of promotion reflecting dominance tendency. While one cannot be sanguine about the ease with which antidiscrimination laws can eradicate this injustice—dominance tendency in individual cases is not easily demonstrated and so neither is misassessment of it—such laws will no doubt go far towards reducing this real discrimination.

The Future

Patriarchy, while perhaps unfair to the woman who is an exception and has a strong dominance tendency, is ultimately 'fair' in the special sense that the sex with the stronger tendency towards dominance dominates. I do not know whether it makes sense to describe the inevitable as 'fair' or 'unfair,' but if it does, then what could be more fair than that the sex that is more willing to sacrifice other satisfactions for dominance should attain it? Those who decry patriarchy like to think of themselves as the *avant garde,* but they most remind me of those Victorians who denied physiological sexual imperatives and saw virtue in such a denial, much as today's environmentalists deny the physiological roots of the male's stronger dominance tendency and see virtue in so doing. A hundred years ago values and attitudes favored 'aggressiveness' and despised sexuality, while today this is reversed. But if there is one thing that the evidence we have examined tells us, it is that values and attitudes are of little causal importance to the institutions whose universality we wish to explain.

None of this implies that there will not be great changes in the future, but only that such changes will not be relevant to the universal institutions discussed here. It is one thing to claim, perhaps correctly, that the realities of increasing population and increasing technology make social life less and less congruent with our physiological natures and quite another to assert, incorrectly, that our physiological natures no longer help to determine our behavior and institutions. It is one thing to point out that the world is overpopulated and quite another to imply that this will somehow lead to the demise of patriarchy. We shall always need to propagate the species; even if contraception eradicates the overpopulation problem, we shall still need to produce a next generation, as did all the societies of the past, and it will still be women who give birth. Even if an artificial substitute for the mother were developed and even if women wanted this substitution to be made at a widespread level (an unlikely probability), patriarchy would continue unless biological adaptation led to the disappearance of sexual hormonal differences. For the hormonal differences alone would still engender patriarchy, male dominance, and male attainment of status.

Let us descend to the level of the probable. There will be changes in the next few centuries, indeed in the next few decades; whether these are 'revolutionary' or minor depends again on whether one sees the glass as being half full or half empty, whether one emphasizes the physiological reality to which social reality conforms or the myriad variations possible within the limitations imposed by the physiological. There is no doubt that the institutions of American society, for example, will soon accommodate large numbers of women who no longer need devote their entire lives to child rearing, as have many societies that needed virtually all of their women in the labor force. While feminists often discuss this possibility in terms that assume that every woman is capable of a career in nuclear physics, and that this is the option every woman should be able to weigh against the emphasis on the home, the reality is that most individuals, male and female, have close to average capabilities and close to average jobs. It is not at all self-evident that most women would choose to devote to such jobs, rather than to their families, the lifelong expenditures of energies which men devote to their jobs and which are necessary for attainment in most occupational areas. It seems likely that most American women will gravitate towards those areas where there is the greatest need and where they need not compete with men—both because no one is now performing those functions and because those areas (social workers, elementary school teachers, and so forth) do not have a particularly high status that would attract male competition. No doubt there will be an increase in the number of women in the lower authority positions and perhaps an increase in the number of women in the higher authority positions in low-status areas. If, for example, day-care centers become a major factor in American life, women will unquestionably fill the overwhelming number of lower-level authority positions and perhaps the higher ones as well. This generalization of motherhood will be possible because the area will have low status for males who will not compete for the positions, because there are no males now filling those roles, and, dare I leave my theoretical position long enough to advance this point, because women will desire these roles and will be better at filling them than men would be. *Any increase in the number of women in high-status positions in high-status areas, however, will be slight and 'token'.* For this is the area in which dominance tendency counts the most, and men will succeed at attaining the high positions of power, status, and authority as they always have in every society.

Nothing I have written should be construed as implying that modern women do not face the most serious problems. Increasing longevity, a reduced desire for large families, the TV dinner, and the fragility of the family in a frantic society create a context in which the potential for female anomie is very great. To an extent, the women's movement has garnered what support it has because, like any social movement, it can replace feelings of individual meaninglessness with feelings of group strength and belonging. If I do not write at length of economic discrimination it is not because such discrimination does not exist, but because, important as this issue is, it is beyond the scope of this book. If I have ignored the residual laws that discriminate between the sexes it is because, whatever their symbolic importance, such laws are obviously not the source of the energy that engenders male attainment. The masculine nature of modern industrial and bureaucratic society and a reduced emphasis on the family create problems of meaning for the women that are only marginally related to laws and other factors which are not inevitable manifestations of male aggression. If the few remaining laws that differentiate between the sexes are removed, it will become clear in time that such laws had merely reflected society's acknowledgment of sexual differences but had not caused them. Equal rights legislation will have little effect on either the inevitable 'discrimination' we discussed earlier or on discriminatory attitudes.

In the near future America may well have a female leader, but we shall never see a time when males fail to attain the overwhelming percentage of top hierarchical positions. What we shall see, and what is most pressing, are opportunities for women, who no longer need devote the major part of their lives to home and children, to enter areas formerly closed to women. There will be an eradication of one-sex occupations.

None of this will satisfy some feminists, but it will, I think, gratify the majority of women, whose frustration does not result from male domination of upper hierarchical positions, but from the lack of a meaningful life. The eradication of one-sex occupations and a degree of opening up of middle-hierarchical positions will go far towards meeting the needs and wants of most women. The woman who wishes to be a police officer is more concerned with a woman's being permitted to become a police officer and a reduction of the prejudice she faces than she is with the percentage of women in the police force. Likewise, there are far more middle than upper positions available (for men or women) in any hierarchy. For the majority (of men or women) the right to persue a career and a good possibility of attaining a respectable middle position permits the choice and achievement required for most people to reach their potential for success. The upper hierarchical positions are, by their nature, attained by only a few. For the reasons discussed in this book, it will always be primarily males who are willing to make the sacrifices necessary to attain these few positions.

In any case, the seriousness of the problems facing women in contemporary society may tempt us to ignore or even deny that dominance tendency determines hierarchical attainment, but we have no justification whatsoever for doing so. It is an American trait to believe that every problem has not just a partial, relative solution, but one that will satisfy every desire. The desire of the majority of women for meaningful work will be satisfied, at least to the extent that it is for men. The desire of some feminists that males no longer dominate will never be satisfied.

Three Methodological Observations

1. Because upper hierarchical position carries high status in every society, we cannot be certain whether it is the hierarchal position itself or the high status attached to it that elicits more strongly from the male the 'need' to attain the position. Given: a. the near-absence of women in *industrial* hierarchies in Scandinavia, and b. the fact it is always the tendency for large parliamentary bodies and the lower of two parliamentary bodies to have somewhat higher percentages of women than do their small and upper equivalents, it would be worth investigating the possibility that, c. position in political hierarchy in Scandinavia has somewhat less status than in other nations, and d. it may be that it is (in all societies) the *status*, rather than the *position*, that attracts the male more strongly. I treat the *position* as the cue and differentiate this from the cue presented by status *per se*. However, if d. is the case, we can simplify the theory presented here: hierarchical attainment becomes simply a special case of status attainment and 'patriarchy' becomes subsumed under 'male attainment'. Parsimony would then suggest that, having reduced 'patriarchy', 'male attain-ment', and 'male dominance' to 'male attainment' and 'male dominance', we try to reduce the two entities to one.

However, having raised the possibility of reducing the three entities to two and two to one, I should add that I very much doubt that we could do either without doing violence to the precision we have striven for.

Our viewing male pursuit of hierarchical position as striving for status (and subsuming 'patriarchy' under 'male attainment') would, as we have just seen, imply that, if hierarchical position were to somehow lose its status (and leaders were *really* seen as '*servants* of the people'), males would no longer strive for the positions. This seems unlikely. There seems to be an element of dominance for its own sake in hierarchical attainment, just as there is in male dominance in male-female encounters and relationships. This would seem to preclude our seeing patriarchy (hierarchies) as simply a special case of male attainment (status).

Likewise, the evidence of both human beings and species closely related to them indicates that male dominance in male-female encounters and relationships arises primarily from behavior that the mere presence of a female elicits from a male, though this usually becomes entwined with considerations of position and status. This would seem to preclude our seeing male dominance in male-female encounters and relationships as simply a special case of male attainment (status).

2. Perhaps I would attempt to cast patriarchy as the outcome of battle for position between pairs of people, male attainment as the outcome of similar battles for status, and male authority as the outcome of battles for dyadic dominance between members of male-female pairings. This would add a degree of parsimony, but, perhaps, at too great a cost in clarity. (In all of these situations, of course, a host of cultural institutions channel and make concrete the realities we discuss, but the institutions always do this because the realities 'precede' the institutions.)

3. If I were beginning this work now, I would probably alter the presentation in the following way: I would use the term 'male dominance' as an umbrella term subsuming 'patriarchy' (hierarchy), 'male attainment' (status), and a new third term, 'male authority', to replace 'male dominance' as I have used the term (the male and female feelings relevant to encounters and relationships between a male and a female, feelings usually, but not always, reflected in formal institutions of dyadic authority). Thus changing the terminology would have the virtue of emphasizing the reality that is common to, that underlies, the three institutions we wish to explain: the stronger tendency of those with male neuro-endocrinological systems to experience the emotions of dominance, and therefore to exhibit the (socially-determined) actions of dominance, when there is the cue of hierarchy, status, of member of the other sex. 'Male dominance' would, depending on context, refer to both the tendency and the configuration of three institutions that is the social manifestation of the tendency. But this terminological change is not so attractive as to induce me to recast all the arguments of this book.

Part *II*
Objections and Implications

Chapter *VI*

The Inadequacy of a Non-Physiological Explanation

The Weight of the Evidence

At its most basic, the hypothesis at the core of the theory presented here simply states that there are neuro-endocrinological differences between men and women that engender different male and female responses to the environment and, therefore, different male and female behavior, and that these differences set limits on, and give direction to, the social institutions whose explanation is the purpose of this book.

Now, it is probably not too bold to say that there is not a single other non-obvious hypothesis in all sociology for which one can invoke both anthropological universality and direct neuro-endocrinological evidence. Is there not something a bit bizarre about contemporary sociology's accepting innumerable dubious conclusions from silly little studies, the inadequacy of which can be spotted with a cursory glance, while rejecting, on ideological grounds, a hypothesis which can draw upon anthropological universality and direct physiological evidence in its support?

Even if one is not totally convinced that patriarchy, male attainment, and male dominance are inevitable, one must acknowledge that the evidence provided *only* by human anthropology, or *only* by human hermaphrodites, or *only* by the direct neuro-endocrinological study of other mammals suggests that it is an exceedingly strong possibility. When all three converging lines of evidence are taken together the argument for a purely environmentalist analysis disintegrates and the physiological hypothesis becomes compelling. Those who then insist on maintaining their belief in an environmentalist analysis whose internal illogic and empirical inadequacy are manifest, while demanding of the infinitely more probable physiological analysis a deductive conclusiveness which is precluded by the very nature of science, must be profoundly influenced by something other than weight of evidence. There is no such thing in all science as deductive conclusiveness, the 'proof' that the radical environmentalist demands. Science deals in 'probabilities' and always acknowledges the possibility that a future observation will demonstrate that a theory is incorrect. A scientific theory can never be 'proved'. Science leaves open the possibility that tomorrow a mountain will float into space or that we shall discover a matriarchy. We have not 'proved' that e $=$ mc^2 or that smoking leads to cancer.

As we have seen, there is one sense in which the scientist does, and should, proceed as if science discovers immutable truths: he states a hypothesis in terms which imply that it will always be true precisely *because* he wishes to specify the conditions under which it will be surrendered. He wants the hypothesis to specify those events which it predicts cannot occur in nature, so that if they do occur the hypothesis will be shown to be incorrect. It was for this reason that I called the first edition of this book *'The Inevitability of Patriarchy'*. The theory presented in this book claims that there could not be a society that lacked patriarchy, and the discovery or development of a society that lacked patriarchy would *ipso facto* demonstrate the incorrectness of the theory presented here.[1]

Because science is always uncertain, always open-ended, continual empirical testing is an integral part of the scientific method. But to invoke this feature of science in order to dismiss the overwhelming likelihood that patriarchy is inevitable is scientifically untenable. Radical interpretation should imply a better way of explaining what is observed, not closing one's eyes so as not to observe. An over-emotional analysis of an intellectual problem which forces people to disregard observation can have only catastrophic results for objective inquiry. That even a few academic intellectuals have accepted the extreme environmentalist analysis with its illogic and its misrepresentation of fact is explicable only in terms of emotional commitment. It is intellectually defensible in no terms at all.

---

1. As we saw in the First Digression, this is a slight oversimplification. A society that has extensive hierarchy, but which is not patriarchal, *would* demonstrate the incorrectness of the theory, but a primitive society that has no hierarchy would not demonstrate the irrelevance of physiological differentiation for any society that does have hierarchy; it would not demonstrate the possibility of a society that has hierarchy, but lacks patriarchy. This is academic, since there is no primitive society that lacks patriarchy. All this can be said, *mutatis mutandis,* of male attainment and male dominance. Thus a society that separated males and females save for brief sexual encounters would not be expected to manifest male dominance (which requires male-female interaction). There has never been such a society.

The insoluble problem with all totally environmental explanations, is not that they necessarily posit logical impossibilities or that they are necessarily internally contradictory, but that they fail to explain empirical reality. There is rarely only one logical theoretical explanation for an observed reality. Because every physiological sex difference which affects behavior will be reflected in every society's social system, one will always be able to say that men and women act the way they do because their society tells them to. Because men have greater dominance tendencies, boys will be socialized towards dominance behavior and girls will be told that it is unladylike to attempt to attain their goals through such behavior. Those who wish to claim that what we tell boys and girls is responsible for differences in behavior between the sexes will always be able to do so. If they are aware that their explaining a thousand virtually disparate observations with a thousand particular explanations rather than with a single explanation commits the serious methodological sin of 'ad-hoccery', and that they must find some underlying factor comparable to the physiological one, they will be able, by means of tortuous, but not illogical, reasoning, to develop a theory that makes no reference to the physiological factor. I have no idea what form such a theory would take, but no doubt it could be developed. For if one were prepared to accept more and more convoluted and irrelevant hypotheses one could still believe in the existence of phlogiston and ether and ignore all the theories of twentieth-century science that explain reality more convincingly.

The Environmentalist's Dilemma

This is what one will be forced to do if one insists on adhering to environmental or economic theory to explain universal patterns of sex-associated dominance behavior. For such a theory cannot suggest a possible *initiative* of patterns that invariably work *in one direction* that is nearly as logically and theoretically compelling as that provided by demonstrable evidence indicating a strong relationship between hormones and behavior. Such environmental theory attempts to deal with the physiological evidence by ignoring it, thereby refusing to acknowledge the determinative influence of sexual hormonal differences not only in humans (with their societal environment), but in the non-human mammals whose endocrine systems are similar to man's and for whom a totally non-hormonal explanation of behavior is patently ridiculous. The denial of the physiological factor takes the form of either ignoring the universality of patriarchy, male dominance, and male attainment and pretending that such universality does not need explanation, or of explaining it in environmental terms that are either, or both, internally illogical or empirically refutable.

My point is not that the boy is not socialized differently from the girl or that this does not run very deep. I do not doubt those environmentalists who claim that by the time an infant is three months old the nature of the socialization it receives from its parents will be determined by its sex; shortly after their birth we dress male infants in blue and female infants in pink. While it is unlikely that this makes much difference to new-born infants, it does show that differential socialization by the parents begins at birth. But this indicates the strength and importance of sexual hormonal reality and the necessity of any society's socialization conforming to this reality. For the environmentalist to demonstrate that the physiological reality does not underlie the directions in which societies socialize the young, he must demonstrate not merely that socialization runs deep, but that it would be possible to socialize boys away from, and girls towards, dominance. No society has ever done this, nor, according to the theory expounded in this book, could any society ever do it.

A few behaviorists have generalized from experiments (which for argument's sake we will assume were as successful as described) in which behavior is altered through high-intensity conditioning, and use this as 'evidence' that male and female behavior has only an environmental, and not a physiological determinant. Now, besides being unable to explain what element in the cultural environment of every society corresponds to this conditioning, this analysis erroneously implies that because high-intensity conditioning can force one to behave as if, even to think as if, one had no 'sex drive,' then these 'drives' are not physiological in nature. Indeed, we know that some people have been forced to behave in this way not as a result of high-intensity conditioning, but simply because of the extremes of a Victorian cultural environment. The real implication of the behaviorists' experiments is not that sexual behavior is environmentally caused, but that, theoretically at least, even the most basic physiologically-rooted tendency can be over-ridden if the conditioning is extreme enough. The important point to remember however is that there is no outside experimenter who can invent any conditioning he likes for society as a whole. The social values by which the members of a society are conditioned are not infinitely variable: they are limited by a population's observation of the behavior of men and women that is differentiated as a result of their differentiated psychophysiology.

This is the environmentalist's dilemma: he faces the task of explaining, without begging the question by invoking socialization, and without invoking the psycho-physiological differentiation that is seen here as the determining factor, why it is the males in every society who attain hierarchical and dyadic dominance, and why no society associates dominance with women. His explanation must be parsimonious and for this he must find a universal factor comparable to the neuro-endocrinological factor. Lastly, and perhaps most importantly, such an explanation must not avoid any relevant physiological evidence and must be plausible.

Alternative Explanations of Universality

There are three commonly-heard explanations of the universality of patriarchy, male attainment, and male dominance that are both parsimonious[2] and avoid invoking neuro-endocrinological differentiation; all three fail both because they lack plausibility when examined closely and because they simply ignore the mass of neuro-endocrinological evidence we have discussed. The explanations are those which emphasize the male's physical strength, the female's maternal role, and the effects of modern technology. (Clearly, no one would deny that these factors have important social implications or that they may increase sex differences, but they fail to explain these sex differences.)

Those who emphasize the universal fact that males are physically bigger and stronger than females not only ignore experimental evidence indicating that, in species in which males dominate, even males which are no larger than females dominate them; they also ignore the fact that among human males there seems to be little correlation between physical strength and attainment—while it is quite obvious that there is a crucial relationship between the kinds of behavior I describe as 'dominance behavior' and attainment.[3]

Indeed, we correctly describe the superior executive as an 'aggressive' man who will 'get to the top' rather than as someone who is physically strong. The importance of dominance tendencies and the behavior they facilitate are implicitly acknowledged by the old-style environmentalist feminist when she

---

2. When I refer to these explanations as parsimonious, I mean only that they are capable of explaining the universal realities in terms of factors that are present in every society, so that these explanations need not offer twenty different explanations of patriarchy in twenty different societies.

3. Although I happen to think that it is the case, it is not implied here that the subtle neuro-endocrinological differences among males influence their attainments. I have stressed the fact that it does not behove one who sees a great between-group difference in some factor as determinative, to see slight within-group differences in this factor as determinative. My point here is merely that when we look at individuals who attain upper hierarchical positions (nearly always males), we see that physical size and strength is irrelevant while 'dominance behavior' is crucial.

emphasizes the differing motivations and behaviors of men and women and incorrectly attributes them entirely to differences in socialization.

The 'physical strength' explanation often acknowledges that physical strength is of little importance to attainment in modern society, but argues that at one time strength was necessary for securing food and for attaining position and that the association of maleness and dominance is maintained to this day. We have discussed the myriad difficulties encountered by all such evolutionary theories, but I should repeat that there are a great many primitive societies in which women do heavier and economically more important (but lower-status) work than men and many societies in which it is the women who secure the food.[4] None of these societies lack the institutions we discuss. The women in them may 'expend more energy' than the men, but not for dominance. It is precisely the sexual difference in the 'motivation' to expend 'energy' for dominance, rather than for some other satisfaction, that is the manifestation of the neuro-endocrinological differentiation we discuss. (If we were to set up an experimental one-generation society of the infant sons of small parents and the infant daughters of large parents [so that the females of this society were as large as the males], we would still find that this society developed into a patriarchy. If, however, we peopled our experimental society with genetic male infants whose fetal masculinization had been blocked and genetic female infants who had accidentally been virilized *in utero,* we would find that the genetic females ruled, that authority was associated with them, that they attained the positions of high status, that they were dominant in dyadic relationships, and that socialization came to conform to all this.) It is true that many societies explain patriarchy by male physical strength but once again I would point out that we look to other societies for empirical evidence, not for an explanation of empirical reality.

Many of these same points lead one to find implausible the explanation which emphasizes the female's maternal role. It seems plausible when one thinks of the traditional American woman whose maternal duties tied her to her home, but implausible when one thinks of the hundreds of societies in which women take off a few days to give birth and then return to the fields, while men continue with their physically less difficult, high-status roles. Again we might ask why these energies are expended in virtually every suprafamilial area except for those associated with dominance; if the women of a society spend their lives doing heavy, non-maternal work in the fields, then their not devoting their

---

4. Mead, *Male and Female,* 195.

'energies' to dominance-related areas cannot be explained by their being in the home. (Securing food is a male task in many other societies, so one cannot argue that women are responsible for securing food and that *this* explains their not attaining dominance.) And again this explanation simply ignores the mass of neuro-endocrinological evidence relevant to dominance. To those who argue that it is not the physical reality of the maternal role, but the 'posture of submissiveness' (in one critic's phrase) which the maternal role allegedly necessitates, we would stress the neuro-endocrinological evidence demonstrating that the hormonally masculinized female, who appears to be a normal female and is socialized as a normal female, manifests the dominance tendency expected of a male; such females are socialized to the 'posture of submissiveness', yet, because they are hormonally male, they exhibit male dominance behavior. Moreover, no explanation emphasizing socialization accounts for male dominance in non-human mammals. Thus, even if men were not larger and stronger than women and even if all women decided not to have children, the neuro-endocrinological differentiation relevant to dominance tendency would be sufficient to guarantee the continuation of patriarchy, male attainment, and male dominance.

This point is important to remember when considering the third alternative explanation of patriarchy, that which emphasizes economic factors and modern technology. Whether such an explanation emphasizes the fact that women can now control reproduction, or the fact that machines now render physical strength unimportant, it implicitly explains patriarchy in terms of causal factors (be they physical strength, maternal roles, or whatever) which have nothing much to do with the causation of patriarchy and are not of sufficient importance to act as a counter-cause.

While some critics of the first edition of this book favored explanations in terms of physical strength or the maternal role, the majority of them supported the economic-technological explanation of patriarchy. They argued that patriarchy (and male attainment and male dominance) are 'no longer necessary' and that they will be eradicated in modern technological society,[5] and they tried to refute the theory presented here by merely ignoring it—in other words by simply *assuming* and *asserting* that economic-technological changes will override the psychophysiological factor. *If* the theory presented here is incorrect,

---

5. For examples of this sort of criticism see: Mary Ellmann, 'Women's Work', *The New York Review of Books* (1st November 1973; 18), Margaret Mead, 'Does the World Belong to Men—Or to Women?' in *Redbook* (October 1973; 46–52) and Eleanor Maccoby's review in *Science* (2nd November 1973, Volume 182, Number 4111).

then these predictions may prove correct. But they give us no reason to doubt the central importance of the psychophysiological by refusing even to consider the argument for its being determinative. There is not much that I can say in reply to such criticisms except to repeat that: 1. There is not an iota of evidence that any change in social, economic, or technological factors significantly reduces the percentage of males in hierarchies. The most modern society is virtually as patriarchal as the most primitive. There is some variation in the degree to which male dominance manifests itself in dyadic and familial relationships (though no society lacks social manifestations of male dominance), but such variation depends more on such factors as the amount of interaction of men and women and the family structure than on modernization. What does vary tremendously, and what is often confused with patriarchy and male dominance and is often invoked in the criticisms under discussion, is the *attitude* of the society towards patriarchy and male dominance. Thus, a hundred years ago our society valued 'aggression' and placed little value on sexuality while today this is reversed. (Similarly traditional China and Russia applauded traditional sex roles, whereas post-revolution China and Russia constantly issued declarations favoring complete sexual equality in the hierarchy.) But these changes in attitudes, like changes in technology, have no effect on the proportion of males in hierarchies. Indeed, the very point of this theory is that no social factor is of much causal importance to patriarchy or can act as a counter-cause to the psychophysiological. Thus, when these critics assert that 'physiology is no longer important', that 'human beings are not animals', and that 'man is sufficiently adaptable to overcome patriarchy', one can only reply with a rather ungracious 'says who?' and a reminder that technological progress and increased adaptability facilitate rather than counteract psychophysiological tendencies. 2. Claims that social change will eradicate the institutions under discussion simply ignore the neuro-endocrinological evidence and the overwhelming likelihood that neuro-endocrinological differentiation, and not any social-technological factor, is the primary causal factor responsible for patriarchy. 3. Societies are not patriarchal because patriarchy is socially 'necessary' or 'good', but because patriarchy is a social manifestation of a sexual psychophysiological differentiation, one which is not significantly reduced by any social or technological change and which will not be significantly reduced as long as males and females are neuro-endocrinologically constituted as they are now. 4. Nearly all of these critics invoked variation in qualities and institutions that have nothing to do with the theory presented here; we discussed the inability of this line of attack to damage the theory in the section entitled 'Grounds for an Empirical Refutation' in Chapter 2 above.

A great many critics committed the fallacy of 'explaining' the institutions I discuss in terms of socialization, thereby begging the question, failing to ask *why* socialization proceeds as it does, and ignoring the possibility that to a great extent socialization reflects observation (boys really *are* more 'aggressive' and girls more nurturant) and that the differentiation of the behavior that is observed is primarily the result of psychophysiological differentiation. Another version of this criticism committed the fallacy of 'explaining' patriarchy in terms of 'patriarchal values', thereby begging the question by failing to explain why such values are 'patriarchal'. We have discussed the difficulties facing these question-begging approaches at great length. It was, incidentally, these critics who most often claimed that the theory presented here is simplistic, reductionist, or deterministic (a criticism considered in the chapter on psychological aspects of psychophysiological differentiation) and criticized the use of the word 'inevitability' in the title of this book's first edition.

Apart from those just referred to, the most commonly-levelled criticism of this book was that which took exception to my not describing sexual psychophysiological differentiation in the terms used by the discipline of the particular critic. Thus, a social psychologist complained that it is one of 'readiness' to learn dominance behavior, a Freudian that it is one of a 'drive' for dominance, a developmental psychologist that it is one of the threshold for dominance behavior, another Freudian that it is one of ego strength (the female's stronger ego does not need shoring up through attainment), a sociologist that it is one of 'need' for dominance, and a therapist that it is one of the 'motivation' for dominance. A number of critics complained that it is qualitative (males have an 'active dominance motivation' and females an equally strong 'passive dominance motivation'), while many others complained that it is instead quantitative.

Some critics ignored the statistical nature of any physiological reality and argued that the exception proves the unimportance of physiological differentiation or that this unimportance is demonstrated by the fact that differences within the sexes are greater than those between the sexes. Others confused gender identity with dominance tendency. Still others, often those who argued that 'patriarchy is no longer necessary', failed to distinguish between direct physiological evidence and more speculative evidence and challenged evolutionary theories and theories of territoriality and male bonding, the correctness of which is irrelevant to the theory presented here. Finally, some critics raised individual points, such as: if I am to argue that physiology determines differences between the sexes, I should also show that the same applies within the sexes; 'feedback' and the fact that environment can alter physiology somehow demonstrate its irrelevance; the fact that suggestion can sometimes channel the psychophysiological somehow demonstrates the determinativeness of social factors, and the fact that the testosterone levels of girls equal that of boys while boys manifest a greater dominance tendency, somehow demonstrates the irrelevance of testosterone to dominance tendency. All of these criticisms are replied to at length in the chapter on physiological differentiation.

Finally a great number of critics argued that the theory presented here, even if correct, would have unfortunate social results. When invoked as an argument for the incorrectness of the theory presented here, this is clearly an *ad consequentium* fallacy. When not used in this way, I can merely repeat that one cannot legitimately argue that the scientific analysis presented here entails any policy of any kind, that my whole argument is that socialization and laws are only of secondary importance to the institutions I attempt to explain, and that I believe that no consideration of the possible effects of a scientific analysis ever justifies its misrepresentation or suppression.

The Fallacy of the Irrelevant Experiment

Few people argue that men and women do not differ in the qualities of temperament and cognition considered in this book. Disagreement concerns the causes of the differentiation, not its existence. The environmentalist does not deny that, for example, males have a lower threshold for dominance behaviour (are 'more aggressive'); he denies that the differentiation has a primarily physiological etiology. There are, however, possible sex differences that this book does not discuss whose *existence* is denied by a line of reasoning, the incorrectness of which is worth discussing here. For subtle versions of this reasoning infect many sociological and psychological studies of sex differences. Perhaps because of the fashionable conclusions they illegitimately reach, it is just such studies that most quickly find their way into newspapers and popular magazines, thereby accelerating the avalanche of misinformation that threatens to inundate us. (I would emphasize that in this section we are discussing only the presence or absence of certain sex differences in temperament and behavior and not the causation—be it primarily physiological or social—of those differences; and that I am not interested here in whether such differences

—which are not those with which we are concerned in the book—exist or not, but only in the logic of a certain attempt to deny that they exist.)

I am referring to the argument which invokes the evidence of a test, survey, or experiment that claims to discriminate a quality (for example a temperamental tendency or a cognitive aptitude), and then to find that the sexes do not differ in the quality, when, in fact, the test demonstrates nothing more than its inability to so discriminate. This problem does not arise when the quality is easily defined and measured. If, to use an absurd example to make the point, the quality we are interested in is height and we wish to know whether males and females differ with reference to this quality (and whether the stereotype that sees men as taller is correct), we need merely to measure a sample group of men and women with a yardstick. The yardstick test does measure the quality we observe as height, and we will find that, indeed, men are taller and that the stereotype is correct. If, however, someone claimed that men were not taller after testing the sample of men and women not with a yardstick, but with a test of the ability to speak French, he would be committing the fallacy that concerns us here; he would be claiming to measure a quality when, in fact, his tool of measurement discriminated another (irrelevant) quality.

Clearly, no one would make this sort of error when discussing a quality as easily described and measured as height. But the psychological and cognitive terms that we use every day—and that are represented in stereotypes such as 'women are more perceptive' and 'men are more logical'—are far more difficult to describe, far more subtle, and far less concrete than a quality like height. As a result, it is more difficult to tell whether a test is testing the stereotyped quality.

Now it is important to note that the psychological and cognitive terms are not *defined* by the tests that claim to measure them; they are operationally defined by our use of them and by the informal tests imposed by our observations. If we say that 'women are perceptive', we do not mean that we have rigorously tested their psychological perception but that, statistically speaking, they display a series of aptitudes that we observe and call perception. Even if we were completely unable to articulate in our attempts to define the term and to describe the aptitudes we observe, this would not render the term meaningless or indicate that we were not observing an empirical reality. For the fact that we independently agree on which people are more perceptive than others means that, even if we cannot articulate the qualities we refer to, we know them when we see them; otherwise there would be no agreement on which people manifest them. Consider, for example, a group of 50 acquaintances. Were we to ask four members of this group to list independently the ten most perceptive (or logical or nurturant) members of the group, there would be agreement of a high statistical significance. This is, *ipso facto,* evidence that the term means *something,* that there is agreement on its meaning, and that we can select those who most strongly exhibit the qualities under consideration. If someone gave a test that he claimed to measure 'perception' to the group of acquaintances and found that those who had been listed by the observer-members as most 'perceptive' scored no higher than other members of the group, we would correctly assume that the test was not measuring the 'perception' observed by the observer-members; the test-giver would have no way of explaining how the observer-members had been able to agree independently on the ten most perceptive members. If we had asked the four observers to list the ten most 'fnorcal' members of the group—even assuming that each observer independently made up a meaning for 'fnorcal' and assessed the members in terms of the meaning—there would be no agreement on which members most exhibited 'fnorcality'. 'Fnorcal', unlike 'perceptive', 'logical', and so forth, has no meaning prior to the test (this is demonstrated by the lack of agreement by the observers) and can be defined only in terms of scoring high on the test of 'fnorcality' (if at all). If some people consistently scored high on a test of 'fnorcality' the definition of 'fnorcality' would be nothing more than 'the ability shown on a test of "fnorcality" '—until we found, as we no doubt would, that 'fnorcality' was a synonym for some word (like 'perception') whose meaning can be established prior to the test; if no regularity were found in tests of 'fnorcality', then the term would lack even a test-operational definition.

Thus when a psychologist announces a test that discriminates logical aptitude and that finds no difference between men and women, he has not necessarily demonstrated that the general belief that men are more logical is incorrect or based on faulty observation. Certainly he has refuted the hypothesis whereby men will score higher on a test that *he* claims measures the quality that the general population terms 'logical aptitude'. Certainly his findings cannot be invoked as evidence that the sexes do differ in the quality that the general population terms 'logical aptitude'. But it may well be that he is presenting us with a subtle version of the attempt to deny a sexual difference in height on the basis of a French test. After all, we do have considerable prior evidence that the sexes do differ in 'logical aptitude' (as the general population uses the term). This evidence includes the stereotype that sees men as 'more logical' (one is hard-pressed to find a strong stereotype that—whether its origins are primarily physiological or social—is not or was not a basically correct observation; there is no stereotype of Japanese as great basketball players or American Jews as great farmers); the tasks that require a strong logical aptitude are primarily performed by men (there are few female mathematicians and theoretical physicists); even most environmentalists do not, when pressed, deny the reality of sexual differences in logical aptitude, but offer a non-physiological explanation of its presence, though often a simple descriptive statement of palpable fact (such as 'women are, on the whole, not as good at math as men') evokes antagonism.[6]

We might make these same points with reference to any test that failed to find a differentiation in a quality for which we had considerable prior evidence.

I realize that the argument I present in this section may strike some readers as trying to have my cake and eat it. Some readers are disturbed by my considering tests that find an expected difference as evidentially more important than tests that do not. To such readers I would make a few additional points: 1. We do demand of a hypothesized sex difference strong prior evidence of the type we have discussed. We do not accept the presence of a sex difference simply because someone claims that it exists. 2. Strong prior evidence leads to the questioning of negative test results in many areas of science. If an illness behaves in many ways like a virus-caused disease, we will not assume that viruses are not involved merely because a test fails to find them; we will often, correctly, assume that the test is too crude to identify the virus and that more discriminating tests will succeed. 3. In reality we are never so inarticulate that our prior definitions are demonstrated only by our agreement and ability to reach an independent empirical identification; we are quite capable of at least roughly defining 'logical aptitude', 'nurturance', and so forth. 4. We always look for tests that can discriminate the quality and reflect the differences indicated by the prior evidence. Most importantly, in reality we nearly always develop such tests. In reality, when tests such as those described in this section fail to find differences, *other* tests can differentiate between the sexes (statistically speaking, of course) on the basis of the quality that prior evidence had indicated to be sexually differentiated—though the newspapers reporting the former tests rarely mention this. When one test finds a difference and another does not, *the two tests do not cancel each other out*. The reasonable assumption is that one test, like that which uses French to measure height, fails to discriminate the quality, while the other, like the yardstick test, does so. After all, it is an empirical fact

---

6. Environmentalists cannot deny the sex difference in this aptitude because, as we shall see, there are many tests that can discriminate it and that do find the sex difference. In this section, however, I wish only to make the point that the lack of such tests would not demonstrate the absence of the sex difference.

that some sex difference is being manifested in the second test.[7] 5. While one cannot assess the adequacy of a test from a newspaper report of it, even a cursory examination of the tests and questionnaires that claim no sex difference with reference to a quality for which there is strong prior evidence of its existence usually exposes their inadequacy. Readers who have taken such tests or answered such questionnaires are no doubt aware of how often they fail to have anything to do with what they claim to measure.

Even though tests of the sort described here are not relevant to the evidence provided in this book, I think the discussion worthwhile. No doubt the reader has reacted with scepticism to popular reports of studies claiming that there are no sex differences in a quality that the reader knows perfectly well to be more strongly represented in one sex, for whatever reason. In all likelihood, such reports were of studies that were unable to discriminate the qualities they claimed to discriminate, and the reader was quite correct to trust his observation.

---

7. When two different researchers administer the *same* test and one finds a sex difference while the other does not, there is a methodological problem of some sort.

Chapter VII

Confusion and Fallacy in the Environmentalist Analysis

The Necessity of Theory

Falsity of assumption cannot be balanced by a doubling of emotional investment. The biochemical realities that lie at the core of all social situations involving men and women cannot be eradicated by claiming that one is not interested in theory. All social and political theory is built on conceptions of the nature of man, and this is true even if the theorist is unaware of this and confuses his ignorance with objectivity. When one accepts the necessity of theory, as one does when one puts forward alternative political, economic, or social systems, one must begin not with a vision of what one would *like* reality to be like, but with observation. One must either accept and explain such observation or demonstrate convincingly that it is not trustworthy or not inevitable. The concept of the 'inherent childishness' of the black man is mistaken not because we *like* to believe that the black man is born the equal of the white, but because observation of this and other societies indicates that the behavior described by whites as 'childish' is not universal but a particular response to a particular environmental situation. Likewise, all those 'inevitable' masculine and feminine characteristics that turn out to be socially rather than physiologically determined can be exposed by anthropology. This has not been accomplished, however, with patriarchy, male dominance, or male attainment of high-status roles and positions, and so the environmentalist must attempt to refute the determinativeness of the physiological factor on a theoretical level. It is pointless for him to ignore the theoretical in order to 'concentrate on the political and the economic'; doing so is analogous to explaining the dearth of women boxing champions by discussing only economic and political discrimination against women boxers. This analogy seems extreme not because there are many more women in the highest positions of power and attainment—

there are not—but because the reader has no emotional resistance to the acknowledgment of male physical strength while he resists with all his energy the reality of the male dominance advantage. If the political and economic systems do not conform to the limitations set by hormonal differentiation, it is incumbent on the feminist to demonstrate this.

The Environmentalist Assumption

The view of man and woman in society that implicitly underlay virtually all the arguments of the feminists of 20 years ago, and remains influential today, is this: there is nothing inherent in the nature of human beings or of society that necessitates any role or task (save those requiring great strength or the ability to give birth) being associated with one sex or the other;[1] there is no natural order

---

1. *"It is time that we realized that the whole structure of male and female personality is entirely imposed by social conditioning.* All the possible traits of human personality have in this conditioning been *arbitrarily* assigned into two categories; thus aggression is masculine, passivity feminine . . ." [Emphasis added]. (Kate Millett, *Barnard Alumnae,* Spring, 1970, 28.) This statement expresses the assumption which underpins all of Dr Millett's *Sexual Politics* (London: Hart-Davis, MacGibbon, 1971). In the four hundred pages of *Sexual Politics* she offers only four bits of evidence in support of this crucial assumption: 1. She quotes Dr Robert Stoller's *definitional* distinction between biological 'sex' and societal 'gender' and leaves the strong impression that Dr Stoller believes that 'sex' need not be relevant to behavior. The true flavor of his thesis is better summarized by Dr Stoller himself a few pages past the point where Dr Millet stopped quoting: "A sex-linked genetic biological tendency towards masculinity in males and femininity in females works silently but effectively from fetal existence on, being overlaid after birth by the effects of environment, influences working more or less in harmony to produce a preponderance of masculinity in men and femininity in women" (Robert Stoller, *Sex and Gender* [London: The Hogarth Press, 1969], 74). The point here is not whether Dr Stoller is correct in his assessment, but that, if scientists are in the kind of disagreement over the importance of sexual biology to behavior which Dr Millett claims they are, one would not think that she would find it necessary to misrepresent the views of a scientist who *does* believe that sexual biology is crucial. 2. Dr Millett includes a footnote that refers the reader to a Rockefeller University publication that is only tangentially relevant to this issue. 3. There is an out-of-context quotation from a work of Dr John Money. We need not examine this here because we have seen that it is Dr Money's own work, more than that of any other scientist working with humans (as opposed to experimental animals), which indicates the crucial importance of sex hormones to behavior. 4. Finally she states that "the best medical research points to the conclusion that sexual stereotypes have no bases in biology". As we have seen, this statement is absolutely indefensible unless one defines *stereotype* not in the terms of probability that the biologist uses but in terms so rigid that the point becomes irrelevant and unless one defines *best medical research* as 'research which points to the conclusion that sexual stereotypes have no bases in biology'. (This assumes that there is some medical research pointing in this direction; my investigations have uncovered none.) If anyone presented a thesis in an uncontroversial area to a graduate department in the social sciences or the physical sciences and attempted to get away with this kind of intellectual dishonesty, he would

of things decreeing that dyadic and social authority must be associated with men, nor is there any reason why it must be men who rule in every society. Patriarchy, matriarchy, and 'equiarchy' are all equally possible and—while every society may invoke 'the natural order of things' to justify its particular system—all the expectations we have of men and women are culturally determined and have nothing to do with any sort of basic male or female nature, and nothing to do with the sort of psychophysiological differentiation which is seen here as determining patriarchy, male attainment, male dominance and the cognitive differentiation that this book attempts to explain.

A clear statement of this assumption which has been accepted by many feminists occurs in John Stuart Mill's *The Subjection of Women*. As an impassioned plea for women's rights Mill's essay is both moving and illuminating. As an attempt to explain the etiology of sexually differentiated behaviour and institutions it is indefensible. One is tempted, given the fact that the author of the essay was Mill, to ascribe its inadequacies to the fact that little of the relevant anthropological evidence, and none of the relevant hormonal evidence, was available at the time. But the weakness of Mill's analysis is attributable even more to the fallacious reasoning that his preconceived conclusions demanded. For example, Mill argues that we can have no conception of the limits of possibility imposed by innate sexual differences, or even of whether such limits exist, because no society has been composed of one sex; thus he does not even attempt to explain why the conceptions of male and female held by his society are not reversed in any other society. Similarly Mill attempts to dismiss the possibility of the determinativeness of innate sexual differences by invoking the irrelevant fact that slave owners defended slavery with the invocation of physiological racial differences that do not exist; this fact is correct, of course, but it casts no more doubt on the likelihood that innate sexual differences are

---

receive ridicule rather than a PhD in literature from Columbia University. When Dr Millett is not energetically planting fallacies among the wild inaccuracies, she is dressing discarded conspiratorial and evolutionary theory in drag and presenting it as new. Her entire analysis is predicated on the belief that stating a disagreeable fact or argument in derisive terms results in alteration of the fact or refutation of the argument. Much of her book consists of an analysis of D.H. Lawrence and other male authors. I would not presume to question the accuracy of Dr Millett's presentation of these authors' representations of women. One wonders, however, whether she intends to imply that these views of women are representative of those held by nearly all male authors (or nearly all men). If not, then why are they relevant? One could 'prove' oppression of the whale by using only *Moby Dick* as evidence. If these representations of women are invoked as representative of those of nearly all male authors, then why do so many of those very individuals who are acknowledged to see most deeply into the nature of things all see the same thing?

determinative to sexual differences in behavior and institutions, than it does on the certainty that physiology is determinative to the ability to give birth.

Four Fallacies

Our comparison of the environmentalist line of reasoning with that of the Victorian is particularly illuminating when we examine environmentalist attempts to explain away the anthropological and physiological evidence we have examined. Virtually every radical environmentalist theoretical argument could be as easily, and no more absurdly, advanced to deny the existence or determinativeness of those physiological sexual factors we loosely refer to as the 'sex drive' and to deny the inevitability of every society's conforming its institutions to this drive. Since there is no exception to the universality of societal conformation to the 'sex drive' one could argue that many individuals deny this drive in themselves, that many men are insecure enough to exaggerate it in a constant attempt to prove its presence, that its universality does not 'prove' that such acknowledgment is inevitable, that we have not proved—and could never prove—with deductive conclusiveness that it exists, that no society has ever even tried to deny to a large number of its members institutional channels for its satisfaction, that the socialization of every society assumes its existence and that capitalists exploit it. This line of reasoning differs from that of the environmentalist only in that the environmentalist has no emotional barrier preventing acknowledgment of the absurdity of Fundamentalist reasoning.

It often used to be suggested that we should ignore the illogic of old-style feminist analyses since it represented merely the 'excesses' that must be expected of a social movement. I do not think one has the right to ask even this of the theorist, but the problem we deal with here is much more serious. For the fallacies we discuss are not peripheral or unimportant, but are central to the entire environmentalist line of reasoning which until recently was endorsed by most feminists. There are great differences among environmentalist writers in tone, in political approach, and in reasonableness; but all those who do not ignore the anthropological and physiological evidence altogether begin with the incorrect assumption that sexual hormonal differences are irrelevant to behavior and institutions, and try to compensate for this incorrect assumption by invoking one or more of four basic lines of fallacious reasoning.

The first of these admits that the evidence is basically correct, but argues that the existence of individuals who do not conform to universal societal norms proves that such norms are not inevitable. We have discussed the pointlessness of invoking the individual exception to disprove the inevitability of the societal rule. As we have seen, statistical inevitability for the whole not only need not, but usually will not, imply inevitability for every individual when physiology is a causal factor; the existence of some women who are taller than some men does not diminish the fact that there is a physiological reason why the men of every society are taller than the women.

The second environmentalist fallacy involves one or more of various lines of reasoning that assume that two entities that have some aspects in common are, therefore, functionally identical; this is the sort of reasoning that sees a man and a table as identical because both have legs. The crucial relevance of male fetal hormonalization to dominance behavior is denied because there are cyclical aspects to both male and female biology. The importance of those types of cognitive and psychological tests that can discriminate between the sexes is denied because other types of cognitive and psychological tests cannot so discriminate. The inevitability of qualitatively different forms of socialization of the sexes is denied because sexual differences in the physiological materials relevant to dominance tendency are quantitative (for example women are not without testosterone nor are they passive; men, too, are vulnerable to the cries of an infant—quantitative and continuous sex differences become qualitative and discrete only when they are manifested in social conceptions). A number of writers have maintained that we cannot tell the sex of a person from his skeletal remains.[2] This is not true, but let us assume that it is. What difference would

---

2. Dr Germaine Greer (*The Female Eunuch*, London: Hart-Davis, MacGibbon, 1970) is something of a master at introducing irrelevant factors and making it sound as if she were proving a point. Her attempt to dismiss physiological considerations appears in her first paragraph. "Perhaps when we have learnt to read the DNA we will be able to see what the information which is common to all members of the female sex really is, but even then it will be a long and tedious argument from biological data to behavior" (15). To the reader who is not knowledgeable in this area this sentence no doubt *sounds* as if it means something. But let us once again use the analogy of boxing. Dr Greer's logic would force us to say that we will have no idea whether biology is relevant to male superiority in boxing until we learn to 'read the DNA'. When we learn to do so we will know *how* the male genetic programme's direction—that the male will develop superior strength—is encoded in the genetic materials, but we hardly need to 'read the DNA' in order to know that it is so encoded. If one considers boxing and agrees that a certain level of strength is a condition for prowess at it, then the biological element is apparent from the greater muscularity of the male; to see the connection between sexual biology and behavior in this area one does not need to 'read the DNA'. Likewise, we know the hormonal evidence relevant to dominance. Nothing much will be added to our knowledge of the *importance* of hormones to dominance when we can precisely describe the genetic etiology of the hormonal development. The use of boxing as an example of behavior to which sexual biology is relevant also allows us to deal with the attempt to dismiss biological considerations by emphasizing that women as well as men produce testosterone (though of course

this make? To say that male and female bones are identical hardly casts doubt on the determinative effect of the male and female hormonal systems. Similarly fallacious reasoning is involved when the feminist points out that women perform roles in other societies which we consider male roles. We have seen that in nearly every case this is because such roles have high status in our society and low status in others, so that in our society men 'use' their energies to attain such roles while in others they use their energies to attain other (high-status) roles. But let us assume that some roles (or qualities) in our society are associated with the male for purely arbitrary reasons and are not related to the factors we have spoken about. Of what importance is this to the question of physiological differentiation? To focus on these aspects rather than on the universality of patriarchy, male dominance, and male attainment of high-status roles in order to deny the importance of sexual differentiation is to mimic the lawyer who argues, 'Certainly you have four witnesses who saw my client commit the crime, but I have twelve who didn't.'

This fallacy has been invoked to deny differences in temperament between men and women; because our society's association of emotional expressiveness and demonstrativeness with the female is reversed in other cultures, innate sexual differences in temperament are denied. This demonstrates that it is by no means inevitable that the men of a society will be 'less emotional' than the women (that the males will be less demonstrative in expressing their male emotions than women are in expressing their female emotions) but it casts no doubt on the possibility of innate differences in male and female hierarchies of emotions.

The third fallacious method of rejecting distasteful evidence is the invocation of a sophistic tool that one might call 'the fallacy of the glancing blow'. In committing this fallacy, those who cannot face the implications of a basically sound theory, reasonable premiss, or trustworthy observation, *totally* dismiss them by focussing only on their excesses and perverted uses, and would have us believe that such a glancing blow is lethal. These excesses and perverted uses are often quite real, and their exposure often quite clever, but there is no more

---

in lesser amounts and not in a context of a 'masculinized' CNS). Women also have muscles (though smaller ones than males), and, just as women are aggressive (though less so than males), so they could box. In both cases the quantitative differences become qualitative when society conforms its socialization practices to biological probability. While some women could no doubt become better boxers than some men, society must, for reasons we have discussed, socialize women away from such behavior. If it did not, if women attempted to attain their goals through force, they would lose in almost every case. That Dr Greer is aware of the theoretical problems in her work is apparent from the fact that whenever contradiction threatens, she abruptly ends the chapter.

reason to reject the basic ideas that lie behind them than there is to reject physics because its predictive power is less than absolute or because 'physicists make bombs'. This fallacy can be seen today in many areas not related to gender. Many reject the possible intellectual validity of psychoanalysis altogether merely because the nature of mind and behavior precludes the attainment of a level of certainty possible for the physical sciences (thereby raising the real possibility that theoretical constructs will become self-fulfilling prophecies). Others reject even the possibility that homosexuality can be meaningfully described as abnormal simply because we now know that a certain amount of the homosexual's unhappiness results not from his homosexuality, but from societal ostracism. Still others declare the whole concept of normality altogether meaningless as a description of an individual's ability to deal with his environment because a distorted definition of normality may be used as a device for political oppression. This is not to say that there can never be valid arguments for rejecting psychoanalysis, accepting homosexuality as normal, or considering all behavior normal, but that such attacks must strike at the heart to be fatal.

Environmentalists sometimes ask us to dismiss the possibility that hormonal differentiation determines behavior and institutions merely because bogus biological arguments have been invoked against women and other groups in the past. As a result they refuse to even consider the hypothesis that the differing hormonal systems of men and women might reasonably be thought to result in differing propensities and behavior merely because a hormone-behavior relationship has never been 'proved' with a certainty that the 'inductive' approach of science can never, even theoretically, achieve. The environmentalist rejection of scientific evidence usually takes the form of branding any work that refers to hormones as 'pseudo-scientific', much as Vice-President Agnew used to refer to any statement he disliked as 'pseudo-intellectual'; environmentalists usually demonstrate about as much understanding of the scientific method as the Vice-President of the intellectual approach. Both tend to refer to any logic that they cannot handle as 'sophistry'.

The glancing-blow evasion occasionally involves invoking an endless number of criticisms, some of which may have a certain validity under certain circumstances, but which cast no doubt on the basic soundness of what is being criticized. For example, critics point out that, in certain types of research, there has been shown to be a tendency for the researcher to overestimate the evidence in support of a hypothesis; this has been invoked to dismiss the findings of anthropologists that patriarchy is universal. This tendency is occasionally relevant when dealing with certain types of sophisticated research, but is hardly relevant to patriarchy (which can be demonstrated by merely counting the number of men and women in positions of suprafamilial authority). In its crudest form, this use of the 'glancing blow' dismisses anthropological evidence because 'all the ethnographers have been men'. The point is not so much that this is not true, but that this criticism betrays the ideological nature of the environmentalist's intellectual approach. Only someone whose commitment is totally ideological could seriously believe that anthropologists would spend years living in other cultures and then misreport the percentages of men and women in authority positions. Furthermore, if an anthropologist were to lie, he would be more likely to lie in the other direction; fame is the sure reward of any anthropologist who discovers a society without patriarchy. This is not to deny that the differing perspectives and mentalities of male and female anthropologists may result in differing interpretations of some of the exceedingly complex aspects of social life, but it is a wild leap to suppose that any anthropologist, male or female, would see matriarchy or female dominance where none exists—and, indeed, no ethnographer ever has. (Moreover, in the last century —before the theoretical and empirical evidence rendered the belief untenable —many anthropologists believed that matriarchies had existed.)

Similarly, in challenging the theory presented here one might attempt to exaggerate such methodological considerations as the difficulty of developing a precise description of the institutional manifestations of male dominance, the lack of standardization in ethnographic studies, the small size of Dr Money's sample, and the dangers that are always implicit in the generalization to the human level of experimental studies of non-human animals. While none of these criticisms is anywhere near lethal even in its own area, each has a partial validity. If the theory presented here rested on the evidence of just one of these areas, then perhaps the challenge, while not overwhelming, would be worthy of serious consideration. But to attempt to dismiss a theory that can sacrifice the evidence from any one of these areas without damaging that provided by the others, is to commit the 'fallacy of the glancing blow'.

The fourth and most crucial of the fallacies involves the confusion of cause and function. We need not involve ourselves in a detailed discussion of causation here; a simple example should suffice. A jockey is small because physiology made him that way. There may be an element of feedback here in that the jockey might well weigh more if society did not reward his weighing as little as possible, but the reasons for his being able to become a jockey are primarily physiological. The function that his size plays in society, its manifestation in his role of jockey, is not physiological, but society's putting his size to use. Likewise, the economic functions that sexual differentiation requires do not cause the differentiation. The physiological element relevant to dominance tendencies will manifest itself in any economic system. It is useless for the Marxist to attempt to disprove the inevitability of male attainment of authority and status positions by demonstrating that males attain such positions in a capitalist society for capitalist reasons, when the same occurs in societies with primitive, feudal, and socialist economies. Because social and economic variables must conform to the physiological, we can change any variable and patriarchy will not be diminished. Political rule is male whether the institutions relevant to private property, control of the means of production, and class stratification are as minimal as possible or as advanced as those found anywhere. It is male whether a society is patrilineal, matrilineal, or bilateral; patrilocal, matrilocal, or neolocal; white, black, or heterogeneous; racist, separatist, or equalitarian; primitive, pre-industrial, or technological; Shintoist, Catholic, or Zoroastrian; monarchical, totalitarian, or democratic; Spartan, Quaker, or Bourbon; ascetic, hedonist, or libertine. It makes no difference whether a society has a value system that specifically forbids women from entering areas of authority or, like Communist China, an ideological and political commitment to equal distribution of authority positions. One cannot 'disprove' the inevitability of physiological factors manifesting themselves by demonstrating the function that they serve in a political or economic system. No system could operate that did not conform to, and utilize, the reality that constitutes it. *In short, the fallacy here is the reasoning that concludes that men rule because of the nature of the political-economic system and ignores the reality that the possible varieties of political-economic systems are limited by, and must conform to, the nature of human beings.*

Incidentally, the reader who is interested in seeing virtually every environmentalist fallacy—both those described here and those discussed in the section on the irrelevant experiment—committed in just a few pages might like to read Naomi Weisstein's ' "Kinder, Küche, Kirche" as Scientific Law: Psychology Constructs the Female', which has appeared in numerous feminist anthologies. Dr Weisstein presents us with a veritable catalogue of the mis-statements of fact and the fallacious reasoning that are the hallmarks of the environmentalist attempt to explain social reality. She proceeds on the assumption that to show that psychological and psychiatric tests are incapable of discriminating between male and female subjects is to show that there are no crucial psychological differences between men and women. It is quite true that there are many psychological tests that do not differentiate men from women in their results because they measure one of the many areas in which men and women do not differ. It is those areas in which men and women do differ that are of interest to us, and a demonstration that they do not differ in other areas is irrelevant; demonstrating that men and women do not differ in memory does not indicate that they do not differ in abstract reasoning. There are many tests on which one sex does far better than the other; the differences in male and female results on these tests cannot be explained by bias on the part of the experimenter because the questions are of the multiple-choice type. If male and female answers to the questions consistently differ, there must be some reason for their doing so. Why they differ is another question; differences in test answers demonstrate only that they do differ. The most important point, however, is this: even if it were true that *no* test were capable of distinguishing between men and women, this might reflect only on the value and capabilities of the tests, not on the presence or absence of male-female differences. (See the section at the end of the previous chapter entitled 'The Fallacy of the Irrelevant Experiment'.)

If Dr. Weisstein asks us to deny that men and women are different in their psychophysiological make-up simply because psychological tests cannot reflect sexual differences, she asks us to deny not merely the evidence advanced in this book and the observations of the psychiatrists she quotes with derision, of our own experience, and of our greatest writers, but those of almost every feminist author as well. For even the pure environmentalist school of feminist authors did not deny the presence of a female world-view and female attitudes; indeed they give us lengthy descriptions of the female mind that differ from those of the psychiatrists quoted by Dr Weisstein not primarily in what is reported, but in the evaluation of what is reported and in the explanation of its causes. Where the psychiatrist admires nurturant attitudes and behavior, which he sees as flowing from a female physiological substrate, the environmentalist authors see submission engendered by social oppression. In the latter part of her essay Dr Weisstein argues not that there are no important male-female behavioral differences, but that such differences are not universal and that the physiological evidence is either faulty or irrelevant. She invokes the finding of S. Schachter and J.E. Singer that the effect of adrenalin on behavior is to an extent a function of suggestion; subjects treated with adrenalin will be euphoric or fearful depending on the actions of others in the room. This is an interesting and valuable fact about adrenalin, though it would seem that anyone who has felt love and fear at different times would know that adrenalin can attach itself to more than one emotion. Absurdity threatens only when one attempts to transfer this insight into the nature of adrenalin to other physiological materials. Would Dr Weisstein have us believe that insulin is as malleable in its effects? Is there any reason at all to believe that the fetal stimulation of the male brain by fetal testicular testosterone and the presence of high levels of testosterone in the adult male are merely physiological catalysts for social suggestion? And again the same question, which invariably asserts itself: if one so argues, why does no society suggest female dominance to its members? (See the section in Chapter 4 above, entitled 'Feedback and Suggestion'.)

That Dr Weisstein was aware of this theoretical problem is apparent from the fact that she claimed that Margaret Mead had discovered a number of societies in which male dominance was not manifested in social institutions; we have seen that Dr Mead went out of her way to deny ever having said this and that, in any case, she would have been wrong if she had said it. Dr Weisstein carries her method to the primate level and invokes all the illogic we were forced to deal with in the discussion of primates. As I have said, it would make no difference at all to the line of reasoning I invoke if dominance in all non-human primates were associated with the female or if it had not been shown that primate male dominance manifests itself even when primates are raised in isolation (thus removing the possibility that primate male aggression can be explained by socialization). But one cannot resist asking why, if there is no physiological basis to the differences in dominance between primate males and females, half the groups of each species of primate are not led by females.

Vulgarized Marxism

This fourth fallacy is central to all those analyses which are derived from Engels's work and all those which treat women as a class. There are, to be sure, a number of Marxist writings on the subject of sex-role differentiation that do not commit this fallacy; these either do not disagree with the theory presented in this essay, or admit that the hormonal factor is relevant, but argue that it need not be; in the latter case we cannot, as we have seen in our discussion of human malleability and the nature of society, logically disprove the theoretical possibility of a society without values, stratification, or status differentiation, but can only point out the utopian nature of such a hypothesized society, repeat that the same argument could be made by the Victorian for the possibility of a society that over-rode the 'sex drive' of the majority of its members, and admit that, if there were no government and no hierarchies of any kind, then there would be no patriarchy. The better-known feminist works of a few decades ago, such as *Sexual Politics, The Female Eunuch,* and Shulamith Firestone's *The Dialectic of Sex*[3] all invoke either aspects of Engels's reasoning or an approach that the authors believe to be an adaptation of a Marxist analysis, but with which, I suspect, no serious Marxist would associate himself. By denying or ignoring sexual hormonal differentiation, these authors force the histories of all human societies into the framework of economic determinism in order to confuse the conformations of economic systems to the reality of male and female physiologies with the physiological determinants of differing sexual roles. While the two latter books show the same ignorance of the relevant anthropological and physiological facts and the same total ignorance of what theory is all about that permeates *Sexual Politics,* Dr Millett's book is the most annoying to the serious scholar; for, unlike *Sexual Politics, The Female Eunuch* and *The Dialectic of Sex* do not try to camouflage their intellectual inadequacy behind a facade of scholarship and a misconception that a profusion of footnotes compensates for a lack of the hard logic and the hard mental work of real scholarship.

Since any analysis of patriarchy must either accept the determinativeness of physiological differentiation or demonstrate that such differentiation need not engender patriarchy, we need not detain ourselves with the specific Marxist analyses that consider only the economic and ignore the physiological. That which views women as a social class is too silly for us to bother with: it is sufficient to point out that the members of one class are not hormonally different from the members of another, and that the individuals of one class do not pair off in head-to-head encounters with the individuals of another (thereby rendering each member of each class more tightly bound to a member of the other class than to any member of his own).

---

3. Shulamith Firestone, *The Dialectic of Sex* (London: Cape, 1971). Miss Firestone's book begins with the advantage (over those of Drs Millett and Greer) of an at least tentative admission that men and women are different from each other. Her acknowledgment of physiology is, however, limited to the woman's reproductive role and no mention is made of the determinative hormonal differentiation. Like Simone de Beauvoir's infinitely better book, *The Second Sex* (London: Cape, 1968), Miss Firestone's book admits the universality of patriarchy without giving the reader any reason to doubt that the forces that have engendered patriarchy will continue to do so. Where Dr de Beauvoir is immune to the criticism that she does not introduce the hormonal evidence we have discussed (little of which had been discovered when Dr de Beauvoir wrote), Miss Firestone chose merely to ignore the evidence that renders her theory irrelevant. Dr de Beauvoir's book fails only when it deals with the etiology of patriarchy, male attainment, and male-dominance; elsewhere it offers a great deal that is of value. Miss Firestone's book is both an unsubstantiated assertion that for some reason physiology is no longer determinative and a fantasy of suggested social changes whose probabilities range from the minuscule to the non-existent.

When the Marxist feminist attempts to deal directly with the question of biology we can expect the arrival of Glancing Blow's ne'er-do-well sibling, Red Herring. In her otherwise commendable piece, 'Women: The Longest Revolution',[4] Juliet Mitchell acknowledges the necessity for the Marxist to deal with the biological factor, but presents this not in terms of hormonal differentiation, but in terms of the family. She implies that the institution of the family, or at least its relevant aspects, may not be inevitable and, therefore, that patriarchy may not be inevitable. Now there are quite strong anthropological arguments for claiming that no society could be built on any other foundation than the family and that, even if one could, the family would represent not oppression of the female but woman's greatest triumph. But this is not my point here. For Dr Mitchell to demonstrate that physiology is not insurmountable, that patriarchy is not inevitable, she must demonstrate that sexual hormonal differentiation does not render patriarchy inevitable. No attack on the family or any other red herring—even if it were successful—could lessen the probability of the correctness of the theory presented here. No analysis that attempts to explain the causation of sex-role behavior or sexually-differentiated institutions in purely economic terms can refute one that uses the hormonal factor to explain the limits of social reality; such an analysis may go far towards clarifying how the roles, socialization, meanings, values, and ideologies of a society conform to the limits set by the hormonal factor or how they vary within those limits, but it cannot explain the limits themselves, much less demonstrate that there are no such limits. Any Marxist attempt to explain patriarchy, male attainment, and male dominance in terms of the economic functions served by these is as absurd as an attempt to explain male boxing superiority by demonstrating that male boxers earn big salaries, that males are socialized towards boxing, or that our ideology associates boxing with males. One might argue that an alternative value system might outlaw boxing (thereby eradicating male attainment in this area), but to then argue that a society could similarly eradicate patriarchy, male attainment, and male dominance by eradicating group values, stratification, government and dyadic dominance is once again to invoke Utopia.

Vulgarized Marxism not only fails theoretically by ignoring all the biological and anthropological evidence; it also fails empirically in that it must explain the failures of each socialist society to reduce patriarchy in terms of each individual socialist society. As we have seen, there is no evidence that

---

4. *New Left Review*, 40 (November–December, 1966), 11–37.

patriarchy, male attainment, or male dominance were ever reduced in socialist societies.

The Failure to Ask 'Why?'

Like those we have just discussed, a number of traditional economic and sociological analyses ignore physiology and cross-cultural anthropology altogether (or treat them with a superficiality that is tantamount to ignoring them) and concentrate on the manifestations of physiology in socialization (boys are encouraged to compete, become scientists, and so forth, while girls are encouraged to develop their nurturant qualities) and in economic reality (males constitute the overwhelming number of politicians, leading businessmen, department chairmen, and scientists). Some of these works, such as Elizabeth Janeway's *Man's World, Woman's Place,* Jessie Bernard's *Women and the Public Interest,* and Cynthia Fuchs Epstein's *Woman's Place* are honest and intelligent, while others are shoddy and a waste of the reader's time. But they are all irrelevant to the general questions addressed in this book; no primarily economic or sociological analysis—no matter how high its quality—can ever explain the causes of patriarchy, male dominance, and male attainment of high-status roles and positions. Such works merely document the presence of these universals in this society, a presence that human physiology renders inevitable in this and every other society. The more the environmentalists produce such documentation, the deeper they dig the grave for their basic assumption that these institutions are not inevitable.

Here we see the ultimate failure of a purely environmentalist analysis. Even the best of these works are grounded in the erroneous assumption that demonstrating that a society attaches different values and expectations to men and women (or showing that men have often said that men and women are different) somehow proves that these different values and expectations are entirely arbitrary and are not the social manifestations of physiology (or that women have behaved in a feminine way simply because men have told them to—in which case one might ask why it is the women of every society who listen to the men and never the other way around). Because these works fail even to acknowledge the problem of causation by asking 'why?' (*Why* does every society socialize boys towards, and girls away from, competition? *Why* are the non-maternal roles of women never given high status by any society? *Why* does every society associate authority with the male? *Why* is it women who are socialized away from the sciences?), they cannot be considered theory, but, at best, merely description. One does not need a sociologist to tell one that boys are dissuaded from playing with dolls or girls from fist-fighting or that most politicians and leading business executives are men. As long as the feminist attempt at theory ignores all the hormonal evidence or simply claims that such evidence is unimportant, as long as it ignores and leaves unexplained the universality of patriarchy, male attainment, and male dominance, and as long as it ignores the fact that no society fails to socialize males towards dominance and females away from dominance, it will illuminate little and explain less.

But to ask why, to look for theory in order to understand rather than selective description in order to justify ideology, to attempt to answer questions rather than to beg them, requires one to lay before the reader all one's facts, assumptions and reasoning, and, only then, all one's conclusions so that—if one is wrong—the reader can track down and identify one's mistake just as the electrician tracks down the short on the circuit board. This is what theory is all about; it differs from what may be a brilliant and perceptive non-theoretical work in that one may choose any sentence and follow its thought to its logical conclusion, do the same with any other sentence, and find that the logical extensions not only do not contradict each other, but create harmonies that explain even more than the two sentences taken individually. This is the minimum requirement of any work demanding to be taken seriously. But this the pure environmentalist dares not do lest the inaccuracy of his facts, the fallaciousness of his reasoning, the incorrectness of his conclusions, and the general inadequacy of his analysis be exposed for all to see.

It is not coincidental that the intellectual background of nearly every author of the older school of feminist anthropological and biological theory (Millett, Greer, Firestone, Figes, Janeway, Mitchell, and, to a lesser extent, de Beauvoir) was literature or art. An author's intellectual background has no logical bearing on the correctness of his analysis, of course, and the last three authors offer much that is illuminating when they are not discussing anthropology and physiology, but no serious female physiologist or anthropologist has offered her support to the theories of these writers.

Third Digression: The Obscurantism of an Inadequate Analysis

The environmentalist analysis is most obviously inadequate when it deals with the manifestations of physiological sex differences discussed in this book. Complex as the areas of patriarchy, male dominance, and male attainment of high-status roles and positions are, however, the intellectual damage caused by the environmentalist analysis is minimized by our ability to explain the mechanisms whereby hormonal reality limits social possibility. In this digression I want to be more speculative and to discuss not these areas, but those in which the potential for obscurity is far greater—areas in which although our present knowledge precludes rigorous explanations of sex differences, the differences we observe may quite possibly be real and inevitable aspects of different 'mental gestalts' flowing from the different physiologies of the sexes.

The refusal to consider the possibility that there is a physiological component of observed sexual differences in the sensitivity necessary for nurturance, perception, superego development and pathology, the nature of sexual arousal, the personalization of reality, the ability to make and remember psychologically significant observations (compare the blurred and obvious description given by the husband with the specific and perceptive observations detailed by the wife when a couple discusses the party they have just attended), the conditions for scientific and artistic genius, and all the other incredibly subtle, inter-related areas for which observation indicates that there are sex differences, is intellectually indefensible until we have some reason to assume that physiology does not play a part. We *know* that sexual physiology is crucial to the areas discussed in my theory and we *know* that men and women think and behave differently, whatever the cause. Therefore, it does not seem unreasonable to suggest that the observed sex differences listed above might represent manifestations of physiological differentiation. In any case, whether these subtle differences are physiologically or socially generated, they do exist, and rejection of *descriptions* because one does not like them is hardly justified. This is not to deny the potential danger of an expectation becoming a self-fulfilling prophecy; however, to reject the validity of all our observations of sex differences for this reason is to commit the 'fallacy of the glancing blow' and to ignore the question of why we have such expectations.

Given its soft intellectual core and its simplistic approach to the complexities of reality, the environmentalist analysis cannot deal with the most interesting aspects of sexual differentiation. For example, feminists often portray the male as viewing woman as 'unprincipled', quote some nineteenth-century misogynist for 'documentation', and then refuse to discuss the whole subject any further. In their idealized version of the male view of possible sexual differences in superego development, they assume the superiority of the line of development of superego sanctions that leads men to the psychiatrist's couch and to fight wars for 'great causes'. This assumption dooms them to unhappiness, but, more importantly for our purposes, it leads them to dismiss from discussion differences that observation begs us to study more closely. Even if one insists on maintaining that psychological development is totally dependent on social factors, one has no intellectual justification for disregarding one's own observation that women fighting a duel for honor strikes us as being absurd, and that it is unimaginable that *Crime and Punishment* could have been written about a woman (or would have been written by a woman).

For the remainder of this section I would like to introduce a number of random thoughts and observations, not as proof of anything, but as an indication of the incredible number of observations of sexual differences we make daily and the likelihood that each of these may have a component that the environmentalist analysis would have us disregard.

a. Examination of the most mundane matters can be illuminating for those willing to look for causation rather than mere description. Let us take the married woman who is referred to as 'Mrs' and wears a wedding ring. Let us say that this woman is angry because married men are not differentiated from single men by terminology and wear wedding rings far less often than do women. Now one needs no 'right' to get angry. But if the woman argues that these distinctions are merely arbitrary or even that they only exist because male strength enables men to enforce them, she is almost certainly wrong. Social expectations are related to physiological reality, to necessities inherent in the very nature of society, and to individual convenience. Even if one insists on maintaining that our expectation that the male will be the sexual aggressor (though by no means necessarily the sexual initiator) is unrelated to the realities of male and female hormonal and anatomical reality, in my view a totally untenable assertion, it should be obvious that the institutions of 'Mrs' and the wedding ring are society's way of indicating to the male which women are potentially available and which are not.

It would not be surprising if the attempt to replace the abbreviations *Miss* and *Mrs* with *Ms* were successful in the business sphere (on letters, for example), but success will have little to do with the intention behind such a move. The function served by differentiation of married from single women is irrelevant for the company that is sending out its monthly bills (or to the male writing to a female stranger about a business matter), and here *Ms* is convenient and possible. Differentiation is important only in face-to-face contact; it is here that the (sexually aggressive) male must know which women are available. This is of paramount importance for society (the family is the basis of every society's organization and status system) and convenient for the individual married woman. The inconvenience that would be suffered by women in a society that did not differentiate between single and married women in some easily observed way would be intolerable. This is reflected in the fact that, to the best of my knowledge, there is no society that does not so differentiate. Because this alone would account for the differentiation between single and married women, there is no need here to go into the complex issue of whether this differentiation would be necessary for far more important societal reasons. The reader might like to consider that it is quite likely that no society that was not based on the family and its role in directing psychophysiological energies, maintaining status, and other vital functions could survive, and that the family could not survive in a society that did not inculcate in its males an inhibition against taking other men's wives, and that did not identify these wives. That there are many cases of adultery is irrelevant; no institution in any society works perfectly—that is why every society has methods of social control. To those who would argue that the breakdown of the institutions of marriage and the family are exactly what they hope for, I would point out that all the evidence of anthropology indicates that society must be based on the family, and the family cannot exist without marriage. Since man cannot exist without society, the breakdown of this society would merely be followed by the rise of another that was also based on marriage and family.

   b. It has been demonstrated that the intelligence levels of husband and wife are among the most highly correlated variables in the American marriage relationship, yet feminists often complain that men refuse to enter relationships with women of equal intelligence because they then feel threatened. If we consider the population as a whole this is untrue. If we limit ourselves to the relatively intellectual segment of the population, I believe that there is some truth in what the feminists say, but that they are telling only half the story. Intellectuals, by definition, place great emphasis on intelligence, and it is natural that, for them, physiologically-generated feelings of men and women relevant to male dominance should manifest themselves here. In other words, it is possible that it is not only male emotions that engender relationships among intellectuals in which the man is the more intelligent; perhaps the woman intellectual, despite her claim to want a large number of men to choose from, is unlikely to select a man over whom she has intellectual dominance (and who will not, therefore, "take the lead" in this crucial area). This thought occurred to me during a discussion with a feminist who, after arguing that dominance was not relevant to her relationships, remarked that she did not find masculine any man who was not more intelligent than she was.

c. For our last example of a situation in which physiological differences between men and women are not readily seen to be crucial but for which they may be determinative, let us consider the observation that most women prefer men taller than themselves for sexual and marital relationships. We know that women search out taller men even though they are perfectly aware that height is irrelevant to all human virtues. Now a superficial, but again possibly totally correct, explanation would see a woman's desire for a taller man as merely a manifestation of our particular social values. But let us assume, again for argument's sake, that the women of every society feel this way; I have no idea whether they do or not. We now have a number of possibilities. We might assume, as I do in this book, that there is no direct CNS imperative which makes a female desire male dominance—the universal female acknowledgment of male dominance being totally attributable to the reality of its existence and the inevitable female response to it—and that her man should be taller than she is; this universal tendency of women may then be merely an inevitable social reflection of the fact that men in every society will be taller than the women, so that the preference of women for taller men merely reflects the fact that a man is 'supposed' to be taller than his woman (because most men are). Or perhaps there is a direct CNS imperative which makes women desire male dominance, but not one which makes them desire a taller man; in which case the association of dominance and size may result from the observation, particularly of the child, that—all other things being equal, which of course they rarely are—size is related to dominance. Again perhaps there is no CNS imperative making women desire male dominance, but one which directs the female to the man who is taller than she is (again all other things being equal); this would make sense in evolutionary terms. Or perhaps there is a CNS imperative which leads women to desire a man who is both dominant and taller.

I do not know how important the physiological factor is in any of the situations discussed in this digression or, when it is important, whether it is direct or indirect. I do know that no one else knows either, and that no one has the right to assume that physiology is irrelevant by automatically accepting the explanation which considers social factors only. It might be worth noting, however, how seldom the aphorisms and proverbs concerning masculine and feminine qualities contradict one another, no matter how disparate the societies that produced them. Could this not be because they have long since penetrated to the cores of our natures to find truths whose physical correlates we are only now discovering? It would hardly be the first time that wisdom preceded knowledge.

Chapter *VIII*

Common Objections to the Theory of Male Dominance

The reader will not be surprised to learn that my work has elicited a *lot* of negative criticism. This is to be expected, whatever the degree of correctness or incorrectness of the work itself.

Empirical analysis in sensitive areas invariably elicits fear, fear that acceptance of its conclusion will compel an unpalatable moral or political position. While such fear is never relevant to the correctness of the feared theory, it may well be that some such criticism *does* demonstrate the incorrectness of the criticized theory, whatever the irrelevance of the fears or the feared consequences that motivate the criticism. When this is the case, it is legitimate criticism; the fact that a critic was moved to criticism because he feared the practical consequences of acceptance of the theory he criticizes has no bearing on the correctness of his criticism, just as it does nothing to support his criticism. Indeed, motivation is irrelevant even in the case of bad criticism. What makes criticism good or bad is not that which motivates it, but that which it is. If it exposes fallacy or error, it is good criticism. If not, it is bad criticism.

Twenty-five Questions to Ask about Any Criticism of the Theory of Male Dominance

I do consider a few critics by name in this book, but any item-by-item survey of the badly-done criticism would drive every reader away. Fortunately, it is possible to respond to all this criticism with a generic list of fallacies and errors and the questions that expose them (in this chapter and in the section in Chapter 3 above entitled 'Seven Claims That Are Neither Assumed Nor Implied'). If the reader finds any critic who avoids all of these fallacies and errors, virtually any one of which is fatal to the criticism containing it, the reader should study the criticism very closely. It is probably correct.

1. *Does the criticism ignore or deny the fact that there is a universal reality to be explained?* Criticism might be successful if it found fallacy or error in an attempted explanation. One need not have an alternative theory, or even grant the empirical reality the criticized theory attempts to explain, if one can show fallacy or error in the criticized theory. However, vague references to 'complexity' and accusations of 'reductionism' do not, for reasons discussed here and in the section below on Green, qualify. Likewise, no invocation of *other* realities that *have* changed (women in the work force, abortion, and so forth) are relevant to the universal empirical realities we wish to explain; in many societies women have always performed full-time economic roles outside the home and have been permitted abortion, but all such societies are patriarchal.

2. *Does the criticism invoke empirical realities that are irrelevant to the empirical claims I make (for instance, variation that has nothing to do with the universals we wish to explain)?* Many critics invoked societies that differ from each other in some behavior or institution other than the behaviors and institutions I attempt to explain. They will, for example, invoke the fact that clothes makers in one society are female, while in another they are male, as somehow casting doubt on the universality of patriarchy. The pointlessness of any such argument can sometimes be disguised when a number of such variations are invoked together in order to insinuate the notion that cultural variation is unlimited. In fact, the extensive degree of variation that does exist should surely lead us to ask why, with all this variation, the institutions *we* attempt to explain are universal.

Many critics have attempted to invoke as refutation variation that does exist, but which the theory I present does not deny. No one doubts the differences between, for example, patriarchy in Saudi Arabia and the United States, but the question I address is why the United States and Saudi Arabia and all other societies are patriarchal. In other words: whenever a criticism speaks of variation from society to society it is speaking of some *other* expectation or institution than those relevant to my work or it is speaking of variation within the limits I discuss.

Such variation is irrelevant here, for the criticism that invokes it is simply a camouflaged version of the doomed attempt to refute by the invocation of "complexity". I attempt to provide a *sufficient* explanation of the universal limits and direction of the institutions we discuss. I do not attempt to explain the (environmentally-explicable) variation falling within the limits. One who wishes to offer a *sufficient* explanation of why the members of every society most of the time eat at least once a day, need invoke only human physiology and is not obligated to explain why Americans eat American food and Chinese eat Chinese food. (*If* contemporary changes plausibly suggested the coming of an exception to universality—suggested that the variation was widening to the point where the former limits were being erased—*then* variation might be causally relevant. But there is no indication that changes in the reality of patriarchy—as opposed to attitudes towards it—approach the extremes long exhibited by some non-modern societies, extremes that fall well within the limits whose causation we attempt to understand.)

The biological equivalent of the futile attempt to refute an explanation of universality by invoking irrelevant variation is seen in its purest form in a work by Richard Lewontin, Steven Rose, and Leon Kamin, *Not in Our Genes.*[1] Lewontin, Rose, and Kamin attempt to cast doubt on the determinativeness of the neuro-endocrinological differences by criticizing research on a host of biological factors that I do not mention. Indeed, nearly all of the authors' discussion of sex differences, which is primarily devoted to an attempt to refute my theory of male dominance, is addressed to irrelevant issues I do not mention: differentiated functions of brain hemispheres, brain size, rates of disease, longevity, and the like. Since such factors play no part in the argument I present, we can, for argument's sake, grant the correctness of what the authors write about these factors.

The authors do make three points that are relevant.

The first is simply a denial of the cross-cultural universality that is the empirical reality we wish to explain.[2] But as I argued at length in Chapter 2 above, neither these authors nor anyone else has managed to find a single example of a human society without patriarchy or male dominance.

The second relevant claim is also incorrect. Lewontin, Rose, and Kamin tell us that women can be medical doctors, a point no one could reasonably dispute, and add that in the Soviet Union the majority of family doctors are women. They then comment that Soviet family doctors have "lower status and lower pay than in the United States, but that is a different point."[3] Lewontin, Rose, and Kamin somehow contrive to overlook the rather elementary fact that this "different point" *is precisely the central point.* Why is lower status *always and everywhere* associated with the (non-maternal) roles women play? Since Lewontin, Rose, and Kamin fail to face this question, they are unable to deal with my answer: that high status elicits from males a greater tendency to do that

---

1. Richard C. Lewontin, Steven Rose, and Leon Kamin, *Not in Our Genes* (New York: Pantheon, 1984).

2. *Op. cit.*, 138.

3. *Op. cit.*, 136.

which is necessary for the attainment of the status. A high-status role like that of family physician in the West does not have high status primarily because it is male; it is male primarily because it has high status, a high status that elicits more strongly from those with male physiologies the behavior required to attain the high status.

The final relevant claim made by Lewontin, Rose, and Kamin is one of misrepresentation. They imply that I hold that there exists a gene for "kissing babies for votes". I have never made any such preposterous assertion. The genetic basis of sex differences manifests itself in different emotional and behavioral tendencies and predispositions; the specific actions in which these are exhibited are determined by social factors. Similarly, one who argues that human beings have a genetically-rooted propensity for drinking liquids is not claiming a gene for buying Hire's Root Beer. The physiologically-rooted behavioral tendency described by the theory I present is one that leads males to more readily choose the actions required for dominance; the specific actions are determined by society, just as society determines the sexual positions that will be used to satisfy our physiologically-rooted tendency to feel sexual arousal.

3. *Does the criticism simply assert that modern technology or the 'changing needs of modern society' will over-ride psychophysiological differentiation?* Margaret Mead and many others grant all of the physiological and anthropological empirical evidence I present and then claim that these factors will no longer be relevant as modern technology and changing human needs come to characterize human life. These criticisms simply ignore the argument that it is the physiological differentiation that determines the behavioral differentiation (and observation of the behavioral differentiation that sets limits on socialization and institutions). We are offered no reason, other than the wish that it be the case, to believe that modern technology and changing need will change the behaviors and institutional limits we discuss, or that economic and technological factors can remain unlimited by, and can override, the psychophysiological causal factors responsible for the behaviors and institutions.

Modernization probably does, for reasons we discuss, set lower as well as upper limits on the status of women—as compared to the limits in various primitive societies. Modernization probably requires that women enter the labor force in large numbers. But there is no evidence that increased numbers of women in the workforce can alter the domination of hierarchies to anything approaching that which would cast doubt on the existence of patriarchy; there are many primitive and modern democratic societies in which women comprise half the workforce, yet all of these are overwhelmingly patriarchal. All modernization guarantees is that no modern society will give women's maternal role the high status it receives in *some* primitive societies.

Similarly, many critics simply assert that, even if sexual physiological differentiation plays a crucial causal behavioral role, "we are human beings and not animals", "we no longer 'need' the biological impulses that have evolved in us", "modern society has different needs from those of pre-modern societies" and, therefore, "we can overcome through will our biological impulses". Now, no doubt this is true for a few individuals in every society (as Catholic priests demonstrate in ours). The environmentalist can always claim that we will override our male and female tendencies in the future, but this environmentalist is as likely to find society meeting his hopes as were the Shakers. There is no evidence that this is possible for the large numbers of people whose behavior determines the culture of a society. The only difference is that those who hope to nullify sexual differences in behavior would abhor—and acknowledge to be impossible—a celibate society like that which appealed to the Shakers.

4. *Does the criticism treat environmental variables such as values and socialization as if they are independent variables, and can act as counterpoise to the physiological?* This is the central flaw of all environmentalist attempts at a sufficient explanation of the sexual differentiation of behavior and institution that we discuss. In treating the limits of the social as the independent variable—rather than a variable whose limits are dependent on the psychophysiological—this criticism ignores the fact that the social is given its limits and direction by the physiological; we do not have the option of socializing people to associate, say, physical strength or dominance behavior more strongly with women or the ability to give birth with men. This failure to understand that a population's observation of a psychophysiological difference between males and females sets limits on possible social expectations of men and women infuses all claims that we can change our expectations and socialization and thereby override the psychophysiological differentiation. We can do so only within the limits imposed by the psychophysiological differentiation. That we *can* do so within the limits imposed by the psychophysiological is evidenced by the variation we do see from society to society.

The environmental variable is never so independent as to be capable of preventing the physiological factor from setting the limits manifested in the universals we wish to explain. It is true that many physiologically-generated tendencies are tendencies to behave in a given way in a given environment. Thus, to use Haldane's example, the respective physiologies of a Jersey and a Highland cow are such that the former will give more milk if the cows are in an

English pasture, while the latter will give more milk if the cows are on a Scottish moor. However, this differs from the human male-female differences we discuss in that the environment of the cows is independent of the cows' physiology; a moor is not a moor because Highland cows are built the way they are.

In the case of humans, the cultural environment is limited by the reality of male-female differences and the population's observation of them. That is why the environment always ratifies the reality of the physiological differentiation. Unlike the laboratory experiment, in which an 'outside experimenter' can set up any expectations and values that seem desirable, societies have no 'outside experimenter'. The expectations and values of a society are limited by the reality of what the population observes. Just as no society could have expectations associating equal height with females, so no society can have expectations associating an equal dominance tendency with females. The range of possibilities on the level of expectation and socialization is limited by constraints imposed on the neuro-endocrinological and neuro-endocrinological-behavioral levels.

5. *Does the criticism confuse cause and function?* Even if we were to accept a caricature of economic determinism and grant that rulers, for economic and political reasons, determine a population's values concerning food, encourage people to buy unhealthy food, and so on, we would still not conclude that the people of all societies eat because rulers want to make a profit. They eat because human physiology is such that people must eat and, let us assume for argument's sake, rulers exploit this. To explain the universality of male dominance in terms of economic factors is like seeing McDonald's's need for profits as the cause of the human need to eat.

6. *Is the point made by a critic also true of the height difference between men and women and does the criticism invoke the correct, but irrelevant, point that within-sex differences are greater than between-sex differences; in other words, does the criticism misunderstand the statistical nature of sex differences?* If so, then it is no argument against my theory of male dominance. Consider, for example, the claim that, for neuro-endocrinological reasons, men more readily exhibit the behavior associated with attainment of upper hierarchical position than do women (that they are, to use the terms a bit more loosely than I like, 'more aggressive' or 'more competitive'). The fact that some women are more aggressive than some men is no more a refutation of this claim than is the fact that some women are taller than some men a refutation of the claim that men are taller than women for inherent physiological reasons. Whenever one speaks

of males and females, one speaks in statistical terms; ignoring this dooms any discussion of the subject to incoherence.

It is only on the societal level that the statistical becomes absolute, as the 'law of large numbers' takes effect (in all societies 'aggression' is more strongly associated with males and socialization and upper hierarchical position is overwhelmingly associated with males). The fact that a criticism of a claimed statistical sex difference is also true of height does *not*, of course, demonstrate that the claimed sex difference is, *in fact*, a manifestation of neuro-endocrinological differentiation; such a demonstration requires additional evidence of the sort presented in this book. But the fact that the critical point raised is also true of height does show that the criticism fails to accomplish its mission of casting doubt on the *possibility* that the sex difference is a manifestation of neuro-endocrinological differentiation.

With reference to virtually any characteristic, the difference between the within-sex extremes (the male with the most and the male with the least or the female with the most and the female with the least) will be greater than the between-sex difference in means. To see this fact as casting doubt on the importance of the between-sex difference is like arguing that—because the difference between the shortest and tallest males (or shortest and tallest females) is much greater than the difference in means of the heights of males and females—the male height advantage has nothing to do with the fact that the best basketball teams are male.

Moreover, those who raise this point fail to note an important fact: a slight difference in means often complements a great difference in the extremes. The height difference between men and women is only a few percent, but virtually all people over six-feet, eight-inches tall are men. This point is crucial in any discussion of the genesis of social expectations and role models; a sex difference in physiologically-rooted aspects of the behavior relevant to dominance of only one-thousandth of a standard deviation would easily account for the institutions we attempt to understand.

More generally: all discussions of sex differences are doomed if we fail to remember that such *differences are virtually always statistical, not absolute*. No one argues that males are not generally taller than females on the grounds that some females are taller than some males nor does anyone argue that such exceptions cast doubt on the physiological basis of the sex difference in height. But, when the discussion turns to physiologically-rooted behavior, many do precisely this.

Anne Fausto-Sterling's *Myths of Gender* is a veritable catalog of the errors that ensue from a failure to treat individual sex differences as statistical realities. Professor Fausto-Sterling writes:

> [Goldberg raises] questions about the competency of *any and all* females to work successfully in positions of leadership, while for women working in other types of jobs, the question is, Should they receive less pay or more restricted job opportunities . . . ? (emphasis in original)[4]

Save for a discussion *en passant*, unrelated to my theory of male dominance, of the association of mathematical skills with males, I have not argued that sex is associated with *competence,* but with attainment of position. Moreover, Fausto-Sterling's reasoning would have us believe that one who pointed out that men are generally taller than women would necessarily be implying that every woman is shorter than every man and that a woman who is six feet tall should not be permitted to serve in a role requiring only such height.

Fausto-Sterling claims that I imply that sex discrimination doesn't exist.[5] What I imply, indeed say outright, is that sex discrimination can and *does* exist precisely because we apply correct expectations about a category of people to individual members of that category to whom the expectations do not apply (exceptions). It is unforgivable discrimination when a man who is no better a mathematician than a woman is favored over the woman. But the incorrect expectation that the man is, in this specific case, the better mathematician is possible precisely *because* men are, in general, better at mathematics than are women (the *cause* of that sex difference being irrelevant here).

Fausto-Sterling's confusion and misrepresentation is best exemplified by this paragraph:

> Steven Goldberg could argue that the finding that professional and managerial women have higher "male" hormone levels than do housewives proves that male hormones are a positive aid in achieving success. Therefore, he might claim, women with naturally higher testosterone levels are more assertive, more masculine, and more likely to achieve in the male arena. That, however, is *not* the conclusion reached by Purifoy and Koopmans. Instead they point to the well established observation: stress lowers testosterone levels.[6]

What is one to make of such a haggis? Note the "could" and "might". Fausto-Sterling hopes to mislead the reader into believing that I make an argument that implies that within-sex differences are relevant to the theory I

---

4. (New York: Basic Books, 1985), 91.
5. *Op. cit.,* 124.
6. *Op. cit.,* 130.

present. She has to misrepresent me, because I have so often made the point that *nothing* in the theory implies that *within-sex* physiology has anything to do with attainment of position and status. There is no implication in my work that neuro-endocrinological differences between men are relevant to attainment by some men and non-attainment by other men (or attainment by some women and not by other women). (I happen to think that within-sex physiological difference *does* play a by no means insignificant role, but the theory of male dominance can assume that this is not the case, and therefore stands or falls independently.)

The neuro-endocrinological effects of stress (which play no role in the theory) would be worth mentioning only if stress could render female and male testosterone levels equal. Stress does not even begin to do so. Moreover, even if *this* were the case, Fausto-Sterling's argument would simply ignore the fact that the fetal preparation of the male Central Nervous System and its effect of sensitizing males to whatever testosterone is present would have an effect even if male and female testosterone levels were the same after birth.

The inadequacy of Fausto-Sterling's arguments is by no means limited to the statistical fallacies. There is the inevitable inapplicable argument about "reductionism" and many of the other fallacious forays discussed here.

7. *Does the criticism invoke patriarchy to explain realities present in some societies, but absent from others?* Such explanations must fail because all societies are patriarchal and a universal factor cannot explain a factor that is not universal. It makes no sense to say that a nation has laws against abortion *because* the nation is patriarchal; some nations don't have such laws, yet they too are patriarchal. And, if the factor that is to be explained *is* universal, then it is usually not *explained* by patriarchy, but merely described by it. One cannot, for example, say that men rule *because* a society is patriarchal; this is what 'patriarchy' *means,* so some other factor—such as some specific physiological aspect of maleness—must be invoked to explain patriarchy.

8. *Does the criticism invoke a false empirical analogy that dooms it from the start?* Common examples include references to slavery or to myth. It is practically *de rigeur* for the environmentalist to claim that my reasoning would justify the belief that slavery is inevitable. In fact, such an argument is dead in its tracks: some societies, actually most societies, have *not* had slavery and this fact immediately refutes any hypothesis that slavery is inevitable.

As it has become more and more obvious that none of the thousands of societies on which we have any direct evidence are exceptions to the universalities I discuss, more and more is made of 'the truth content of myth'. Myths have truth content in the moral and psychological sense that the Bible does. They no more represent literal truth than do they demonstrate that cyclops *really* existed.

9. *Does the criticism present socialization as the cause of the behavior differences and the institutions we wish to explain?* If so, then the criticism neither explains anything nor casts doubt on the criticized causal explanation. The critic merely rephrases the question, which becomes: 'Why do all societies have expectations of a more easily-released male aggression and why do they socialize their members to expect this?' In other words, such explanations fail to ask the central question of why every society's socialization associates dominance behavior with males. Such arguments are equivalent to one claiming that men can more readily grow moustaches than women *because* little girls are told that facial hair is unfeminine.

This, incidentally, is the problem with 'explanations' emphasizing the fact that English speaks of human beings as 'man' and of 'businessmen'. Even if it were true that all languages everywhere did the same, the question would still be why they do this. Once some prior reason is given, the issue of language becomes irrelevant. (In fact, of course, many languages do not do this, yet they are all spoken in patriarchal societies.)

Socialization often increases any sex difference when it serves its function of providing specific channels for (amorphous) psychophysiological tendencies (physiology accounts for males' more easily-released violent behavior and the female's more easily-released maternal behavior, but there are no genes for firing a rifle or changing a diaper). Likewise, socialization can make concrete the statistical, and this often leads to discrimination (the statistical greater male aggression becomes 'men are aggressive; women are passive'). But invocation of these facts does not obviate the need to answer the central question: Why does the socialization and discrimination we discuss work in the same direction in every society?

10. *Does the criticism confuse attitudes and values concerning a reality with the reality itself?* Not long ago in our society, most women and men approved of the association of dominance and maleness. (See any of hundreds of 1930s movies in which it is clear that women are drawn to the man who 'takes the lead'.) Today many do not. When attitudes and values play an important causal role—as in the case of premarital sex—*then* change in attitude or value engenders change in the reality. But attitudes and values play no important role in the causation of the universal realities we discuss or in a sufficient explanation of the universality. One finds diametrically-opposed attitudes and values relevant to the institutions as one goes from one ethnographic society to

another, but one always finds the institutions. Attitudes may determine how happy we are with what we are, but they cannot, with reference to male dominance, determine what we are. What we are, with reference to the behaviors we discuss, is a function not of attitudes, or the 'needs of modern society', but of a. the differing physiologies of males and females; b. the differing behavioral responses to the environment engendered by these differing physiologies; and c. the social realities that are limited and given their direction by the population's observation of these physiologically-rooted behavioral realities.

11. *Does the criticism misunderstand the relevance of research on the physiological mechanism to the theory I present?* The theory of male dominance does not generalize from the direct physiological evidence of the relevant mechanism, but predicts that such evidence of the mechanism exists or will be discovered. I do not generalize from the biological evidence, but—in effect— predict that the biological evidence that explains the universalities will be found. (The prediction is of course retrodiction—the neuro-endocrinological evidence is already here—but the methodological point is the same.) Demonstration of cross-cultural universality makes the argument for a neuro-endocrinological explanation far stronger than does the biological evidence alone.

In other words, the physiologist or neuro-endocrinologist might quite likely acknowledge the clear relationship between sexually-differentiated neuro-endocrinological factors and sexually-differentiated behavior, but will refrain from speculating about the relevance of this to society. This represents both a laudable scientific conservatism and an acknowledgement that the physiologist or neuro-endocrinologist doesn't know anything about the relevant cross-cultural evidence. When informed of the cross-cultural evidence that alone would justify the strong suspicion that a physiological factor gives direction and limits to behavior and institution, the physiologist or neuro-endocrinologist will grant that the likelihood of correctness of the theory increases greatly.

Even if we did not at present have *any* of the evidence of the nature of the physiological mechanism, the inability of environmental explanations to explain the cross-cultural anthropological evidence would render the most probable explanation one that posited an as yet undiscovered physiologically-rooted mechanism.

12. *Does the criticism give lip-service acknowledgment to the role of physiological differentiation and then ignore this acknowledgment?* The reader should note that it is by an analysis itself, and not a mere lip-service acknowledgment

of the importance of physiological differentiation, that the analysis's view of the role of physiology should be assessed. A work that claims that it does not deny the role of physiology—but then proceeds to treat the over-representation of males in positions of power as exclusively representing discrimination—is, in fact, denying the role of physiology. A lip-service acknowledgment of the role of physiology does not immunize such a work against the contradictions inherent in a denial of the physiological.

The theory makes no assumption that there is any female physiological factor, complementing the dominance tendency of the male, that motivates the female to search for, and prefer, a dominant male. Male tendencies alone would be sufficient to explain that which we wish to explain. Despite current ideology, however, it may well be that there is a 'wired in' female preference for a dominant male. The male primate who ranks low in an all-male hierarchy (and who happens also to be as small as a female) rises to the top when placed in an all-female hierarchy. While this can be explained entirely in terms of male psychophysiology, it may be that female physiology is such that it acts on the male to increase his dominance tendency. In other words, the female role in engendering the male dominance behavior might well be a volitional one. If one looks at the actual behavior, rather than the ideological proclamations, of women, even feminist women, one could make a strong argument for this applying to human beings as well. A picture of the female playing an equal role in the 'dance' has the positive effect of replacing a social perception of female passivity with an active submission that, certainly on the level of coital behavior, is more satisfactorily concordant with our experience and observation. But none of this plays any part in the theory I present.

13. *Does the criticism invoke a general criticism of evolutionary and sociobiological theories, irrelevant or false analogies with studies of race, or ethological investigation of primates in their natural environments?* Such criticisms attempt to dismiss the strongest of theories emphasizing biology by subsuming all biological theories under one heading and dismissing all such theories as if they all exhibited the weaknesses of the weakest. This attempt to set up a straw man fails because all of the other theories are irrelevant to this book; the factors they discuss play no role in the argument I make. I take men and women as they are, in fact, physiologically constructed and make no attempt to explain why they have evolved over millions of years to this state. It is not incumbent upon someone who wishes to explain why men are better basketball players than women to explain how males evolved greater height. Likewise, while I find much sociobiological work fertile and fascinating, if often

highly speculative, I avoid introducing such work because the theory I present does not require it. Finally: ethological evidence fully supports the theory I present, but it elicits methodological charges of anthropomorphism; I can omit such evidence, and avoid such methodological arguments, because, I believe, the evidence I do invoke is more than sufficient to confirm the theory.

Likewise, criticisms that equate the argument I make with those seeing a genetic basis to racial IQ differences fail for at least three reasons.

a. They simply *assume* the incorrectness of the IQ arguments, thereby making an analogy to a possibly incorrect assumption. Even if it were the case that my argument were entirely analogous to the IQ argument, such a criticism of my argument would be telling only if the critic could demonstrate that the IQ argument is incorrect. The critic never attempts to demonstrate this, but merely assumes that no one would entertain the thought that the IQ argument is correct. In any case, since the analogy the critic attempts to make is false, it is irrelevant whether the IQ argument is correct or incorrect.

b. They ignore the evidential difference between an argument that can invoke universality in a world of varied societies that are half male and half female and one that is based primarily on one minority living under one cultural setting.

c. They fail to distinguish between a claimed difference in 'motivation' and a claimed difference in aptitude.

Those who raise any or all of these criticisms often refer to the theory I present as 'reductionist'. I discuss this point below.

14. *Does the criticism confuse sex-associated behavior with gender identity?* There is no confusion as widespread in the sociological literature on sex differences as that concerning 'gender identity'. We have discussed this at length earlier. Here I can merely state the central point: gender identity (to simplify somewhat, but without distortion) is one's continuing self-conception as male or female. Many sociologists have claimed that gender identity has a purely social causation. I believe this to represent a woeful misunderstanding of the pioneering work of John Money, but for our purposes we can grant—for argument's sake and for argument's sake alone—that gender identity has a purely social causation. We can grant this because it is *not* gender identity, but male and female *behavior,* that is here argued to be associated with sexual neuro-endocrinological development and that is posited here as causally crucial to the sexual differentiation of behavior responsible for the institutions we discuss.

This can be seen clearly if we consider chromosomal female fetuses hormonally masculinized *in utero*. When masculinization is not too extensive, the newborn's Central Nervous System is masculinized, but the anatomy is female and socialization conforms to anatomy. In other words, no one has any reason to doubt that the child is a perfectly normal girl and the parents treat her as such. We can grant, for argument's sake, that, in these individuals, gender identity is determined by socialization alone and is as female as is that of the normal female. What is relevant here is the fact that the behavior of these individuals is—statistically speaking—far more like that found in hormonally normal males than in hormonally normal females. This cannot be explained in terms of socialization, because the socialization is female. It should be stressed that the issue is not whether the tendency of these hormonally masculinized females to behave in ways associated with hormonally normal males is 'good' or 'bad': the point is that these females *do* behave in ways associated with males and that this cannot be explained without invoking the hormonalization. It is this behavior (behavior whose neuro-endocrinological origin is attested to by an enormous volume of evidence from a varied range of scientific disciplines), and not gender identity, that is ultimately responsible for the institutions we discuss.

Put another way: It does not matter whether these hormonally masculinized individuals see themselves as males trapped in female bodies (have male gender identities) or as females who are 'extreme tomboys' or 'aggressive'. What matters here is that the behavior is that usually exhibited more strongly by males—despite the female anatomy, female socialization, and even female gender identity. This cannot be explained without seeing the hormonalization as determinative.

This distinction can be elucidated by looking closely at the one of John Money's subjects most often invoked by sociologists as demonstrating the social nature of sexual differentiation—a hormonally normal male who was castrated in a circumcision accident. This male was surgically (but not, until puberty, hormonally) feminized and socialized as a female. Let us, for argument's sake, agree with the sociologists' assertion that this individual's gender identity was that of a normal female—that it was the result of socialization. The point that is relevant to our discussion is the behavior, not the gender identity, of this individual. Money makes it clear that this individual was "often the dominant one in a girl's group" and exhibited "tomboy" behavior, tendencies that cannot be explained in terms of the socialization, which was female.

I do not mean to make a lot of this one case. I mention this case only because a good number of sociologists, who realize that all the other cases discussed by Money obviously imply the importance of sexual hormonalization to behavior, treat this case as if it argues for the unimportance of hormonalization to behavior. For the reasons we have discussed, this is mistaken.

15.   *Does the criticism argue that hormones are so 'suggestible' that it is not the hormones, but society's instructions to the hormones, that determines behavior?* Environmentalists are fond of invoking Stanley Schacter's well-known finding that the behavioral effects of epinephrine can, under experimental conditions, reflect suggestion: individuals given adrenaline will feel fearful or exhilarated, depending on the behavior of others in the room. This finding will not surprise readers who have felt fear at one time and romantic love at another. As an argument against the psychological and behavioral directions given by the male hormone, this fails for reasons similar to that mentioned above. Even if we ignore the fact that fetally differentiated Central Nervous System sensitivity to whatever testosterone is present is clearly relevant in the case of testosterone, but not clearly relevant in the case of adrenaline, and even if we ignore the dubious assumption that the effects of testosterone are as malleable as those of epinephrine, we still face the central problem with this argument: In Schacter's experiment it is clear where the suggested behavior came from: the outside experimenter (Schacter and his assistants). But who are the 'outside experimenters' in every society that has ever existed? Why is it always the case that dominance is suggested to males? Once one must invoke some other factor (for example, male physical strength) to explain why it is always males who dominate, then the entire issue of suggestibility is rendered an irrelevant mediator and one must defend the causal determinativeness of the newly introduced factor.

16.   *Is 'feedback' (or 'interaction') invoked as evidence for the possibility of the environmental causal parity?* It is sometimes argued that environmental factors a. 'feed back' to the physiological and that this b. makes possible an equalizing or overcoming of the original physiological tendencies. The a. argument is undoubtedly true to some extent, but the environmental forces feeding back—the expectations and values of the population—were themselves limited by the original physiological-behavioral reality.

Aside from its inability to explain why the physiological effects of feedback are so small, this 'explanation' fails to explain why feedback never results in a society with females exhibiting dominance behavior as readily as do males. The answer is that the environmental component that is 'feeding back' to the physiological component of the causation has already itself been given direction and limits by the physiological. (In the long, long evolutionary sense, of course, physiology owes its nature to environmental selection, but this environmental influence takes tens of millions of years and its effects on human male-female differences were set in the species that preceded us millions of years ago.)

To choose a non-behavioral example, the expectation that males are physically stronger than females arises from the male physiology that makes males physically stronger than females. This expectation may feed back (for example, through male weight lifting) to increase the strength difference. But it could not be the case that the social-environmental factor that fed back was an expectation of greater female strength; physiology determines that it will be greater male strength that a population will observe and this will set limits of possibility on expectations and values. This is why the environmentalist emphasis on 'feedback' and 'interaction' cannot succeed in demonstrating the causal equality of social factors. That there is no need to posit causal equality (for a sufficient explanation of universality) is obvious from the fact that the institutions we discuss are universal; if feedback were causally equal, there would not be the universality of the institutions for us to explain. The issue of feedback begs the question: Why does feedback never undo that which the initial physiology does?

17. *Does the criticism make the error of assuming that, because pre-pubertal boys and girls have roughly equal testosterone levels, the boy's greater dominance behavior must have a purely social causation?* In all likelihood, boys more often exhibit the male behavior because their fetal Central Nervous System development has sensitized them more to whatever testosterone is present. But let us assume that this is not the case and that the boys' male behavior is entirely the result of imitation of adults and of socialization. It is the behavioral effects of adult male hormonalization—in which the male testosterone level greatly exceeds that of the female—that accounts for the adult behavior to which the boy is socialized. (There are many physiological events that are not manifested until puberty; the hormonalization of which we speak accounts for the fact that boys do not have facial hair, while men do.)

These points, incidentally, make clear why the fact that each sex has some amounts of the hormones associated with the other sex does not demonstrate the unimportance of the hormones: the levels are different and, more important, so are the fetally-prepared CNS structures with which the hormones interact.

18. *Does the criticism dismiss my work as 'reductionist', 'deterministic' or 'simplistic'?* Scientific explanations are *supposed* to be reductionist, deterministic

(if describing superquantum realities), and parsimonious. The charge that a theory is 'reductionist', 'deterministic', or 'simplistic' has disparaging force only if the theory attempts to explain an empirical reality it is incapable of explaining. A theory that does this is one that claims sufficiency when it cannot deliver it. This *would* be the case if I were to claim to explain differences between patriarchy in Saudi Arabia and patriarchy in the United States.

However, none of the critics who use these terms even attempts to offer an example of my claiming to explain any empirical reality I cannot explain. It is not merely that the critic cannot show that I do this; such critics have no interest in wrestling with the facts and reasoning of the theory. The critic wishes to find some general concept that will justify dismissing the theory without having to show that anything is incorrect in it. Thus the critic invokes a concept that is justifiably invoked against *other* theories and ignores the fact that it cannot be so invoked here. The reader can be certain that a critic is taking this tack if the critic claims that I fail to understand the 'complexity' of the issue, but gives no example of this 'complexity' that I attempt to explain but fail to explain. The universality of universal institutions—the limits that constrain possibility in every society—is as simple as an empirical reality can be. The criticism that denies an explanation of universal limits on the ground that the explanation does not explain variation within those limits—variation that the theory does not claim to explain—cannot refute that which it wishes to refute.

19. *Does the criticism fault my claim that patriarchy is inevitable on the grounds that this claim rejects the possibility of a non-patriarchal society?* This criticism confuses the scientific sin of refusing to acknowledge an empirical reality with a rejection of the possibility of a future empirical event. Rejecting a specific future empirical possibility is precisely what a scientific hypothesis is supposed to do. It is only such a rejection that enables the hypothesis to specify the conditions under which it will be surrendered.

20. *Is the criticism based on an explanation that is unparsimonious?* An explanation of patriarchy that gives causal primacy to capitalism in capitalist societies, feudalism in feudal societies, and so on, while not literally illogical, is so obviously *ad hoc* as to be implausible in the extreme.

21. *If the criticism offers a parsimonious alternative—like explanations invoking female maternal roles or male physical strength—does the criticism simply ignore the direct psychophysiological evidence and much of the social evidence?* Many criticisms simply ignore the direct psychophysiological evidence of the behavioral effects of neuro-endocrinological reversal, as well as the evidence of

the many societies in which women work harder and longer outside the home than do the men. Such evidence suggests that it is behavior, far more than physical strength, that correlates with dominance.

22. *Does the criticism change definitions in order to avoid unpalatable empirical realities?* Much 'feminist social science' is not even bad reasoning about empirical questions, but empty or confused discussion that substitutes terminology for explanation. One would be hard-put to find another group that talked so much about science without doing any science. (There are, of course, many women scientists who do science; but these women never make the arguments made by the 'feminist scientists'.)

Consider, for example, the myriad social science versions of 'reconceptualization'. Unable to deny that dominance behavior, as usually defined, is associated with males in every society, many feminist writers have redefined 'dominance' in such a way that it no longer refers to the behavior whose universality we wish to explain. Having done this, they can then claim that 'male dominance' (as they use the term) is not universal. The problem with this is that one cannot erase an empirical reality by changing its name. One may call a tree an 'elephant', but one must then find another way to distinguish trees from those fat animals with skinny tails, and it would be reckless to conclude that these animals have roots, bark, and leaves. If the environmentalists wish to use the word 'dominance' to refer to some reality other than that which we refer to, then they must select some other word to refer to the reality to which we refer. No semantic sleight-of-hand can legitimately be used to deny the existence of an empirical reality that exists.

23. *Does the criticism mistakenly believe that a finding by one study is called into doubt by a null finding of a study using a different methodology?* Feminist writings are replete with claims that Smith's finding that males are more aggressive conflicts with Jones's finding that they aren't. *If* Smith and Jones had used the same methodology, then there would be a problem, but this is rarely the case. The usual situation is that Smith used a methodology sufficiently fine-textured to discriminate a sexual difference, while Jones did not.

If, for example, you claim that men are taller than women and I claim that they are not, a look at the evidence we each present is clearly called for. If we find that you measured men and women with a yardstick with inch measurements, while I used a yardstick capable of measuring only to the nearest yard—a quantitative insensitivity, or used no yardstick, but asked questions about American history—a qualitative insensitivity, it would be clear that your study used appropriate measurements, while mine did not.

This fallacy is found most often in discussion of sexual differences in cognitive aptitudes. It is often claimed, for example, that an aptitude test measuring 'mathematical ability' and finding no difference refutes a different test that does find a difference (and whose results correlate with various forms of mathematical success). In fact, the first test fails where the second succeeds.

24. *Does the criticism require that we attain the impossible before suspecting that it is impossible?* Even John Stuart Mill made the mistake of implying that we cannot suspect that the behavioral sex differences we discuss are rooted in physiological sex differences until we have a society in which there are no such sex differences. This makes as much sense as saying that we will not know if physiology is relevant to the fact that it's women who can give birth until we have a society in which men give birth too.

25. *Is the criticism one that addresses not the argument, but the alleged motivation of the one making the argument or the (putative) consequences of a belief in the argument's correctness?* If so, then clearly it is irrelevant to the correctness or incorrectness of the argument it criticizes. If the theory I present is incorrect, then the critic need merely show where it is incorrect. But *this* the critic must do if he is to legitimately reject the argument.

If bias on the part of a theorist renders his theory fallacious or in error, one need merely point out the fallacy or error. If one cannot do this, then it would not matter if the theorist *were* biased. Bias of the theorist is relevant only to the extent that it biases his theory and an *ad hominem* attack on the theorist unsupported by evidence that there is anything wrong with the theory is just beside the point. Likewise, even if it were true that belief in a theory would have the most horrendous practical results, this would have nothing to do with the correctness of the theory.

In science, as in libel, truth is the perfect defense, and nature will give you a lift only if you're going her way.

An Aside on the Role of Neuro-endocrinological and Experimental Evidence

Journalists writing about my work have often asked neuro-endocrinologists, physiological psychologists, and other research scientists their opinion of the role of sexual physiological differences in the causation of sexually differentiated behavior and institution.

This is, of course, perfectly reasonable. However, a crucial point gets inadvertently omitted when my work is represented by the questions asked by the journalists: the questions posed to the research scientists invariably imply that my work proceeds from the physiological level to the social level.

Now, this is true of my description of the causal chain involved; it is precisely the point of this book that sexual physiological differentiation generates sexual differences in behavior which are observed by the population and are incorporated in expectation, socialization, and institution (all but the last being statistical realities).

However this direction, from the physiological to the institutional, was *not* the direction of the reasoning used for the development of the theory. The theory was developed in precisely the opposite direction: the universality of the limits that define patriarchy was established from the anthropological evidence (sexually-differentiated behavior was seen as the explanation of the universality of expectation, socialization, and institution) and it was *predicted* that there would be found hereditary physiological differences between the sexes that best explain the universalities of behavior, expectation, and institution. The 'prediction' is, of course, retrodiction—volumes of neuro-endocrinological evidence have long been available—but the methodological point is the same.

When the journalist asks the research scientist his opinion of the role of sexual physiological differences in the causation of sexually differentiated behavior and institution, he invariably implies that the primary evidence I invoke is the physiological. In other words, the research scientist is led to conclude that I merely generalize from the physiological, rather than predict the physiological on the basis of its manifestations on the institutional and behavioral levels.

When, as is the case, the research scientist is asked, in effect, to generalize from just the physiological evidence, he is understandably reticent; his reluctance to generalize is owing to the fact that the experimentalist, as experimentalist, lacks the evidence required for generalization. Thus, when you ask the experimentalist who has demonstrated the importance of male hormonalization to male behavior in hamsters to assess the relevance of his findings to human beings, he will say something to this effect: 'It is clear, from the medical-neuro-endocrinological study of human beings and of animals analogous to human beings in the system being studied, that the effects of male hormonalization in human beings are similar to that which we have found. But if you ask me about the human behavioral and social implications of this, I cannot say. One must consider not merely the effects of hormonalization on human behavior, but also the effects of the resulting behavior on the social environment, the effects of the social environment on physiology, the feedback that echoes from the social back to the other levels, and subsequent interactions of all of these.'

This is an admirable acknowledgment on the part of the experimentalist of the lack of the sort of evidence required for generalization (the evidence, for example, of anthropological universality). There is, of course, no reason why the experimentalist should know about the universality of the behaviors and institutions we discuss. When, however, you tell the experimentalist that in all of the thousands of societies we have studied, with all their varied social environments, dominance is associated with males and that the institutions of dominance always reflect this, the experimentalist will probably acknowledge that this new evidence enormously increases the likelihood that the universal institutions are manifestations of the neuro-endocrinological differentiation investigated on a nonhuman level. The concordance of explanations at different levels is precisely what science searches for. Prediction on the social, cross-cultural level is impossible for the experimentalist, then, because the experi-mentalist doesn't know anything about the evidence provided by the social level, the evidence that must be combined with the experimental evidence if one is to make predictions to the social level. But the experimentalist should acknowledge—and the majority do acknowledge—that demonstration of cross-cultural universality and the behavior relevant to it extends our knowledge of the effects of differentiated hormonalization to a point that the experimental evidence alone could not predict.

It is often the case that the perimeters of a given discipline or science impose limits on explanation and prediction that are overcome when we consider the evidence provided by a number of disciplines. It is often the case that a number of logically possible explanations permitted within the limits of one discipline are ruled out when the evidence of other disciplines is considered. The causal determinativeness of human physiological differentia-tion to the universality of patriarchy, male attainment, and male dominance cannot be predicted by evidence from the experimental level alone. But when the evidence of cross-cultural universality—and the evidence of the behavioral and social realities that mediate the physiological and the cross-cultural—are all considered along with this experimental evidence, and when the inadequacy of purely environmental explanations is demonstrated—then the likelihood of a physiological causal determinativeness increases enormously (as the research scientist acknowledges, at least in private).

Despite this, non-scientists who dislike the implications of all of this evidence often merely assert the irrelevance of hormonalization to the behavior of men and women. In so doing, they are, in effect, making incorrect predictions about what we find on the social level; they in effect make the claim that the institutions we discuss will not be found to be universal or that the universality can be as well explained without reference to sexual physiological differentiation.

Thus, many who dislike the implications of the experimental studies attempt to dismiss these with the claim that 'people are not animals'. They do not, however, abstain from using any of the thousands of medications, knowledge of whose safety and efficacy is dependent on the reliability of similar experimental studies. The safety of such medications is, like the evidence we have discussed, predicated on the ability of studies of nonhuman animals, and medical studies of human beings, to identify the effects of chemical substances on human functioning. The most obvious relevance of an experimental finding is, of course, to the animal being studied. But very few study the hamster just to find out about the hamster. In the back of nearly every experimentalist's mind is the ultimate relevance of his finding to human beings.

Even those who deny merely that current experimental evidence provides any relevant information and who demand ever more specific evidence merely obfuscate findings they do not like. One can always demand finer and finer points between the correlates included in an explanation and can refuse to accept a hypothesis by demanding explanation down to the quantum level. Likewise, one can always argue that, examined to sufficiently fine structure, all empirical realities are merely correlates and that cause and effect is illusory. But one who does these things can have no reason to believe that any statement about the world is more likely to be true than any other, and this can be a handicap.

The Appeal to Variation and 'Complexity': The Case of Philip Green

A stratagem of evading the empirical question demanding an answer—why are patriarchy, male attainment, and male dominance universal?—is perhaps most clearly embodied in Philip Green's *The Pursuit of Inequality*.[7] Green is quite candid in his attempt to justify this dismissal of the evidence: he expresses

---

7. New York: Pantheon, 1981.

his conception of objectivity when he writes that the proper approach to studying the evidence relevant to the empirical reality would be to "remain studiedly neutral by refusing to study it at all"[8] Because, Green writes, "we cannot arrange to study the kinds of societies different from those that already exist",[9] this approach would have us remain silent on the causation of precisely those realities that are so powerful that they set limits on social possibility (thereby *precluding* the possibility of the "different" society Green sees as necessary before we can consider the causation involved). Green's reasoning would forbid us to suspect, until men start giving birth, that physiology has anything to do with its being women who give birth and its being women who are associated with birth by society's institutions.

Green's book is an attempt to refute explanations that conclude that physiology is of primary causal importance. All of the points Green makes fall into one or another categories of fallacy and error.

1.   Green devotes much of his book to *ad hominem* and *ad consequentium* arguments that a. depict each theorist whose theory he dislikes as motivated by a desire to maintain the political *status quo* and b. invoke putative social consequences of a belief that the theory is true.

Neither the motivations of the theorist nor the putative consequences of an acceptance of his theory are relevant to the correctness of the theory. If a theorist's motivations or desires for practical consequences do not lead him to fallacy or error in his theory, then—even were the motivations and desires what Green claims they are—the motivations and desires are irrelevant. If motivations or desires for practical consequences *do* lead to fallacy or error in the theory, then these can be directly exposed, with no speculations required of the irrelevant issues of a. why the theorist committed the fallacy or error, and b. the alleged social consequences that could result from acceptance of his theory. But it is *only* by exposure of fallacy or error in the theory that doubt can be cast on the theory. *Ad hominem* and *ad consequentiam* accusations are no more than claims implying that there is such fallacy or error that provide no evidence whatever in support of the claim of fallacy or error.

2.   Green attempts to nullify the strongest arguments by attacking the weakest; thus, he fails to distinguish among: a. evolutionary arguments (such as many sociobiological theories, which are far stronger than Green implies, but which are irrelevant here); b. theories invoking statistical and other evidence

---

8. *Op. cit.*, 126.
9. *Op. cit.*, 126.

implying a physiological factor, but not specifying it (such as those theories arguing the importance of physiological factors to intelligence); and c. theories capable of *specifying* the physiological causal mechanisms and giving evidence of their behavioral effects. The theory of male dominance is an example of c. In reality, the *development* of the theory presented here was like those in b. It was argued that the evidence of universality in so varied a world, and the inadequacy of environmental explanations of the universality, force us to consider likely a physiological sufficient cause, with the discovery of the physiological specifics being a *prediction* that such a physiological mechanism will be discovered or, as is the case, will be found to have already been discovered.

This point is crucial because, while this book may be of interest to sociobiologists and evolutionary scientists, it makes no evolutionary claims itself. In other words, *Why Men Rule* does not attempt to explain how males and females evolved the physiologies they did; it takes the physiologies as given. This sort of argument is, by its nature, far less speculative, far more testable, and, if it passes the test, far more persuasive than is evolutionary theory. Thus, Green's many criticisms of analyses that base their claims of the importance of physiological differentiation to sexually-differentiated behavior on evolutionary arguments would be irrelevant to my argument even if Green's criticisms were correct.

3.   Two points that should be too obvious to mention are implicitly and explicitly denied by Green.

Whenever we speak of male-female differences in behavior we speak in statistical terms. Even when one speaks of a virtually purely physiologically-caused property like height, one finds many exceptions (many women taller than many men). When one speaks of behavior—which has familial and other environmental causal roots as well—one certainly expects exceptions. But social expectations and values reflect the statistical reality of large numbers—entire populations—and, on this level, the statistical and continuous becomes absolute.

Before the first edition of this book appeared, I guessed that critics would make the false claim that I argue that because the institutions we discuss are universal, therefore they are inevitable. Green claims that I argue that universality entails inevitability and then refers to such an argument as an "astonishing *non sequitur*" (which it is, but not one I committed). I have never argued that universality entails inevitability; I argue that, when thousands of independent societies, with all their impressive variation, always conform to an invariance (the limits and directions of the institutions we discuss), common sense and parsimony suggest a common factor that is responsible for the invariance.

To make the point as clearly as I can: universality does not *demonstrate* inevitability any more than the fact that the sun has appeared every morning for billions of years *demonstrates* that it will appear tomorrow. But, just as the billions of years of the sun's appearing each morning may suggest the existence of a mechanism explaining that regularity and indicating the strong likelihood that the sun will appear tomorrow, so the universality of patriarchy suggests the existence of a mechanism explaining that universality and indicating the strong likelihood that the universality will continue. Inevitability is not a deduction from universality (which is necessary, but not sufficient, for inevitability); it is the hypothetical mechanism suggested by universality that renders likely the inevitability, once that hypothetical mechanism has been examined and corroborated.

Universality in a world of such seemingly infinite variation as that exhibited by the Jivaro, the Pygmy, the Inuit, the Swede, the Japanese, and the American certainly suggests the likelihood of an underlying reality that sets limits of possibility on social variation. The evidence demands that we look at this possibility, and it will be ignored only by those for whom the possibility is unacceptable. In science no possibility is unacceptable.

4.   Green takes the tack of endlessly invoking 'variation and complexity' in differing political systems. Such variation is irrelevant to the limits we wish to explain (because all the variation and complexity falls within the limits.) No one denies the myriad differences among, for example, small hunter-gatherer society, a twelfth-century monarchy, and a contemporary democracy. It is only the relevance of these differences to universality that is denied. Indeed, it is the astonishing degree of variation of all other institutions that renders even more astonishing the universality of those few institutions that are universal. To be relevant, the variation would have to be such that one of these societies failed to exhibit the institutions we attempt to explain. And none does.

The fact that the hunter-gatherer society is ruled by a chief and a council of elders, the monarchy by a king and nobles, and the democracy by a President and a Congress is irrelevant. What is relevant to this book is that leadership in all these societies is male.

Green could not avoid noticing that his emphasis on variation and complexity would lead the reader to ask: What is the relevance of all this *variation* and complexity to the *unvarying* universality of patriarchy, male attainment, and male dominance? Green therefore writes as if there were no empirical reality to explain: "the most that [biological theory] has 'proved' is the unequal likelihood of male success in the quest for one particular and very untypical kind of political office in one particular kind of political society".[10]

This statement, which tends to divert attention from fact that it is the universality we wish to explain, is as utterly untrue as is Lewontin, Rose, and Kamin's similar attempt to deny the reality of universality. But even if we translate the sentence as 'patriarchy is universal, but Goldberg "proves" only that biology is relevant in just one type of society', the statement is both insupportable and dubious. For, given the universality, there is no reason for, and every reason against, distinguishing one of these societies from the others. Whatever the nature of the political (and social and economic) system, whatever the nature of the culture, the hierarchies are overwhelmingly filled by males—not merely in "one untypical kind of political office in one particular kind of political society", but in every kind of political office in every type of society (except in gender-segregated hierarchies, which are always subordinate to a male institution.)

Green uses examples almost exclusively from modern industrial societies, examples representing a small portion of the range of actual variation; but even the differences among modern societies over the past century (and no doubt after the next century) are small when compared to existing differences among all the thousands of societies that have existed. And even this great variation never obtains in the case of the institutions we discuss.

Green comes close to acknowledging the central role of the male dominance tendency:

> Of course, women lose out dramatically . . . in the process of recruitment for positions of authority, including candidacy for political office.[11]

Why do women "lose out dramatically . . . in the process of recruitment for positions of authority" in every society? I would say that this is because males are—for psychophysiological reasons—more strongly 'motivated'[12] to behave in

---

10. *Op. cit.*, 146.
11. *Op. cit.*, 139.
12. For simplicity's sake, in this section I refer to the male 'need' and 'motivation'. As I have mentioned elsewhere, one is free to distinguish the male and female behavior in any qualitative or quantitative way one chooses, as long as the model reflects the empirical reality of the difference. The empiricist in me prefers the stylistically heinous: 'lower male threshold for the release of dominance behavior in an environment that elicits (cues) dominance behavior'.

the ways associated with attainment of position in their given societies and are willing to sacrifice more to attain position. Society recognizes and institutionalizes this.

Green suggests that males discourage female participation in order to maintain the male political dominance. Why is it always males who are in a position to do this? Even the explanations positing the determinativeness of male size or the female's maternal role fail 'only' on empirical grounds; they at least give us a noncircular causal explanation, even if it is one that has been refuted by observation.

> [Goldberg's] proposition is irrelevant to the choice of members of a primarily deliberative body; of an administrative bureaucracy, a judicial system, or any other set of positions filled according to real or alleged merit; of ideologically defined delegates to an assembly, or tribunal. . . . Needless to say, his 'theory' is also irrelevant to an explanation of how power is attained in hereditary monarchies.[13]

If Goldberg's "proposition is irrelevant to the choice of members of a primarily deliberative body, administrative bureaucracy, judicial system . . .", how come the proposition correctly predicts one hundred percent of the time that it will be overwhelmingly males who are members of the "primarily deliberative body", "administrative bureaucracy", or "judicial system", no matter what the *method* used by any given "deliberative body", "administrative bureaucracy", or "judicial system"?

My answer is that, for psychophysiological reasons, males are, in every society, more strongly 'motivated' to behave in whatever ways are appropriate for attainment in that society, to do and learn what is necessary for attainment, and to sacrifice other rewards and pleasures in favor of dominance and attainment. (*If* I had claimed to distinguish *between* two deliberative bodies, and so on, to explain their different methods or structures, *then* Green would have a point. But I have made no such claim.)

Green wanders even further from the relevant when he invokes not *forms* of government that differ in ways that are irrelevant here, but specific political issues. He seems to think that the fact that males fill the hierarchical positions in every society somehow implies that the men of one society will always agree with the men of another on every issue:

---

13. *Op. cit.*, 146.

> The biological theorist will have to explain what it is about the biology of Swedish men or Japanese men . . . that made those nations pioneers in the legalizing of abortion on demand.[14]

That is nonsense. The only thing that the "biological theorist" has to explain is why Sweden and Japan and every other society are ruled by males. And this is precisely what the "biological theorist" does and what Green seems to be completely unable to attempt. Why the men and women of one nation support a right to abortion and those of another do not is an example of the variation that this 'biological theorist' does not attempt to explain.

All of Green's examples are either: a. irrelevant because they invoke realities that have nothing to do with the realities we attempt to explain, or b. supportive of the very argument Green wishes to refute. Thus, for example, Green makes much of women's suffrage and the current feminist movement and sees these as somehow casting doubt on my argument. This despite the fact that these movements have not significantly altered the percentage of men in upper hierarchical positions, a failure that is precisely the prediction I have consistently made. (Female hierarchical attainment—in political, though not corporate, hierarchies—in Scandinavian nations has long far surpassed anything we are experiencing in the United States. Yet even this Scandinavian reality does not begin to support an argument that the Scandinavian nations are exceptions to universality; these Scandinavian nations still maintain official bodies devoted to their unsuccessful attempt to reduce overwhelming male domination of hierarchies. As we have seen, none of these nations casts doubt on the continuing primacy of patriarchy.)

Subtleties of variation are, of course, important in other contexts. If one's interest is in explaining variation within the limits, variation of the sort of which Green speaks, then causal variation is required. If, for example, we wished to explain, say, differences between patriarchy in the United States (with its relatively egalitarian legal system) and patriarchy in a traditional Moslem country (with its prohibition of women's participation in many areas of life) or between self-conceptions of men and women in these societies, *then*, of course, variations of meanings, conscious perceptions, values, and the like would be crucial. Such differences *do* involve all of the complexities of which Green writes. But, for an explanation of the limits within which every society's customs and institutions fall, these are irrelevant; no differences of meaning,

---

14. *Op. cit.*, 138.

conscious perception, values, and the like have resulted in a society lacking patriarchy or failing to associate dominance behavior with men.

Let us say that we wish to understand why every society has customs of eating. After demonstrating that every society *does* have such customs, we would suggest that there was probably some physiological reason for this. When we were able to demonstrate the actual physiology involved, we would consider the case as being as closed as a case can be in science.

Green, on the other hand, would presumably invoke the quintillion subtleties concerning food—meanings, taboos, meals-per-day, religious significance, and the like—and claim that the undeniable variation and complexity of these somehow refutes the claim that human physiology sufficiently explains the limits within which all such variation falls (why every society institutionalizes at least one meal a day, has one or another institutions of food collection, and so forth). If, on the other hand, one wishes to understand why Americans eat American food with forks and Chinese eat Chinese food with chopsticks or why one people eats dog and another doesn't, then the answer is probably not rooted in physiology.

Because variation can never explain consistency, it behooves Green to show that there is an exception to the consistency or to provide an alternate explanation of the consistency. If Green could show that there was or is an exceptional society, one that did not exhibit the limits and in which males did not dominate, then he would have a powerful argument. But this cannot be done. For all the seemingly infinite variation exhibited by societies as disparate as those I have mentioned, no society lacks the universals. Unless he were to dispute this fact, which he does not, Green has little alternative, if he wants to keep some semblance of an argument going, than to invoke the irrelevant.[15]

5.   Green's 'subtlety and complexity' arguments are as ineffective when he discusses variation in the behavior that mediates the psychophysiological and the institutional as when he discusses variation in the institutional.

We have seen that, when Green discusses social and political systems, he focuses exclusively on differences between different society's systems as if this

---

15. There are many contemporary *predictions and wishes* that assume that changes in attitudes will manifest themselves in equality of position and status. But there is no evidence that this is happening and we have no reason to believe that it ever will. Attitudes (such as whether a population looks favorably or unfavorably on the universal institutions) are causally unimportant to the institutions we discuss. The astonished response to this claim on the part of those who predict an end to patriarchy is not a function of the evidence, but of their wish that this be the case. Such is the power of wish over those for whom curiosity is not the strongest motivation for addressing the issue.

variation somehow undercut, rather than emphasized, the fact that all of these systems, whatever their differences, are patriarchal. Likewise, when discussing the various behaviors that are associated with dominance in various societies, he treats as an unimportant coincidence the fact that such behaviors are always more strongly associated with males.

Time and again Green conjures up the inevitable variation and "immense range of complexly differentiated political, social, and economic behaviors"[16] and argues that these preclude prediction that fails to take into account all their subtlety and complexity (and that, since there is no way of taking all this subtlety and complexity into account, there is nothing we can say on the subject).

All these differences make no difference: whatever the nature of the dominance behavior and whatever the form of government, the former is associated with males and the latter is filled with males. It is this fact that it is our purpose to explain. And the most plausible explanation, even if we lacked the direct evidence of the behavioral effects of physiological factors, would be one positing a 'common denominator' of the various specific forms of dominance behavior. The 'common denominator' is the male's greater 'motivation' to learn what is necessary and do what is necessary for attainment and dominance, and the behavior that this 'motivation' generates. This male tendency sets limits of possibility on social behavior and institutions. (The most important environmental element responsible for the limits is the perception of the sexual difference by a society's men and women: expectations and values must, if they are to be taken seriously, tend towards concordance with observation; a society could no more fail to associate dominance behavior with men than it could fail to associate height with men.)

There is a perfect correlation on the societal level between expectations associating the behavior required for attainment of position with males (despite the variation from society to society in what this behavior is). This astonishing correlation has no persuasive effect on Green. I would be persuaded of Green's objections if he could find a single society in which dominance and attainment behavior were not associated with males and in which males did not dominate.

The basic problem with Green's position is that all the complexity he cites is irrelevant because we can fully explain what we wish to explain—the universality—without any need whatever for considering all this complexity. The complexity fails to explain anything required for that which we wish to

---

16. *Op. cit.,* 130.

explain because the complexity all falls within the observed empirical limits we want to explain. On the basis of sexual physiology *alone* we are able to predict the limits between which the institutions of every society fall.

Green's line of reasoning is analogous to one that denies the physiological roots of our tendency to become sexually-aroused on the grounds that favored sexual position varies among societies. A theory positing the physiological basis of sexual arousal need not make any claim about the position in which a society's members express this arousal. The theory simply says that the members of every society will react to certain environmental situations with one or another behavior from a fairly narrow range of behaviors and that they must because this is what they are. This is attested to by the very subtlety and complexity of the ways that we have developed for expressing what we are, ways that always fall within the limits imposed by the physiologically-generated impulses that make us what we are.

The fact that sexual behavior consists of one position in one society, another in a second, and still another in a third does not cast any doubt on the physiological basis of the impulse that leads to one or another of these positions. However, Green would, were he making the argument analogous to that he makes in criticizing this book, argue that the fact that one society exhibits 'missionary position behavior' and another 'man-behind behavior' demonstrates that physiology has nothing to do with the fact that the peoples of all societies have intercourse.

6. When Green glances at some of the thousands of studies on sex differences surveyed by Maccoby and Jacklin,[17] he finds, as does any reader, that various researchers conceptualize a. similar behaviors in different terms and b. different behaviors in similar terms.

Now, if one imposes an absolutely literal interpretation on all of these disparate studies one can argue—absurdly though not literally illogically—that, say, all studies using a term like 'aggression' are comparable and all studies using different terminologies are incomparable. This is what one will do if he wishes to avoid the obvious conclusion he is led to by the studies. This is what Green does.

If, however, one is even vaguely objective in assessing these studies, he will conclude that running through all of the relevant studies is a finding of a

---

17. Eleanor E. Maccoby and Carol N. Jacklin, *The Psychology of Sex Differences* (Stanford: Stanford University Press, 1974). See also these authors, *The Development of Sex Differences* (Stanford: Stanford University Press, 1966).

general male dominance tendency in hierarchical, status and (male-female) dyadic situations.

Maccoby and Jacklin clearly would prefer interpretations that would sever physical 'aggression' from 'dominance' and would distinguish forms of dominance behavior with sufficient fineness to emphasize elements of attainment other than dominance behavior. Their problem is that they are too good at what they do and too clear-headed to permit anything approaching Green's strategy. Indeed, Maccoby had earlier very plainly stated the import of the evidence:

> there is good reason to believe that boys are innately more aggressive than girls—and I mean aggressive in the broader sense, not just as it implies fighting, but as it implies dominance and initiative as well.[18]

Many of the studies consider behaviors that do call on tendencies and abilities *in addition to* those we discuss. Green attempts to use this fact, as well as the multiplicity of terms, models, and the like, to deny the obvious thread that runs through the male behaviors observed (in those studies having anything at all to do with the issue).

Green's approach is analogous to that taken by those who deny that there is such a thing as 'G' intelligence on the grounds that its manifestations each require additional elements (which is why there are highly-intelligent people with *relatively* lower specific abilities like mathematical facility or literary insight). But strong correlations among these, to say nothing of everyone's observation that some people are more intelligent than others (an observation that is supported by a high correlation between people's intuitive assessments and the IQ scores of the assessed) lead nearly everyone to realize that there is such a thing as 'intelligence' and that intelligence—whatever its cause—is a necessary condition for the various specific aptitudes. "Nearly everyone" here includes laymen who daily observe the world and specialists who devote their lives to the issue and the methodology for studying it. It does not include all sociologists.

Neither in the case of intelligence nor in that of dominance behavior does this attempt to invoke additional necessary elements, or multiplicity of methodological terms and practices, obscure the obvious: there is a common denominator running through the behaviors and this common denominator explains consistencies of behavior and, ultimately, institution otherwise inexplicable.

---

18. Eleanor E. Maccoby, 'Woman's Intellect', in *The Potential of Women*, Seymour M. Farber and Roger H. Wilson, eds. (New York: McGraw-Hill, 1963), 37.

Were Green looking at competitiveness in, say, games, sports, status competitions, and politics, he would deny the relevance of a general competitiveness and would insist that the behavior relevant to each was completely independent of the others. Most of us would say that, while each of these do have necessary conditions not relevant to the others, a general competitiveness is relevant to success—indeed virtually necessary for success—in each.

The point of all this is that anyone looking at the evidence will see that a host of behaviors exhibited differentially by males and females manifest, in addition to qualities unique to each, a much stronger male tendency to exhibit dominance behavior.

At times Green seems to all but acknowledge this, but claims that psychophysiological differentiation is of only minor importance. The evidence yields no support for this claim; the differentiation is important enough to generate the universals we wish to explain. But, even if there were some sense in which the differentiation is minor in the way that the carburetor is a 'minor' part of the automobile, the universal institutions would represent an extreme dependence on initial conditions that renders a society lacking the institutions about as likely as a functioning 1959 Impala without a carburetor.

But for the most part Green simply ignores the evidence and asks questions like, "why are we supposed to believe that men actually have these [dominance] emotions and needs in greater strength than do women?"[18] Because this is the message of the concordant evidence of cross-cultural observation, our knowledge of the effects of neuro-endocrinological differentiation, and the experience of all of the members of every society on Earth, not the least of whom are the environmentalists who detest it and mistakenly deny its physiological roots.

7. A typical example of Green's approach: Green demands a specificity of behavioral effects of physiology that no theory emphasizing physiologically-generated impulse claims or would claim. Thus, for example, consider Green's attempt to deny the obvious conclusion of the fact that females hormonally-masculinized *in utero* and *socialized as girls by parents who don't doubt that they are girls* exhibit the behavior associated with males, including a desire for male clothes. Green claims, let us assume correctly, that "in some cultures males wear the equivalents of dresses and females the equivalents of slacks".[19] He then argues that this contradicts the implication of the importance of hormones to sexually-differentiated behavior. Green's criticism implies that the theories he

---

18. Green, *op. cit.*, 128.
19. *Op. cit.*, 145.

criticizes hold that physiology engenders a specific male desire for slacks-as-slacks and a specific female desire for dresses-as-dresses. Yet I have made clear time and again that the effect of physiological differentiation is a generalized impulse whose specific manifestations are determined by the customs of the society, customs that fall within limits of possibility imposed by the differentiation of impulse. Green forgets that there is a question to be answered: why do these hormonally-masculinized females socialized as *females* choose clothes that their society associates with *males* and why do they exhibit a wide range of behaviors associated with *males?*

Green repeatedly asserts that there is no evidence that hormones are correlated with human behavior. There is such a wealth of evidence of the relationship between hormonal masculinization and dominance behavior (even if one uses only human evidence) that one must assume that Green refers to a *within-sex* neuro-endocrinological-behavioral connection. But even so, there is nothing in the theory presented here requiring that hormones have anything to do with the greater dominance behavior of one man as opposed to another man (or one woman as opposed to another woman). It would hardly be surprising if the small differences within-sex were not important, while the large differences between-sex were: size is unimportant to being a good football lineman once you weigh 270 pounds, but this hardly leads to the conclusion that size is unimportant to being a good football lineman.[20]

It will not surprise the reader to learn that Green dismisses all of the experimental study of the relationship of physiology and behavior in animals out of hand. The reader who is sufficiently tenacious to compare the evidence I have presented with Green's attempt to assert it away—and who does not deny the possibility that the study of animals similar to us in the relevant ways just *might* tell us something about ourselves—will see how unwarranted are Green's attempts to dismiss the evidence.

As difficult to believe as it is, it *does* seem that, having asserted away all of the evidence provided by experimentation on non-human animals, Green is simply asserting away virtually all of the evidence provided by scientific and medical study of normal human beings and human hermaphrodites and all of the other evidence provided by human beings and discussed above. No degree of similarity of the effects of fetal and neonatal hormones on behavior in normal

---

20. I happen to believe that sufficiently fine measurements *will* eventually distinguish *among* men or *among* women on the basis of a significant correlation between physiology and dominance behavior. But here I assume that there is no such correlation within-sex. All that is relevant to this book is the between-sex difference on the hereditary and behavioral levels.

human beings and hermaphroditic human beings can lead Green to doubt the correctness of his rejecting out of hand all such evidence.

8. Green makes the obvious point that physical aggression does not "necessarily" lead to dominance. Of course it doesn't *necessarily* lead to dominance. It often leads to jail. No manifestation of a strong 'need' to dominate—physical or not—*necessarily* leads to dominance or attainment.

The point is not that this 'need' is sufficient, but that it is necessary (or, more precisely, a 'strong facilitator'), and the more 'open' the society—the more democratic and unbiased and the less hereditarian the society—the more can this 'need' determine who attains position and status. Those for whom this 'need' is less pressing, for whom it ranks lower in the hierarchy of desires and therefore motivates them less to learn and do what is, in their respective societies, necessary for dominance and attainment, will, statistically speaking, be less likely to attain position and status. Likewise, no doubt some who fail will be found to have a strong dominance tendency, but that is irrelevant. The claim is not that a much stronger-than-average dominance tendency is sufficient for attainment of high position and status, but that this *independently-defined* tendency is necessary.[22] This is evidenced by all formal and informal observations of position and status. Indeed, observation of this difference is implicit in the feminist denunciation of the male tendency.[23]

Were Green attempting to refute the claim that professional basketball players tend to be tall, he would argue that tallness does not necessarily make one a good basketball player and that many tall people are not good basketball players. Both of these things are true and irrelevant. The issue is not whether tall people tend to be professional basketball players, but whether professional basketball players tend to be tall people. Likewise, the issue is not the percentage of males who attain positions of dominance, but a. the percentage of those who attain the positions who are male and b. the role male physiology

---

22. The comparison in dominance behavior is between those in the upper positions and those not in these positions. At some point one can always filter out even the most powerful causal factor (as we saw in our example of linemen who weigh more than 270 pounds). There are many other requirements for high position, so when one has narrowed the population being considered, relatively subtle differences in dominance tendency become as unimportant as the weight differences among the linemen who weigh 270 or more.

23. When I first wrote on male-female differences, I tried to make clear that 'aggression' referred not merely to physical aggression, but—much more importantly for our purposes—also to 'aggression' as it is used in phrases like 'he's an aggressive businessman', a usage that comes very close, especially in its implication of competitiveness, to the meaning of dominance behavior. However, I soon dropped the word 'aggression' completely, in favor of 'dominance tendency'.

plays in explaining why those who attain the positions are everywhere overwhelmingly males.

Moreover, Green consistently confuses physical aggression and dominance tendency in other ways. He ignores the important point that this book sees male physical aggression as simply one of many manifestations of the male's dominance tendency, one that is *relatively* rarely necessary to invoke and that is, usually, invoked only as a last resort.

9.   Green represents the theory I present as primarily a theory of the effects of lesser female "leadership *capabilities*",[24] when it should be clear to any reader that the crucial effect of physiological differentiation posited is a lower male threshold for the *attainment* of position. The issue of *capability* for leadership is irrelevant to the theory (except insofar as one must attain a position before capability becomes an issue). Whether the male tendencies render men more, equally, or less qualified for any particular task, role, or position is a question unrelated to the theory we discuss here.

10.   Green implies that the theory is tautological; he seems to believe that, to the extent that *Why Men Rule* leaves unspecified the behavior by which dominance is attained in specific societies, it says no more than that men attain dominance because they attain dominance. But this is a woefully misrepresentative caricature of the theory. The theory states that: a. those who attain dominance in every society will tend to come from a *specifiable* and *identifiable* group of people (males) with *specifiable* and *identifiable* physiological characteristics; b. these characteristics give them a lower threshold for the release of dominance behavior, however it be exhibited in the particular society, and a lower threshold for the elicitation of dominance behavior that is acknowledged and *identifiable* in every society, by proverbs, songs, jokes, by psychological tests, and, in general, by the observation of the members of every society; and c. this psychophysiological reality engenders more strongly in males the behavior required in a given society for dominance and attainment and is *independently identifiable* as such; and d. this behavior results in its being males who attain position and status, a claim that *predicts* that this behavior will everywhere be associated with attainment (by *observation* and psychological *test*) and will be associated with males.

Perhaps what concerns Green is the fact that the theory does not specify the behavior required for dominance in each particular society. Where the male physiology and the lower threshold for exhibiting dominance behavior is

---

24. Green, *op. cit.*, 127.

universal, the specific behavior required is socially defined by each particular society (within limits of possibility). As we have seen, the same thing is true of the sexual 'drive'. Physiology engenders the tendency to feel sexual arousal; society determines which positions will be used to satisfy sexual arousal.

Admittedly I have not tried to identify, for each of thousands of societies, the behavior which mediates the physiological and the institutional. But I do grant that all refutation would require is that Green give us an example of just one society in which the behavior, socialization, values, and the like (and the resulting attainment) are not more strongly associated with males. The fact that neither Green nor anyone else can do this implicitly concedes that there is no such society. In other words, *Why Men Rule* does indeed claim that in every society one or another independently specifiable and discoverable behaviors can be shown to be associated with attainment and that in every society the behavior—whichever it be in any given society—will be found to be associated with males.

The fact that we must look to the specific societies to see the specific forms that the behavior takes no more renders the point 'tautological' than does the fact that different societies favor different sexual positions render tautological the claim that sexual arousal is a function of a physiologically-rooted tendency. Whether one is concerned with the skills and abilities that must be developed if one is to attain dominance or with the specific sexual positions, one is concerned with institutions that are clearly specifiable and identifiable (society by society) independently of the results they explain.

11. I have tended, in this discussion, to proceed as if the actual behavior required for dominance in society were so varied that the specific behavior cannot be specified in general. In other words, I have proceeded as if dominance went to the physically strongest in one society, the most-learned in another, and the most friendly in a third, with five thousand different behaviors attaining dominance in five thousand different societies.

I have proceeded in this way because, for the sufficient theory I propose, it is perfectly legitimate to do so (as I have just attempted to demonstrate). In reality, however, it is far from the case that the required behavior is as varied as all that or as difficult to specify in a way that describes the required behavior in all societies. For not only is it a simple matter to test for dominance behavior, competitiveness, and the like, but it is simple to measure hierarchies of the individual values of men and women (the desire for position and status relative to desire for the other rewards and pleasures the society offers), the willingness to sacrifice other rewards for dominance, the refusal to back down in the face of opposition, and the like, and to show that some of these are associated with attainment and dominance in every society.

If, for example, it were shown that the women of all societies put dominance lower in their hierarchy of desires than did men in theirs, and that desire for dominance were associated with attainment of dominance, it would certainly make sense to see this as going far towards explaining male attainment of position, status, and dyadic dominance.[25] This would not, in itself, demonstrate that *physiology* explained the association of dominance behavior with males, but that is not the issue here. The issue here is the importance of dominance behavior to attainment and the association of dominance behavior with males. The issue of *cause* concerns the evidence we have discussed above and the inadequacy of environmental explanations of the association of dominance behavior with males.

The "refusal to back down" just mentioned gives an insight far deeper than the superficial image of a physical fight. Men and women both would, in the abstract, choose to attain all good things (love, health, protection of children, relaxation, dominance, wealth, and all of life's other satisfactions). In the abstract, people would fight equally hard for each of life's rewards. But precisely what we are talking about here is individuals' hierarchies of desires, their ranking of the desires when forced to choose. The male's stronger "dominance tendency" is equivalent to—in essence, is—a desire for dominance that ranks higher in the male's hierarchy of desires than does the female's desire for dominance rank in the females' hierarchy of desires. Thus, males are, on this view, more willing to endure pain, frustration, and the like, to learn what they must and do what they must for attainment and dominance, while females— statistically speaking as always—are more willing to endure such pain, frustration, and the like for familial reasons, for children, for love, and so forth, but not as much for dominance.[26]

---

25. It may well be that women exhibit these characteristics just as strongly when, for example, protecting the endangered infant, but it is precisely the point that male physiology is such that *hierarchy, status,* and *member of the other sex* elicit such behavior more strongly from males. In any case, it is irrelevant to our concerns whether it is true that maternal impulses generate tendencies this strong.

26. However, dominance may be more complex than wealth or other aims in that there may be a strong female desire for dominant males. The evidence of real behavior—as opposed to that of ideology and poll—justifies the suspicion that this is the case. The tendency of even many feminists to select males of higher status might imply that the female attitude towards male attainment and dominance is more complex, with a desire for dominance being subordinated to a desire for a dominant male. Whether this is the case is not relevant to the theory: the lower male threshold alone would be sufficient to explain that which we wish to explain.

I think that this will seem, to those willing to subordinate ideology to understanding, to be a very accurate picture of the statistical realities we encounter when living in the real world, with its real men and women.

12.   To be sure, it is often the case that the association of position and status with men becomes institutionalized. As I have mentioned, this results in a societal ratification and reification, a concretization, of the male physiological 'advantage' that renders male attainment of position and status nearly automatic. (Similarly, the statistical, continuous, and quantitative greater male tendency to exhibit dominance behavior becomes concretized into the absolute, discrete, and qualitative, 'men are aggressive; women are passive'.) The clearest example of such institutionalization is the hereditary monarchy, which always has rules of succession favoring appointment of a king over appointment of a queen (as we, but not Green, would predict).

To be sure, other factors often preclude many men and women from attaining position no matter what their physiology or behavior (for example the black in South Africa in 1980). But, within the group otherwise permitted position and status, it is always and everywhere predominantly males who attain the position and status.

And, to be sure, this institutionalization will make attainment more difficult for the woman who is the equal (in dominance tendency) of a man who attains. To be sure, whatever can be done to limit this undesirable outcome should be done. But the empirical question remains: why is it *male* attainment that is institutionalized?

13.   Although Green implies a failure of my theory to explain the empirical reality it attempts to explain, he is not obliged to offer an alternative explanation. (Indeed, since he barely acknowledges the reality, it would be unlikely that he would offer any explanation of it.) One need not have an answer in order to argue that another answer is incorrect.

However, the reader who is unimpressed by Green's argument, and who finds *Why Men Rule* persuasive, will require of Green an at least equally persuasive alternative, environmental theory. As we have seen elsewhere in this book, neither Green nor anyone else can provide an alternative theory that, even if it managed to avoid the fallacy and misrepresentation that characterize such alternative theories (and even if we ignore such theories' neglect of the psychophysiological evidence), avoid being implausible.

14.   Green refers to Eleanor Leacock's criticism of the first edition of this book in the "March, 1975" *American Anthropologist* and writes that "there has been no response to her critique as far as one could tell". The March 1975

American Anthropologist is not the issue in which Leacock's criticism appeared, but the issue *in which my response to Leacock appeared*. Let us just say that Green 'could not tell' whether there had been a response to Leacock because he did not actually open the issue of *American Anthropologist* he was holding. But I can't help wondering why he was holding *that* issue if he believed that there was no response to Leacock's (much earlier) criticism.

15.   Finally, it is worth repeating that one can always ask further questions of any theory. Indeed, one should; this is precisely how science proceeds. But, assuming that the theory passes the tests demonstrating that it does explain that which it claims to explain, the purpose of such questions is, in addition to constantly testing the theory, to refine the theory, rendering the theory capable of explaining an even wider area of reality or explaining with greater precision that which it explains.

When a theory is capable of invoking various *independent* lines of evidence, when it explains successfully and parsimoniously a wide range of disparate facts by demonstrating the element they have in common, when all of its many parts are concordant and predictive (if, inevitably, not complete down to the last detail), and when it passes the test of every prediction and retrodiction it makes, then the theory has a good claim to acceptance. An objector can keep on demanding further explanation, down to the quantum level, but his doing so serves only to anchor him in darkness while the rest of us struggle towards the light.

Part III

Cognitive Differentiation

Possible Sexual Differentiation in Cognitive Aptitudes

Introductory Note

I have purposely separated the theoretical considerations advanced in this chapter and the next from the theory of the inevitability of patriarchy proper in order to emphasize as strongly as possible the fact that the validity of the theory in no way depends on the correctness of these two chapters, and would in no way be affected if they were completely incorrect. Thus far I have discussed institutions that can be demonstrated to be both universal and explicable in terms of an observable physiological factor. The existence of universality and the physiological factor have made it possible to present a theory as the only reasonable explanation of patriarchy, male dominance, and male attainment; this may tend to obscure the fact that it is exceedingly rare for any one theory to be the only reasonable explanation of the reality it attempts to explain. It is far more common for a number of conflicting theories to be both internally logical and congruent with empirical reality; in these cases acceptance results not from total destruction of all alternative theories, but from a slightly better ability to persuade. This process is hindered when one of two conflicting theories meets enormous emotional resistance while the other is in accord with what most people would like to believe. We often demand of the first theory a virtually deductive conclusiveness while we embrace the second even if its chances of being correct are very slight. In these two chapters I argue that there is a physiological basis to certain differences in cognition between men and women. I do not attach to these hypotheses anything like the probability of correctness that I attach to the theory of the inevitability of patriarchy. For our discussion of cognitive differences we have neither the extensive cross-cultural evidence nor the direct physiological evidence that we were able to invoke in the discussion of patriarchy. The explanation of cognitive differences presented here, like any alternative, totally environmental explanation, attempts to persuade by presenting a configuration of logically interrelated hypotheses which can explain the evidence that we do have. I do not deny that one could present a totally environmental explanation of the cognitive differences I discuss nor that such an explanation could conceivably be correct. But I do think that the explanation that posits the importance of physiological differentiation is considerably more logically compelling, considerably more in accord with experience, and considerably more likely to be correct than the explanation that does not.

Readers who are familiar with Eleanor Maccoby's criticism of my work in Science[1] *will note that these chapters have been revised in response to criticisms— in my view misconceived and incorrect—made by Dr Maccoby. Since I assume that other readers will be unacquainted with her article and will be put off by the 'Dr Maccoby says I said X, but in fact I said Y' approach appropriate for journals, I have, with a few exceptions, clarified the points criticized by Dr Maccoby without referring to the* Science *article. Readers who question whether I have responded to all her criticisms need merely read her article after reading these chapters.*

Sexual Differentiation in Modes of Cognition

For all that has been said so far to be correct, it is only necessary that there should be one physiological difference between men and women: that which is responsible for the male's greater dominance tendency. But we know very well that, whatever the cause of the differences (whether physiological differentiation is involved or not) we can observe additional differences between men and women. 'Men are more logical', 'women are more psychologically perceptive', 'women are more gentle and nurturant'—these are but a few of the stereotyped qualities attributed to men and women.

Now, I shall argue that every stereotype is 'true' in that it represents an observation, but it may be quite incorrect in the *explanation* it offers of the behavior it *observes*. We shall discuss this further below. My point here is merely that there is always a strong sense in which a stereotype is true; it is, whether we like it or not, an observation of reality. To ignore a stereotype, to pretend that it is not true in the sense we discuss, or assume without evidence

---

1. *Science* (2nd November 1973) Volume 182, Number 4111. Unless another reference is given, reference to Maccoby in this chapter refers to the *Science* article. Dr Maccoby's criticisms of the theory of patriarchy were more or less the standard criticisms. I attempt to demonstrate the inadequacy of these criticisms throughout this edition.

that the observed behavior must have a purely social explanation, is to proceed in the opposite direction from that which science demands. Science demands that we make observations and then attempt to explain them by evidence, not by wish and ideology.

In this chapter I consider the stereotype 'Men are more logical than women'. I would have much preferred to use a stereotype in which women are superior, since this would have the positive effect of balancing a book that might appear to the superficial reader to favor men. However, throughout this book I have assumed that any work of this kind will be attacked at its weakest point. As my guiding principle I have refused to use any but the strongest evidence and have omitted many interesting and reasonable, but less strongly supportable, arguments. Thus, my not arguing for the correctness of the stereotype of women as more psychologically perceptive than men does not indicate any doubt that the stereotype is correct, but merely reflects the fact that, although we recognize this superior female aptitude daily, psychological perception is far harder to measure than logical-mathematical aptitudes. We simply do not have the hard evidence to support the (undoubtedly correct) stereotype. (There is some hard evidence of a female superiority in various verbal aptitudes, but the evidence is more ambiguous and not sufficiently invulnerable to be used as the basis of the argument to be put forth here.)

With this in mind, let us consider the stereotype according to which rigorous, logical thinking represents 'thinking like a man'.[2]

I shall suggest that there can be no doubt about the basic correctness of the stereotype as *observation* and then will suggest that there is considerable logical evidence, and some suggestive physiological evidence, indicating that the sexual difference that is observed is rooted in sexual physiological differentiation.

Evidence for the Correctness of the Stereotype

Bearing all this in mind, let us consider the chess champion, rather than the politicians and businessmen we have considered so far. I am assuming

---

2. The 'logic' referred to in this chapter has nothing whatsoever to do with 'unemotionality'. It may possibly be true that our assumption that women are more emotionally demonstrative than men is reversed in some other societies. I might point out, however, that, while this does indicate that emotional demonstrativeness depends on socialization, it in no way refutes the hypothesis that males and females have different hierarchies of emotional responses and that these are universal and rooted in physiological differentiation. All that the anthropological literature justifies our positing in the way of emotional variation is that the degree to which males will demonstrate male emotions and the degree to which females will demonstrate female emotions depends on social factors.

throughout this chapter that the only necessary condition for chess genius is an extraordinary aptitude for dealing with high-level abstraction.

The term 'necessary condition' refers to the relationship between a. the aptitude for abstraction and b. the ability to do high-level work in mathematics, composing, etc. Clearly it is impossible for one who lacks a. to do b. The term is also appropriate to describe the relationship between male physiology and genius in mathematics, chess, musical composition, and so forth; since there has never been a female of high genius in these areas, we can speak of the 'necessary' role of male physiology until we do find a female of genius. However, when we speak of the relationship between male physiology and an ability to do high-level, but not genius-level, work in mathematics, and so on, it is necessary to speak of male physiology as being a powerful facilitator rather than a 'necessary condition' (or 'condition', which is the same thing in this context); this is because there are some, very few, women who possess the abstraction aptitude necessary for high-level, but not genius-level work in these areas. We would, likewise, use the term 'facilitator' if we were speaking of the relationship of male physiology to the ability to lift 300 pounds. It should be clear that 'genius' in these chapters refers to a level of aptitude demonstrated by only twenty or thirty people in the history of each of the intellectual, scientific, and artistic areas discussed.

I realize that the reader might invoke other necessary conditions (aggression, physical endurance, mental endurance, and the ability to control emotions). I acknowledge this but suggest that the necessary condition of an aptitude for abstraction that is found in some (very few) men and no women precludes a woman from being a chess genius. This aptitude is as essential to a chess champion as strength is to a boxing champion. However, if the reader is bothered by the existence of other necessary conditions for chess genius—if, for example, he believes that aggression, but *not* abstraction aptitude explains male superiority—he may substitute genius in mathematics, philosophy, legal theory, or composing music wherever I use chess genius, and the logic of this chapter is unaffected. But if he also argues that male dominance behavior does not have a physiological basis, he must be able to explain why there are very few women aggressive enough to attain parity with the best male chess players and why we socialize women away from chess. He cannot explain such socialization as being analogous to the socialization of women away from boxing (as I do) because this would admit that the socialization conforms to a physiological male advantage. Furthermore, while each of the areas of genius listed above has conditions for genius that are unique to it, the only obvious condition that all of the areas have in common is an aptitude for dealing with high-level abstractions.

In earlier editions of this book, I stated, correctly, that there had never been a female chess grandmaster. There are now several, and in 1992 Judith Polgar became the youngest person ever to achieve the grandmaster title. Polgar is now seriously spoken of as a possible future contender for World Chess Champion. An accurate account of the achievements of the three remarkable Polgar sisters, to an accompaniment of shrill environmentalist rhetoric, is given by Cathy Forbes.[5] The Polgars' feats have been given enormous publicity because they are women, and the media treatment of the Polgars well illustrates the fact that there exists in our culture a powerful hunger to believe that gender differences in cognitive aptitudes are exclusively cultural.

So far, the Polgars' performance gives us no grounds to abandon the theory that men are innately superior chessplayers. The point I made in earlier editions still stands: women produce, not only far fewer leading chessplayers than men do, but *far fewer in proportion to the number of active female chessplayers*. Furthermore, despite her truly magnificent playing record, Judith Polgar has yet to demonstrate that she is capable of 'genius', defined as membership of the 20 or 30 greatest of all time. Since there is evidence that girls peak earlier than boys in conceptual skills, it is even possible (though it would be disappointing) that a few years hence, Judith Polgar will no longer be seriously viewed as world championship material. She is so viewed now because it's assumed that she will continue to improve at the rate typical of male chessplayers of her age.

Forbes often overstates what can be inferred from the Polgar phenomenon, for example: "Females can play chess as well as any man." Strictly speaking, this is absurd: nearly all *males* are unable to "play chess as well as any man." But even if it be taken to mean that Judith Polgar can at this point in time play chess consistently as well as any currently active male player, it is false. As of January 1993, Judith Polgar, the highest-rated woman player *of all time*, tied for 53rd in the world ranking of *currently active* players. (Chess ratings are objective magnitudes derived by averaging recent results.)

Everyone agrees that the Polgar sisters' remarkable chess performance is in part due to the training methods of their dedicated father, who actually begat them with the intention of turning them into chess 'geniuses' by intensive 'hot-housing', and who pursued this goal relentlessly. To date, we do not know

---

5. Cathy Forbes, *The Polgar Sisters: Training or Genius?* (New York: Henry Holt, 1992).

what the results of similar hot-house training methods would be upon boys. And there is the possibility that hot-housing is able to create child prodigies who for the most part will not continue to improve much in their late teens and early twenties.

Forbes often draws attention to motivational hazards for female chessplayers, such as their possible reluctance to beat their boyfriends or husbands at chess, and it's quite clear that Forbes takes for granted the false premiss that *motivation* (as opposed to capability) is very likely to be exclusively environmentally determined. It should by now be clear to the reader of this book that if, in the future, substantial evidence were to accumulate that women's poorer performance at chess were primarily due to different motivation rather than different capacity for chess thinking, this would not imply that the poorer performance were any less physiological and inborn.

Environmentalists contend that the absence of women from the highest levels of chess attainment merely reflects the fact that girls are socialized away from chess while boys are encouraged to excel in this area. As is so often the case with such 'explanations' this is merely begging the question, and forces us to ask *why* girls are socialized away from chess; it is equivalent to saying that boxing champions are all male *because* girls are socialized away from boxing.

A better environmental argument would see male chess (or mathematical, or similar) superiority as resulting from the fact that women are socialized away from competing with men in many areas where dominance behavior is a necessary condition for attainment (they are so socialized for good reason, as we have seen) and that women carry the noncompetitive attitude into the nonaggressive area of chess (or mathematics, or similar areas) where dominance behavior is unnecessary for attainment. It is conceivable that this generalization of avoidance of competition explains male chess (or mathematical, or similar) dominance, and it is true that it is less certain that men have a physiological advantage that makes them more likely to be better chess players or scientists or composers than that they have one which will lead them to bureaucratic positions of power in the worlds of chess, science, and music. However, as we shall see, there is considerable evidence for the view that men may have a physiological superiority in these areas. It is quite likely that the serial unfolding of the male genetic programme affects the male CNS in such a way that the male really does develop potentials a woman does not (just as a woman develops potentials a male does not). If chess were the only area in which we could examine differences in behavior, we would have no logically compelling reason to favor the physiological explanation over the 'non-competitive' explanation or vice versa.

However, we can test these lines of reasoning when we examine possible explanations why Eleanor Maccoby and Roberta Oetzel found, in a survey of 20 studies of correlations between sex and mathematical reasoning aptitude, that when children are tested (13 studies) there are no consistent differences between boys and girls, but when adult men and women are tested (six studies—one of the 20 studies was of mentally retarded people and is not relevant here) men always did far better than women. These studies were of tests given to thousands of people, and there can be no doubt that they expose real sex differences in aptitude. One might argue that the differences flow from socialization rather than differences in physiology, but one cannot argue that they do not exist.[4] The between-sex differences here are as great as the between-sex differences in height and far greater than any other sexual differences in cognitive aptitudes.

The feminist will say that by the time they are at college girls have been socialized to see mathematics as unfeminine. To assume that this is true still does not explain why the great mathematicians have all been men. Why has the socialization proceeded in this way? Why is mathematics unfeminine instead of feminine? There does not appear to be anything in the nature of mathematics that would automatically lead it to be considered masculine. Why then do we not tell little boys that mathematics is 'girls' stuff'? The answer cannot be merely that women have internalized the noncompetitive mandate that applies only to areas in which dominance behavior leads to attainment. For women equal or surpass men on all cognitive tests not related to mathematical reasoning or associated aptitudes. If the fact that in America sixth-grade girls are the equals of sixth-grade boys in arithmetic, but twelfth-grade girls have an inferior mathematical aptitude to twelfth-grade boys is explained as a manifestation of the older girls' having internalized a norm against females competing with males, why do the twelfth-grade girls equal males in all areas for which the narrow aptitudes relevant to logical abstraction are not necessary?

---

4. That such differences in aptitude exist is demonstrated beyond question in Eleanor E. Maccoby, *The Development of Sex Differences* (Stanford: Stanford University Press, 1966). Of particular interest here is Dr Oetzel's summary of the results of hundreds of testing studies of sexual differences; H.A. Witkin, *et. al.*, *Psychological Differentiation* (New York: Wiley and Sons, 1962); David Wechsler, *The Measurement and Appraisal of Adult Intelligence* (Baltimore: Williams and Wilkins, 1958); and Bernard Berelson and Gary A. Steiner, *Human Behavior: An Inventory of Scientific Findings* (New York: Harcourt, Brace and World, 1964).

One might invoke the fact that men are more likely to have taken logic or mathematics courses, but this is irrelevant for three reasons. Firstly, these tests measure aptitude, and perception on an abstract level, not knowledge or skill. Secondly, male superiority seems to be maintained even when mathematical backgrounds are equalized; this is surprising since, if the pressures dissuading women from entering mathematics were really all that great, one would expect that only the very best women would take mathematics (i.e., the elective mathematics course would have women from only the top ten percent of women, but men from the top 30 percent of men), and that this would decrease or eliminate the male superiority when mathematics students only are tested (even though the male superiority is real and will manifest itself whenever men and women from the same percentiles of their respective sexes are tested). The fact that women in mathematics courses seem to do as badly relative to men as women in the general population indicates either that the social pressures dissuading women from going into mathematics are not all that great or that the sex differences at the top of the statistical curve are even greater than at the middle. Most importantly, to argue that society encourages men to study mathematics and dissuades women from doing so, begs the question, for the basic question remains: why does society not encourage women and discourage men if not because men long ago demonstrated their superiority here, and the population has long since observed this and noted it in a stereotype. (Similarly: on the quantitative aptitude section of the Graduate Record Examination, a score that places one in the 90th percentile among women places one only in the 68th percentile among men.)

I define the 'aptitude for logic and abstraction' discussed here *operationally* as the aptitude that is measured by the tests we have discussed. I do so because, in the article referred to in the introductory note to this chapter, Dr Maccoby bases most of her argument on a statement that is rendered incomprehensible by her own research: "there are tests of logical reasoning and abstract thinking and the sexes do not differ on them." Clearly, the tests referred to by Dr Maccoby, whichever they are, cannot measure the aptitude measured by the tests we have discussed, which *do* always find a sexual difference in aptitude. Moreover, whatever Dr Maccoby's tests are measuring, they are not measuring an aptitude necessary for attainment in mathematics, chess, or composing; for clearly there is a sexual difference in the aptitude necessary for mathematics, chess, and musical composition (whatever its causes). If Dr Maccoby is merely objecting to my terming the aptitude measured by the tests to which I refer 'logic'. I am perfectly willing to call this operationally-defined aptitude anything she likes. It is the empirical reality of the measurable sexual differentiation in the aptitude and the manifestations of this differentiation that are of scientific interest.

To summarize the argument presented thus far, there are three empirical facts demanding explanation: 1. There have been no women of genius, and very few of considerable talent, in chess, mathematics, composing, and other pursuits for which a high-level abstracting aptitude is a necessary condition (while there have been many women of genius in literature and the performing arts); 2. The tests we have discussed find a great difference in male and female aptitudes for this sort of abstraction; 3. A greater male abstracting ability has been observed so often by the general population that it has become the stereotype that 'men are more logical than women' and that a certain type of rigorous, abstract thinking represents 'thinking like a man'. I suggest that the tests and the stereotype measure and reflect male superiority in an aptitude that is a necessary condition for genius in mathematics and related areas, and a great advantage for even the lesser ability that is necessary for the usual professional work in these areas. I would stress, as always, that we are speaking in statistical terms, but remind the reader that these are sufficient to explain why all those most gifted with this aptitude are men (as all the tallest people are men) and why most of those in the upper quarter in terms of this aptitude, are men (as are most of those in the upper quarter in terms of height). Furthermore, while I attach to the hypothesis a far lower probability than I would to the likelihood that male dominance behavior has physiological roots, I suggest that there is strong logical evidence, and some suggestive physiological evidence, that male superiority in this aptitude is rooted in physiology.

Dr Maccoby makes the intriguing suggestion that the individuals who score the highest in the tests I discuss, while males, are not the most masculine of males. In the terms I have used, this means nothing, because I have not distinguished more masculine from less masculine men; these terms have no meaning in my discussion unless 'more masculine' is taken merely to mean 'higher scoring' (on the tests *I* discuss. I assume that what Dr Maccoby has in mind is some social psychological test of 'masculinity' and that what she is saying is that those men who score highest on the tests I discuss are not necessarily those who score highest on tests of 'masculinity'. I have already discussed at length the reasons for my considering social-psychological tests of this kind of dubious value in 'The Fallacy of the Irrelevant Experiment' in

Chapter 6 above), but let us assume, for argument's sake, that Dr Maccoby is correct in saying that the males who score highest in tests to which I refer are not those who score highest in tests of 'masculinity'. All that I am arguing is that physiological maleness is a necessary condition (or, to be more cautious, a great advantage) for a high-level aptitude for abstraction. It is quite possible that there are *additional* necessary factors that, for some reason, cannot be met by the 'most masculine' of men. We might remember the analogy of boxing: male physical strength is a necessary condition for boxing superiority, but the most masculine males (in terms of physical strength—weight lifters) cannot become the best boxers because there are other necessary conditions (speed, agility) that extreme strength precludes. Thus, just as the best boxers will be males, but not the most masculine males in terms of physical strength, so, perhaps, will those who score highest in the tests I discuss be males, but not the 'most masculine of males' in terms of either hormones or any other correlative criterion. That there is no necessary condition for test superiority or mathematical genius that males lack is clear from the fact that the individuals who do best on the tests, and the individuals who manifest the genius, are men; this is the empirical reality we are attempting to explain.

The direct physiological evidence is too extensive to be discussed here[5] and in any case my interest is primarily in the logical aspects of the causes of cognitive differentiation. This would, I think, suggest quite strongly, though not conclusively, that it has its roots in physiological differentiation even if we had no direct physiological evidence at all. We do, however, have at least the beginnings of such evidence. Dr Money writes:

> It is, of course, still too early to make any sweeping generalizations from [the] findings. But Katharina Dalton's work,[6] taken together with our own, strongly suggests that androgens, synthetic progestenic hormones, and progesterone [which has an androgenic chemical structure], given prenatally, do produce an increase in intelligence and eventual academic performance. They do so on both males and females but only when the fetuses are subjected to the hormones in excess at a critical time of their development in the uterus.[7]

---

5. Evidence is rapidly accumulating for innate cognitive differences between the sexes. For a readable and accurate survey of recent findings, see Ann Moir and David Jessel, *Brain Sex: The Real Difference between Men and Women* (New York: Dell, 1992).

6. Katharina Dalton, 'Antenatal Progesterone and Intelligence', *British Journal of Psychiatry*, (114, 1968), 1377–82.

7. John Money, 'Prenatal Hormones and Intelligence: A Possible Relationship', *Impact of Science on Society*, XXI, 289

I repeat that we are not speaking here about intelligence in all its different forms—neither sex is 'more intelligent' than the other—but only of one aspect of intelligence.[8]

Environmentalist Objections and the Validity of Stereotypes

Two objections are likely to be raised by environmentalists. The first asks why, if physiological differentiation underlies male superiority in the tests we have discussed, boys do not do better than girls (why does male superiority not assert itself before puberty?). After pointing out that the purely social explanation does not explain this either (why does socialization take so long to work?), I would suggest that there are two answers that are compatible with the physiological explanation. The less interesting is that there is a male superiority even before puberty, but the aptitude for abstraction is not sufficiently developed to manifest itself in the tests and is not called upon in the arithmetic tests that are given to prepubertal children. The more probable explanation is that prepubertal males are not superior to prepubertal females and that pubertal masculinization is responsible for pubertal and adult male superiority. This is, after all, the case with male 'superiority' in growing facial hair and in height, so there would be nothing surprising about this being the case with a cognitive aptitude as well.

The environmentalist is also likely to object that the line of reasoning I invoke could be used to justify the most damaging stereotypes. This is correct only if 'justify' means nothing more than that the stereotype observes an existing reality. The reasoning I have employed never justifies the *assumption* that the behavior that is described in the stereotype is rooted in physiology. The existence of the stereotype demonstrates only that there is something to explain; it does not explain it, nor does it tell us whether physiology is involved.

No stereotype is 'arbitrary' or incorrect as observation; every stereotype is 'real' in that it observes a behavior or propensity that is, in reality, more

---

8. In her *Science* article Dr Maccoby writes, rather inexplicably, that "sex hormones may be implicated in intellectual development, but . . . there is no reason to believe that male hormones are more associated with high levels of intellectual abilities than female hormones are . . ." If we are referring to the one, and only, intellectual ability discussed in this book, then there certainly is reason to believe that male hormones *are* associated with high intellectual aptitude to a greater extent than are female hormones. (The question is whether the male hormones play a causal role.) If hormones play a causal role in the development of the aptitude, it is certainly male hormones that do so, since it is males who manifest a high aptitude. It does not make much sense to posit the importance of the female hormone (or, less grossly, female physiological development) when the empirical reality that is to be examined is a *male* superiority.

associated with the stereotyped group than with other groups (whatever its causes). There are many ways in which a stereotype can lead to unfairness. It is unfair when applied to a member of the stereotyped group who does not exhibit the stereotyped characteristics. In some cases this can involve unfairness to the majority of the members of the group; the stereotype associating crime with American blacks is correct in that the crime rate for American blacks is higher than for non-blacks, but it is unfair when applied to the vast majority of blacks, who never commit a crime. A stereotype is often unfair in its evaluation of the observed behavior; one man's 'business acumen' is a stereotype's 'cunning'. A stereotype is most unfair when it confuses observation with explanation and becomes self-extending, as when it explains the greater black criminality in terms of bogus physiological causes, and is then used to justify the environmental discriminations that are its real cause. This circular process is accelerated by the awful truth that people will tend to believe what their society says about them, whether correct or not.

Environmentalists will point out, correctly, that male sterotypes of women serve psychological functions (as do all sterotypes). Once one has internalized a value one will feel threatened when its basis is challenged, but this anxiety has no bearing on the correctness or incorrectness of the observations that underlie it or on the relevance to them of physiology.[9]

How does the environmentalist explain the fact that women equal or surpass men in all test areas not related to dominance and abstract reasoning? Why does 'avoidance of competition' not assert itself here? Why is rigorous thinking, but not perceptive thinking, referred to as 'thinking like a man'? Why is the stereotype 'women are illogical' and not 'women are inarticulate' or

---

9. A man is far more emotionally threatened by the thought of losing a physical fight to a woman than he is of losing to another man. He is more threatened precisely because the expectation is that a man will never lose a fight to a woman, and that even engaging a woman in a physical fight is unfair. The fact that he feels threatened hardly demonstrates that the assumption on which the expectation rests—that men are physically stronger than women—is incorrect or unrelated to physiologically generated differences. Likewise, the sergeant who derives his meaning from the soldiering to which he has devoted his life, who has spent years learning the tasks and expectations that define this role, and sees it as a masculine one that women could not fill as well as men and that no society could socialize women to fill as well as men, will feel threatened to the quick by the assertion that male aggression is not innately greater than female aggression, and that a society could develop in which women were socialized to be more aggressive than men; his feeling of insecurity may indicate something about his sense of certainty, but it casts no doubt on the correctness of his assumption that males are more aggressive and that no society could socialize its women to be as aggressive as its men.

'women are unperceptive'? Is it not an unbelievably specialized form of oppression that generates an inferiority in one narrow area of cognition and in no other?

Our conviction that there is a physiological reason for male superiority in the aptitudes necessary for mathematical reasoning cannot be as great as the certainty that there is a physiological basis for male success in *attaining* positions for which dominance behavior leads to attainment. For when we discuss mental properties we are dealing in part with hypothetical physiological elements (as opposed to the specifiable hormonal elements relevant to dominance) and in part with a limited amount of cross-cultural data (as opposed to the demonstrable universality of patriarchy). Nonetheless, the evidence of logic and observation of sex differences in aptitudes in our own society does, as we have seen, indicate a physiologically-rooted male superiority in this area.

The implication here is not that socialization is irrelevant to the development of sex differences in cognitive aptitudes or that there have not been serious attempts to describe these differences as a function totally of socialization and not of physiological differentiation.[10] It is that there are strong, though not conclusive, indications that such socialization reflects sexual physiological differences in cognitive aptitudes.

One might construct a model that admits the relevance of CNS factors but sees these as a result of environmental factors. It has been suggested, for example, that the experience of judging the trajectory of a football is an environmental demand that engenders in boys a CNS development which could be developed in girls if they were exposed to it. Given the absence of cross-cultural evidence here (we do not know the cognitive aptitudes of males and females in other societies as we know their authority and status situations), this explanation is enticing, but not very convincing. We know too much about the relevance of fetal hormonalization to CNS development for a totally environmental explanation to be acceptable. No one would deny the possibility that the boy's activities may facilitate and increase 'male' cognitive aptitudes just as they increase his muscularity, but this point is relevant to the adult factors we are discussing only if there is not a CNS reality that accounts for these being a *boy's* activities.

---

10. See, for example, Walter Mischel, 'A Social-Learning View of Sex Differences in Behavior', in Maccoby, *The Development of Sex Differences*, 56–81.

There have been a few sociological studies which have concluded that sex differences in the aptitude we discuss result from purely social factors. In every case these commit the fallacy we have discussed at length in the section entitled 'The Fallacy of the Irrelevant Experiment' or the fallacy of merely showing that boys are socialized towards, and girls away from, mathematics without asking why or considering the possibility that socialization reflects a male mathematical superiority that is rooted in physiology.

None of this implies that changes in socialization and education could not tend to reduce male superiority in mathematical reasoning; even if this superiority results directly from CNS circuitry the male advantage could, theoretically, be eliminated if girls were massively socialized towards improvement and boys were socialized away from it (just as the adult male's innately superior physical strength could be eliminated, in theory, if all women spent several hours a day in intensive physical training and all men remained sedentary). For our purposes this theoretical possibility is irrelevant if cognitive sex differences result directly from differing CNS circuitries or even from differing socialization caused by different dominance tendencies. For differences that flow from physiological differentiation are observed by a population and this sets limits on expectations and socialization.

Social Implications of Sexual Cognitive Differences

None of what has been said so far, even if entirely correct, justifies discrimination. It would be as absurd and unjustified to argue that a woman who has a high mathematical aptitude has in fact a low mathematical aptitude just because she is a woman, as it would be to argue that the six-foot woman is really only five feet tall because most women are shorter than most men. As with dominance tendency, everything I say here refers to statistical realities, and it is always wrong to judge the individual by the statistical characteristics of his group. Laws that limit such discrimination are, it seems to me, good laws. But it would be unrealistic to believe that cognitive differences of the type I have discussed are relevant only at the highest levels, and it would be utopian to believe that laws, which may go far towards preventing occupational discrimination, will have much effect on the stereotypes of men and women.

There are a number of reasons for this, the most obvious of which is that, however misused they may be, the stereotypes are, in the sense we have discussed, correct. Although a woman of mathematical ability meets discouragement where a male of no greater ability meets encouragement, it is true that she is far more of an exception for her sex than the male is for his. The woman is not 'unfeminine' in any derogatory sense, but only in the statistical sense that she manifests an aptitude that is more usually found in a man. Even if the male superiority were limited to the upper levels (and there were no difference in logical aptitude as far as most men and women were concerned) we would still expect there to be a stereotype. For the small group at the top (the scientists, mathematicians, and philosophers who most strongly manifest this aptitude) is infinitely the most important for the development of the stereotype. But the male superiority exists not merely at the top, but at least, for the upper halves of each sex.[11]

A final point relevant to genius should be made here. Whatever the variable under consideration, whether it be a tendency that is desirable or undesirable or one on which the male and female averages are the same or different, it is nearly always the case that variation is greater for the males; the highest and lowest tend to be males. This sex difference in degree of variation may be in part hereditary. This will be folded into almost any complex experience, so that males tend to be at the very top (as well as at the very bottom). There is no reason to assume that this general truth is not applicable to the question of genius.

---

11. It is not clear whether the male superiority is maintained throughout the entire range. Some studies indicate that males in the upper half of the group of males are superior to females in the upper half of the group of females, while for the lower halves this is reversed. Even if this is correct (some studies find the male advantage throughout the range) it is of little importance to the stereotype. The men and women in the upper halves of their respective sexes far more often exhibit the aptitude we discuss and are in the occupations that demand it. It is observation of these individuals that determines the stereotype. Abstract thought plays little part in the lives of men and women whose logical aptitudes are low.

High Genius in the Arts and Sciences

As is the case with sexual cognitive differences, it is not possible to explain the preponderance of male genius in the arts and sciences with the compelling logic with which one can explain patriarchy, male dominance, and male attainment of high-status roles. It is admittedly difficult even to define genius. Genius is not intelligence, though it is certainly correlated with it and a high intelligence is certainly a necessary condition for genius in mathematics and the hard sciences. ('Intelligence' here is operationally defined as the scores made on an IQ test, scores that correlate highly with people's intuitive assessments of each other's 'intelligence'.) It is probably impossible for someone with an IQ of 70 to possess genius of any kind, but we know of too many people with IQs of 180 who have manifested no semblance of genius, and too many undeniable geniuses whose IQs have not been extraordinarily high, to equate genius with intelligence. It is doubly difficult to identify the physiological factors associated with genius.

Nonetheless, it is difficult to ignore the fact that all the Aristotles, the Leonardos, the Bachs, the Einsteins, and the Capablancas (and their counterparts in other cultures) have been men despite the fact that half of the members of each of their societies were women.[1] In the performing arts one might well argue that the greatest women have been equal to the greatest men. *Perhaps* in

---

1. No doubt the reader thinks of Marie Curie. While I understand that doing so will seem like quibbling to many, I suggest that: 1. even if Curie were the greatest of all theoretical scientists, this would not lead us to conclude that male physiology is not important to the abstracting aptitude we discuss (though it would force us to speak of a statistical physiological 'facilitator' rather than a 'necessary condition'). The discovery of a nine-foot tall woman would not lead us to deny the role of physiology in an explanation of why, statistically speaking, males are taller than females. 2. Madame Curie, one of the greatest of experimental scientists, was not a theoretical scientist of the first rank. While she, like any great experimentalist, had to have a fine theoretical mind, she would certainly not rank with the great theoretical scientists.

literature one might claim that Baroness Murasaki, Jane Austen, George Eliot, and the Brontës were the equals of Homer, Dante, Shakespeare, and Dostoevsky. But there is not a single woman whose genius has approached that of any number of men in philosophy, mathematics, composing, or theorizing of any kind. Even in these areas—except perhaps for composing—there have been a few women at the level below that of the greatest genius, but this is irrelevant unless one is prepared to argue that not only is Suzanne Langer the equal of a Kant or an Aristotle, but that in being the equal of these men she is not merely an exception, but an exception which demolishes the entire statistical rule. For even if genius in these areas resulted *solely* from physiological factors, we would expect that, as is the case with height, there would be a number of women who manifested greater ability than all but a very few men, but none who manifested the ability of the very greatest men.[2]

One might argue that the arts which are considered feminine in other cultures are equal to, or not comparable to, those under discussion but this would make no difference unless it could be demonstrated that the arts and sciences discussed here are associated with women in some other culture; this cannot be done. One can argue that the pottery designs created by women in a society in which this art is associated with them are as creative as Einstein's theory, but this casts no doubt on the relevance of CNS development to scientific genius. I am not saying that masculine creative genius is superior to feminine creative genius—at no point in this book do I say or imply that any masculine quality is superior to any feminine quality—only that it is different. It is more sensible for feminists to argue, as many now do, that our society overrates manifestations of male genius and underrates manifestations of female genius than to argue that there are not differences in the aptitudes of the sexes.

However, I am not discussing here different male and female arts, or even implying that male art is different from female art. It certainly seems that great novels written by women are different from those written by men in the worlds

---

2. I have looked for some hard evidence that mathematicians, composers, philosophers, chess champions, and so forth share an extraordinary aptitude for high-level abstractions that is not possessed by great novelists and performing artists. There seems to be no hard evidence because researchers in the area feel, no doubt correctly, that the hypothesis is so self-evidently true that it would be a waste of time testing it. Thus, while I have no doubt that the assumption is correct, it must be admitted that I *assume* that mathematicians, etc. would score far higher in the tests we discuss than would novelists of equivalent reputation. It is not irrelevant here that the biographies of chess champions, composers, and mathematicians often describe their subjects as manifesting a great ability in each other's fields of activity.

they present and the way they present them; this would make sense, and I would suggest that the commonly-heard claim that one cannot tell a paragraph written by a woman from one written by a man is true only for the sort of non-experiential writing found in academic journals. But for the sake of this discussion, we may assume that a great novel written by a female is identical to one written by a male; certainly a mathematical theorem does not reflect the sex of its creator. We are only discussing the relative numbers of male and female geniuses, and not the differences between them.

Note that the further one moves from those areas in which an aptitude for dealing with pure abstractions is obviously necessary to those in which it is not a necessary condition for genius, the more women there are who approach the level of great genius. Moreover, these differences are maintained as one descends from the level of genius; the history of literature is replete with the names of first-class women writers, but it is doubtful that there has ever been a woman composer who could be considered much above average. It seems likely that the aptitude for dealing with logical abstractions is a condition for genius in composing, philosophy, theorizing, and mathematics. We have seen that male superiority in this aptitude is undeniable, and there is considerable reason to believe that this results from male physiology.

If an exceedingly high-level ability to deal with abstractions is a condition for genius in mathematics, philosophy, and chess, but not for genius in literature or the performing arts, we would expect women to attain the level of genius in literature or the performing arts, but not in mathematics, philosophy, and chess. This is precisely the case. If this reasoning is correct, then it follows that society will always associate with men genius in those areas for which the high-level abstractive aptitude is a condition, and that informal socialization will always conform to this. As with the woman whose dominance tendency equals that of the average man, the rare woman who does possess these abilities will meet resistance where a man of equal abilities will meet encouragement; but, as with the dominant woman, this is the price one unfortunately pays for being an exception. If male physiology does contribute to the male ability to compose, then women composers will always be such exceptions. (I do not know where painting falls on the continuum, whether closer to logic—mathematics—composing—science—philosophy or literature—the performing arts. It is interesting, however, that Sir Kenneth Clark noted that the more "mathematical" or "architectural"—his words—a form or style of painting, the greater the disparity between the numbers of men and women excelling in it.)

I do not deny that one could conceivably develop some explanation of male success in these areas without invoking any physiological factor; perhaps some economic and social factors direct women towards those areas that demand less ability at theorizing. It is true that the ethnographic materials that were so helpful in documenting universal sex differences in dominance and authority are not much help here; we are dealing primarily with science and art in the Western world, China, Japan, and India. Nonetheless, this covers a fairly broad spectrum of different historical times with quite different value systems. Science and musical composition have often had fairly low status, yet even in such times the scientists and composers were men. There have been a great number of women poets and writers ever since Sappho; why have there not been an equal number of women composers and scientists? Furthermore, there would seem to be nothing in composing music (or in the sciences for that matter) that would automatically lead society to associate it with men. Dominance does not give men any head start here, nor is there any obvious connection between composing music and economic reward (which, one might argue, could have led men to forbid women to enter this area). If no male physiological element is relevant here, what has directed women towards those artistic areas in which an ability to deal with abstractions is less necessary? Why does society not associate composing with women if not because men have proved better composers (even when women were strongly encouraged to develop excellence in musical *performance);* why have men always been the better composers if not because they have a greater potential? Any environmental answer to these questions must relate specifically to the differences between composing (or science or philosophy) on the one hand, and literature or the performing arts on the other; for any *general* explanation that one might hypothesize (concerning woman's self-image or the time and energies consumed by the maternal role, for example) will not be able to explain why so many women have excelled in the literary area and in the performing arts. Moreover, an explanation which emphasizes the demands of the maternal role fails to explain the demonstrated superiority of young, single, adult males over young, single, adult females in abstract reasoning. Explanations which emphasize the necessity of training in some of these areas cannot deal with the fact that composing, chess, and mathematical aptitudes are precisely the three aptitudes that assert themselves earliest and with least training. To say that this is true, but that women have nonetheless been dissuaded from composing and have been urged by society to enter the performing arts is to beg the question.

Why have they been so dissuaded and so urged if not because their potential, relative to that of men, is far greater in the latter area?

A similar question might be asked of those who argue that the absence of women from areas for which an aptitude for dealing with abstractions is a condition for genius results from differential socialization which is not so much relevant to the particular creative area, as to the aptitudes which are necessary conditions for genius in these areas. In other words, if one argues that the point is not so much that women are socialized away from composing, but that their socialization does not encourage the aptitude for dealing with abstractions that is a condition for composing genius, one must explain why girls are so socialized if this does not conform to the reality of a physiological male superiority in the aptitude for dealing with abstractions. One will then face the contradictions we discussed in the last chapter. Note that we are speaking here of only one necessary condition for mathematical (and related) genius. There are other necessary conditions, for some of which males have no advantage at all. These are irrelevant to our present discussion because the absence of the first necessary condition precludes genius; that is what a necessary condition is.

Thus, none of what I have said so far concerns other qualities that are associated with males. It assumes, for example, that dominance behavior has nothing to do with the fact that the geniuses we have been discussing were male. However, many of those who have written about male genius, and women writers in particular, have considered a male quality that would seem to be akin to dominance behavior to be crucial. Usually this quality is described as 'aggression', and while the term is not, and cannot be, rigorously defined, in this context it is clearly meant to refer to an obsessive concentration and dedication to their work, the sort of lifelong burst of speed which enabled Balzac to spend 16 hours a day standing at his desk. It is perhaps crazy to write for 16 hours a day, but it is a craziness that seems to possess men more than women. Elizabeth Hardwick has pointed out than even the greatest women writers have not exhibited this.[3]

I do not think it inconceivable that the psychophysiological factors relevant to dominance tendencies play a role here. If they do, then the difference they make will be magnified through interaction with society. It may be, for example, that the greater male 'aggression', when stifled by the father (or

---

3. Elizabeth Hardwick, *A View of My Own* (New York: Farrar, Strauss, and Cudahy, 1962), 181.

maternal uncle in matrilineal societies), becomes the 'energy' that drives the male genius harder than the female genius even in those areas for which an aptitude for great abstraction is not a necessary condition. This would be one, but only one, possible explanation of why there are fewer female than male geniuses even in literature, and it would be compatible with the fact that there are some women of genius in literature (there are some women with the necessary 'aggression' for literary genius, but none with the abstracting aptitude necessary for mathematical genius). This must all be described in virtually metaphysical terms (I would not like to have to define 'energy' and 'aggression' here), and the reader will have to decide whether the idea presented in this paragraph is fertile or meaningless. None of this conflicts with other explanations of the preponderance of male geniuses, such as that which suggests that the female partakes in true creation (which may reduce the need for substitute—artistic—creation) while the male must look for a substitute. Nor does it deny that the various forms of discrimination against women increase the male-female discrepancy.

However, none of these additional explanations are necessary for a general explanation of the preponderance of males in mathematics and related fields (though they are necessary for an explanation of the preponderance of males in literature and the performing arts). *For the fact that only males (a very few males) possess the extraordinary aptitude for abstraction that is a necessary condition for genius in mathematics and related fields, and the fact that far more males than females possess the high aptitude for abstraction that is a necessary condition for near-genius in those fields, virtually precludes the possibility of female genius in these areas and guarantees a preponderance of males in the group at the near-genius level.* (Again, this is perfectly analogous to height, a quality whose etiology is *overwhelmingly* physiological; all people over eight feet tall, nearly all people over seven feet tall, and the vast majority of people over six feet tall are men.)

I suspect that those who explain male genius in environmental terms have never had the fortune to be exposed to a mind of genius for long. It is inconceivable that anyone who has could maintain the belief that genius is often held back by social factors. If genius is not given form by context it will make its own. It is this aggressive reordering of context that *is* genius. It is simply unimaginable that context, whether the intellectual matrix facing the genius or the social and economic factors touching his life, could dissuade him. One could describe the Newtonian world that Einstein destroyed or the unspeakable handicaps overcome by so many of the great minds; one could show that minorities whose inferiority was assumed by all around them have produced men of unquestionable genius. But it must be admitted that if one adheres to the metaphysical assertion that there is something inherent in every society's view of women that precludes the manifestation of an intellectual genius for which women have the biological potential, one cannot be disproved. Such an assertion is termed 'metaphysical' because it is not falsifiable. Whenever those who make such assertions specify a *concrete* social element that accounts for the dearth of female genius one can usually demonstrate that there have been any number of male geniuses who have overcome the posited obstacle. As long as one merely invokes 'society's view of women' as the element that precludes the manifestation of female genius, one's argument does not take the risk of identifying any imaginable observations which would falsify it.

Part IV

The Meaning of Male and Female

═ Chapter *XI* ═

Male and Female

Introductory Note

So far, this book has presented a scientific analysis. It has attempted to demonstrate and explain statistical empirical relationships between sexual physiological differentiation and sexual differentiation in modes of cognition, emotional tendencies, behaviors, and institutions. If this analysis is correct, if the male's greater dominance tendencies and tendency for 'logical' thought, and the female's greater nurturance tendencies and tendency for psychological insight are rooted in male and female physiologies, then the general stereotypes of masculinity and femininity would seem to be justified (as would the assumption that these differences are rooted in physiological differences).

I hope the reader understands that I have focussed on the masculine elements for two reasons: 1. It is these which are relevant to the universal institutions, the explanation of which is the primary purpose of this book, and would be sufficient to explain them even if women were nothing more than less-masculine men. 2. The hard evidence for a physiological basis for the female's greater nurturance tendencies and the female's greater psychological aptitudes is far less extensive than that for the physiological basis of the male tendencies. While I do not doubt that such evidence will be forthcoming soon, I have—in anticipation of a less than totally friendly response to an analysis that places such emphasis on the physiological roots of behavior—refrained from using any but the most powerful evidence.

In any case, I think it appropriate to try to put all this in some sort of social and philosophical context. If the reader believes that the analysis presented so far is incorrect, then he will find this chapter pointless. If he believes that the analysis is correct, then he may find helpful this attempt to find a meaning in the realities I have attempted to demonstrate and explain, or he may find a very different meaning for himself. In any case, this chapter merely assumes the correctness of the analysis presented to this point and does not present further argument for the correctness of the analysis.

Understanding Male and Female

To understand why so many men and women now seem to find their traditional roles meaningless, perhaps one should not begin with the content of roles that were capable of providing meaning in the past, but with the failure of contemporary American society to inculcate in its members the feeling that its value system, its way of defining reality, is correct and meaningful. It is this ability, rather than the specific characteristics of the value system or its 'humaneness', that is the precondition for a society's survival and is relevant to the members' feelings of meaninglessness and isolation that are inevitable if they have no shared meaning. When a society loses its ability to inculcate values its members fall into the abyss. Traditions evaporate, as they must when the values on which they were founded seem meaningless, and they take all sense of continuity with them. Children no longer provide a sense of the future, for values are the link we have with our children, and if we have no values—values based on intelligence infused with experience, not ideological proclamations supported by utopian fantasy—then we sacrifice our future for their contempt. In the abyss some will have the strength to become 'the calm in the centre of the whirlwind', but many will lack the faith, the strength, the courage, the will, and the imagination to create their own meaning. Having received no values from their society and having themselves created nothing worthy of passing on to their children, they will rail against everything in sight save the image in the mirror.

Liberation is an experience of personal salvation that implies power over oneself. It is far more than the attainment of social and economic freedom. Those who have found a well of pure meaning have no need to drown everyone in it. The priest does not frantically ignore physiological evidence by arguing that the 'sex drive' is merely an arbitrary social value or that we could expect many people to choose celibacy; he acknowledges the power of this 'drive' while himself answering a more compelling call. Likewise, any woman who feels that her sense of meaning is satisfied in areas not usually considered feminine need not justify this to anyone. She can never hope to live in a society that does not attach feminine expectations to women, but if she has the courage she will overcome the attitudinal discrimination that she will undeniably face. Certainly such discrimination is less threatening to one's liberation than the obsessive hatred of an enemy who serves only to symbolize one's inner turmoil, the avoidance of the battles for one's own existence, or the inevitably futile attempt to substitute group strength for individual psychic weakness. I do not deny the value of the woman who devotes her life to a career rather than to children; there is no need for her to misrepresent physiology, anthropology, and psychology in order to rationalize an unnecessary defense.

Ultimately every examined life can be interpreted as a disaster; looking closely enough we can always discover psychological and social forces that could provide fuel for unlimited rage. For every intelligent and creative woman there are ten men who must stumble through life without the aid of intelligence or creativity. But no life can transcend its own disasters unless it celebrates its uniqueness and contributes that which only it can contribute. Life is perverted if one is constantly reacting, never initiating, but always allowing rage to define it.

Too often such a definition shapes the lives of radical environmentalists. Too often we fail to ask men and women to face the battles of their own existence; we merely inquire as to which form of societal oppression it is that is causing their desperation, and accept their exaggeration of external oppressions, oppressions that they use to camouflage the terrors that one must face alone because such terrors are inherent in existence. This is not only sad, but dangerous. When a moral urgency is superimposed on an emotional immaturity, as it is when an affluent, educated generation grows up without ever being forced to learn that life's choices offer rewards that are mutually exclusive, fanaticism is more probable than altruism. The alacrity with which environmentalists invent some 'facts' and reject or accept others on the basis of their emotional appeal is illusion in the guise of intellectual investigation. Invocation of this illusion as rationalization is self-indulgence parading as virtue. There is no doubt that our society demands some new answers quickly. But the readiness of many to translate nearly any new idea immediately into action does not demonstrate rational response or even pragmatic desperation, but betrays an emotional development so stunted that they are forced to navigate life on one engine; the intellect is twisted to serve the stabilizing function of inculcating meaning, a function that is usually performed in part by the emotions. Who but children who combine an intellectual egalitarianism (which views every individual's ideas as equally valid and accepts one idea over another on the basis of its ideological value and its perceived sincerity) with an emotional elitism that derides as delusory false consciousness the emotional satisfactions of all the world's men and women, could be so petulant as to attempt to justify their longing contempt for the eternal sources of joy with an analysis built of ignorance and held together by fallacy? Who but children whose lifelong nurturance on material things has cursed them with the inability to discover the small joys that define happiness, could have failed to learn that imperfection is inherent in any institution? To confuse this inevitable imperfection with the reasons for the institution's inevitability is unintelligent. To hope for the perfection of any institution or for its disappearance because imperfection is inevitable is utopian.

Happiness is determined—to a great extent, though certainly not completely—by the degree to which society grants high status to the roles one fills; when society sees what you do as being of importance, so, most of the time, do you. Thus, it seems to me quite likely that both men and women were happier in earlier times, when female roles were given high status and few women ever thought of entering the suprafamilial arena; but such times have long since passed and there is no case for legal discrimination in any areas not concerned with violence and potential violence. But here we are not talking about laws, but feelings, feelings which are rooted in our natures.

Both men and women—even the ones who rail against it—feel that the husband 'allows' and 'protects'. Here the difference between those who strive for equal pay for equal work and those who reject the validity of their own feelings and observations and accept the environmentalist analysis is seen in bold relief. For the former, the question of patriarchy and dominance is unimportant. For the latter, it is crucial; the environmentalist's aversion to the possibility of male dominance being inevitable stems from finding this possibility psychologically intolerable. Indeed, feminist literature emphasizes this area far more than it does real economic discrimination. Economic discrimination is abhorrent because it is artificial. When we speak of male dominance we are speaking of the feelings of both men and women that the man selected by the woman 'allows' and 'protects', feelings motivating the actions and determining the institutions of every society without exception. It is these masculine and feminine feelings, the emotional manifestations of our biologies and the emotional prerequisites of political power, that prescribe the limits of sexual roles and social possibility. As long as societies are composed of human beings these feelings will be inevitable. To judge them is not merely stupid, it is a contemptuous attack on our own natures.

The central role will forever belong to women; they set the rhythm of things. Women everywhere are aware that sublimation is an ignorance of the center; one of the most stunning regularities one notices when studying cross-cultural data closely is the extent to which women in all societies view male preoccupation with dominance and suprafamilial pursuits in the same way as the wife in Western society views her husband's obsession with professional football—with a loving condescension and an understanding that men embrace the surrogate and forget the source. Nature has bestowed on women the biological abilities and psychophysiological propensities that enable the species to sustain itself. Men must forever stand at the periphery, questing after the surrogate powers, creativity, and meaning that nature has not seen fit to make innate functions of *their* physiology. Each man knows that he can never again be the most important person in another's life for long, and that he must reassert superiority in enough areas often enough to justify nature's allowing him to stay. There is no alternative; this is simply the way it is. At the bottom of it all, man's job is to protect woman, and woman's is to protect her infant; in nature all else is luxury. There are some feminists who try to have it both ways; they deny the importance of the physiological basis of the behavior of the sexes, yet blame the world's woes on the male characteristics of its leaders. The latter hypothesis is correct, and we find that we are trapped in what could be the final irony: the physiological factors that underlie women's life-sustaining abilities— the qualities most vital to the survival of our species—preclude them from ever manifesting the psychological predisposition or the obsessive need of power, necessary for the attainment of significant amounts of political power.

It is not merely that the line separating the male's aggression from the child's demandingness is a thin one; the aggression is inseparable from its childish component. What is lacking in the male is an acceptance that radiates from all women save those few who are driven to deny their greatest source of strength. Perhaps this female wisdom comes from resignation to the reality of male dominance; more likely it is a harmonic of the woman's knowledge that ultimately she is the one who matters. As a result, while there are more brilliant men than brilliant women and more powerful men than powerful women, there are more good women than good men. Women are not dependent on male brilliance for their deepest sources of strength, but men are dependent on female strength. Few women have been ruined by men; female endurance survives. Many men, however, have been destroyed by women who did not understand or did not care to understand, male fragility.

It is well here to remember that what I term the male's 'dominance tendency' can be as well conceptualized as a 'drive' or a 'need'. This makes clear the vulnerability that is the other name of power. Every motivation is, by its nature, both an energy and a vulnerability. It is not that a motivation can be one or the other; they are the same thing.

In any case, the central fact is that men and women are different from each other, from the gene to the thought to the act, and that the emotions that underpin masculinity and femininity, that make reality as experienced by the male eternally different from that experienced by the female, flow from the biological natures of man and woman. This is the one fact that the radical environmentalist cannot admit. For to admit this would be to admit that the liberations of men and women must proceed along different and complementary lines, and that the women of every society have taken the paths they have not because they were forced by men but because they have followed their own imperatives. Neither I, nor, I gather, the vast majority of women, can imagine why any woman would *want* to deny the biological basis of the enormous powers inherent in women's role as directors of society's emotional resources; to do so demands that one accept the male belief that power has to do with action rather than feeling. But whatever the reasons, denial does not indicate that there was a choice. If we have learned nothing else from the wisdom of every culture, we should have learned by now that one cannot transcend one's fate until one has accepted it. Women who deny their natures, who accept men's second-hand definitions and covet a state of second-rate manhood, are forever condemned— to paraphrase Ingrid Bengis's wonderful phrase—to argue against their own juices. For all the injustices committed in attempts to enforce bogus biological laws, roles associated with gender have been primarily the result rather than the cause of sexual differences. Sex is the single most decisive determinant of personal identity; it is the first thing we notice about another person and the last thing we forget. Just as it is criminal for others to limit one's identity by invoking arbitrary limitations in the name of nature, so it is terribly self-destructive to refuse to accept one's own nature and the joys and powers it invests.

I have presented the theory advanced in this book in terms that in no way depend on my own feelings and attitudes. This is how a scientific theory should be presented. However, I must admit that as I developed the theory I was often forced to stand back, incredulous that there really are people who have journeyed so far from themselves that they can truly believe that their most basic impulses have nothing to do with their most basic natures. I remain astounded that there are people who can believe that their experiences with their children, in sexual encounters, and in psychological relationships are not given their direction by the hormones that run through them. The experience of men is that there are few women who can outfight them and few who can outargue them, but that when a woman uses feminine means she can command a loyalty that no amount of dominance behavior ever could. The experience of women is that the violence men often seek out is terrifying and overpowering, but that by using the feminine means that nature gave her, a woman can deal with the most powerful man as an equal. Are not these sexual differences manifested and described in the works of our greatest writers, the members of our species whom we have acknowledged to have the greatest insight into our natures? Is not the usual practice of ignoring the theoretical contradiction at the heart of each environmentalist work in order to concentrate on feminist insight, of treating feminist theorists as we would treat women in a coed football game, both insulting to serious women scholars and pointless; can we really expect a better vision from one who is facing away from nature?[1]

Is not an analysis that denies these differences an unspeakable insult to the women of all societies—societies that would not have survived had their women not asserted their female energies? A true feminist movement that genuinely believes in the uniqueness of women yearns to discover rather than deny the biological factors within women which make them unique.

It does not matter for purposes of the scientific analysis presented in this book whether one answers yes or no to these questions, but I do want to make it clear that, as I hope the reader realizes by now, I believe the evidence indicates that women follow their own psychophysiological imperatives and that they would not choose to compete for the goals that men devote their lives to attaining. Women have more important things to do. Men are aware of this and that is why in this and every other society they look to women for gentleness, kindness, and love, for refuge from a world of pain and force, for safety from their own excesses. In every society a basic male motivation is the feeling that the women and children must be protected. But a woman cannot have it both ways: if she wishes to sacrifice all this, what she will get in return is the right to meet men on male terms. She will lose.

---

1. Among the most gratifying experiences I had in writing this book was receiving the support of serious women scholars who had to hide the contempt they felt towards 'feminist' (extreme environmentalist) 'scholarship' lest they be portrayed as female 'Uncle Toms'. These women were well aware that the cowardly male academic tendency to publicly accept environmentalist analyses while privately despising them threatened to cast doubt on the value of even the most valuable work done by serious women scholars.

Alleged Exceptions to the Universality of Patriarchy and Male Dominance

In this Appendix I consider every society I have ever heard suggested as a possible example of a society that failed to exhibit patriarchy, male attainment, or male dominance. It is not without significance that in no case has the anthropologist who studied the group alleged it to be an exception. The claim is invariably made by someone, rarely an anthropologist, with an ideological interest in finding such an exceptional society. This is perfectly legitimate if the exception *is* an exception. However, whenever one returns to the source cited by the author one finds that the society described is in no way an exception. Unless otherwise noted, *the source I quote or refer to is the same as that invoked by the author claiming it to demonstrate an exception.* When I do not quote or refer to the source invoked by the author it is because it is unpublished, in which case I rely on the best available source. *Stephens* refers to William N. Stephens, *The Family In Cross-Cultural Perspective* (New York: Holt, Rinehart, and Winston, 1963).

Agta (and related Philippine Negrito groups)

The Hunting Agta (the only Agta relevant here) are a loosely-knit Philippine Negrito group numbering its members in the hundreds. The Agta live in separate groups of three to five nuclear families for ten months of the year, moving every seven to ten days. They live in groups of eight to ten nuclear families during the other two months.

Morice Vanoverberg, 'Negritos of The Northern Luzon' in *Anthropos* 20:

The father is recognized as the head of the family. (424)

John Garvan, *The Negritos of The Philippines,* ed. Hermann Hochegger, (Wiener Beitrage Zur Kulturgeschichte Und Linguistik, Band XIV, Horn: F. Berger, 1963):

> [The Husband] is regarded by the wife as her superior . . . (90)
> [I]n no case did I find other than an aged man acting as chief. (151)

Jean Treloggen Peterson, *An Ecological Perspective on The Economic and Social Behavior of Agta Hunter-Gatherers, Northeastern Luzon, Philippines* (PhD Dissertation, 1974):

> Peterson reports that leadership is "informal" and based on "special knowledge" and "experience". Yet virtually every example of leadership she gives is by a male. (See, for example, pages 16–18.)

Daisy Y. Novel-Morales and James Monan, *A Primer on The Negritos of The Philippines* (Manila: Business for Social Progress, 1979):

> In essence the political life of the Negrito is an uncomplicated system based largely on respect for age. In the family the father assumes the role of governor of family affairs while at the level of the band the elder men exert control over affairs which are usually of adjunctive nature. (123)

A chapter in a feminist anthology[1] has been invoked by one writer as demonstrating a lack of male dominance among the Agta. ('Woman The Hunter' by Agnes Estioko-Griffin and P. Bion Griffin, 121–151 of Frances Dahlberg, *Woman The Gatherer;* New Haven: Yale University Press, 1981).

Even a literal reading of this chapter fails to support the claim that the Agta lack male dominance, an assertion not made by the authors. The authors' primary concern is merely to show that Agta women are the equals of men at hunting. They do not even demonstrate this. They do not show that men and

---

1. The fact that this appeared in a feminist anthology would, of course, be irrelevant if it were a theoretical interpretation of the empirical evidence of others (as this book is). In such theoretical works the political or other subjective impulses of an author are relevant only to the extent that they result in illogic or misrepresentation, and these can be exposed by analysis and resort to the evidence invoked. But when the evidence itself is the claimed observation of the author, so that we are asked to take the word of the author, then possible bias rooted in wish can immunize itself against exposure. (Even if it were practical to launch a second anthropological project to check the claims of the first, the original ethnographer could claim that the realities observed had changed over time.) Fortunately, in the present case and in all other cases I know of, even the wish that there be a society lacking the institutions we discuss has not generated an ethnographic work that provides—even in a literal reading—evidence of a society lacking the institutions.

women hunt in equal numbers, only that those women who do hunt do so as well as those men who hunt. (In another work by one of the two authors it is explicitly stated that all men, but only some of the women, hunt. See P. Bion Griffin, 'Forager Land and Resource Use in The Humid Tropics: The Agta of Northeastern Luzon', in *Past and Present in Hunter-Gatherer Societies.*) Let us grant that the women who do hunt are as capable hunters as are the more numerous men who hunt; those women who are six feet tall are as tall as those men who are six feet tall; this does not demonstrate that women equal men in height or that the causes of height are not primarily physiological. More important, the issue of hunting is irrelevant to the theory of male dominance; it is relevant only for those who (incorrectly) see patriarchy, male attainment, and male dominance as rooted in economic factors. While such factors no doubt are relevant to variation in these institutions, they are not their primary cause; for the institutions exist whatever the economic system and whatever the method of food acquisition, its family system, or any other variable.

Far less do the authors demonstrate an absence of male dominance. To be fair, they claim only that Agta women "have considerable authority in decision making in the family and residential groups" (121), that "their freedom of choice in sex and marriage seems to support the hypothesis of an egalitarian society", and that "clearly only a beginning has been made in understanding women's position in Agta society" (140). Since women in the United States, and in any number of other modern and primitive societies for which no one doubts the existence of the institutions we discuss, "have considerable authority in decision making in the family and residential groups" and "freedom of choice in sex and marriage", these realities would hardly support a claim that this one society lacks the institutions found in all others (even if the authors had made that claim).

The authors acknowledge that their study "is based on inadequately quantified data, on questions incompletely answered and an insufficient length of participant observation in the field" (140). This does not represent undue modesty: the authors provide no evidence other than that mentioned to support a claim that the Agta lack male dominance and their observation of the relevant Agta was limited to a few "brief visits" (147) which seem to have totalled less than two weeks.

The authors acknowledge that the relevant Agta "are not dissimilar to other present and past Philippine Negritos" (122). As the works quoted above— works invoked by Estioko-Griffin and Griffin—demonstrate, no argument can be made that the Philippine Negritos fail to exhibit the institutions we discuss.

Alorese

Cora Du Bois, *The People of Alor: A Social-Psychological Study of an East Indian Island* (Minneapolis: University of Minnesota Press, 1944):

> [M]arriage means for women far greater economic responsibility in a social system that does not grant them status recognition equal to that of men while at the same time it places on them greater and more monotonous burdens of labor. (114)

Balonda

A few readers of the first edition of this book remembered reading of David Livingstone's description of his encounter with a Balonda female chief and wondered whether the Balonda might represent an exception to male dominance or even to patriarchy. They did not give sources. Reference to the available sources indicates that the chief whom Livingstone met was the sister of the (male) "greatest Balonda chief". Since this is the only mention of a female chief, I think it fair to assume that much of the status and power of the female chief (which so impressed Livingstone) was owing to her relationship to the greatest chief, and not to a general female equality of authority. See David Livingstone, *Missionary Travels and Researches in South Africa* (London: John Murray, 1857).

Bamenda

Phyllis M. Kaberry, *Women of the Grassfields* (London: Her Majesty's Stationery Office; Colonial Research Publications, Number 14, 1952):

> Women are not eligible for the headship of kin or political groups. (148)

Bantoc

See above, pages 43–44.

Batek (See also: Semai and Semang)

Kirk Michael Endicott, *Batek Negrito Economy and Social Organization* (Cambridge, Ma. Unpublished PhD thesis, 1974).

The Batek comprise relatively nomadic groups the size of a few extended families. The total number of people in all these groups combined is in the hundreds. As is the case in a few other 'societies' lacking much organization above the familial level, the line between 'patriarchy' (which, by definition, requires hierarchy) and male dominance (which refers to male-female and familial relationships) becomes blurred. In the *relative* absence of hierarchy, decision-making becomes more informal and more a function of male dominance. That this is the case with the Batek is clear from Endicott's work.

> Wives usually go where their husbands want to go and the men seem to prefer their own home areas. If the women could choose, there would probably be a slight uxorilocal bias. (239) [Note: Though most Batek were monogamous, men were permitted to have more than one wife.]
>
> The Batek have a system of headmanship which appears to go back some time. There are at least seven men in the Aring and Lebir Valleys today who are commonly regarded as *penghulu* ('headmen') and they have in their genealogy several generations of *penghulu, menteri* ('ministers' or 'chiefs'), *panglima* ('war captains'), and even a *raja* ('king'). Although the Batek, especially the younger ones, claim that ordinary persons . . . must obey a *penghulu,* that he can order them to do things, in fact the influence of the *penghulu* is purely advisory. . . . The main duty of the *penghulu* is to deal with outsiders. (244–45) [Note: In other words, the authority is more the informal authority of male dominance than the formal authority of patriarchy. From Endicott's own description, moreover, it is not clear that even this is the case; when Endicott is quoting the Batek, rather than giving his interpretation, the male dominance seems virtually formal.]
>
> The position of the *penghulu* descends to the sons of previous *penghulu,* ideally in order of birth. If the *penghulu* has no sons, it goes to his next oldest brother and then to his sons in order. (246)

It is not entirely clear in Endicott's work how the Batek relate to the Semang. However, throughout his work Endicott quotes Schubesta as if that which is true of the Semang is true of the Batek. As we have seen in our discussion of Whyte, Schubesta wrote that, among the Semang, "In each family the father alone is a respected person" and "The head of a Semang local group [is a male]". The same may be said of the Semai.

Berbers

Stephens implies that it is "possible" that the Berbers do not associate familial authority with the male. He indicates that the ethnographic materials do *not* imply that the Berbers fail to associate familial authority with the male (301); his basis for raising the possibility that they may be an exception is information obtained in an interview with a graduate student in archaeology who had observed a particular Berber group in the Rif Mountains while on an archaeological dig (personal communication). Since the informant has not published on this subject, it is not possible to demonstrate in her own words that the group she observed does not represent an exception to the universality of male dominance. Furthermore, the term *Berber* refers to a large number of social groups whose languages are similar. Since there is no way of knowing which of the Rif Mountain groups was observed, it is not possible to invoke someone else's ethnographic study of the group. One would doubt the absence of male dominance simply because all Berber groups are Moslem. Moreover, Murdock, in his compilation covering all Berber groups writes: "Nuclear families are reported to be independent social groups only among the Mzab [not a Rif group]. *Elsewhere* they are aggregated into patrilocal extended families, *each with a patriarchal head"* [Emphasis added] (George Peter Murdock, *Africa: Its People and Their Cultural History* [New York: McGraw-Hill, 1959], 117).

Bribri

See above, page 43.

Catal Hüyük

A poet had suggested that the excavation at Catal Hüyük provides evidence of a neolithic group that was female-headed. In a letter to the *New York Review of Books* (4th October 1973, 37–8), Steven Webster responded:

> . . . as Mellaart [the leader of the excavation] would be the first to admit, the archaeological evidence of female oriented ritual at Catal Hüyük is no more a substantial demonstration of matriarchy than some future excavations of a contemporary shrine of *La Virgen de Guadalupe* (or some other cult of the Madonna) might uncover . . .

Filipinos

C.L. Hunt, 'Female Occupational Roles and Urban Sex Ratios in the United States, Japan, and the Philippines' in *Social Forces*, Volume 43, Number 3, March 1965:

> This combination of patterns has brought the Filipino woman to a point where, although denied some of the adventurous freedom of the male, she may be even better prepared for economic competition. The acceptance of the boredom of

routine work may be seen as part of 'patient suffering' which is said to characterize the Filipino female to a greater extent than the male. Her responsible role in the household means that the wife is charged with practical affairs while the husband is concerned to a greater extent with ritualistic activity which maintains prestige. (144)

Fore

Shirley Glasse (Lindenbaum), *The Social Life of Women in the South Fore* (Mimeographed. Department of Public Health, Territory of Papua and New Guinea. 1963):

> At marriage a Fore woman . . . is expected to be . . . an obedient spouse, a prolific childbearer, and generous with gifts of food to her affines and her husband's friends. (1)

Gahuku-Gama

See above, page 35.

Hopi

Edward P. Dozier, 'The Hopi-Tewa of Arizona', University of California Publication in *American-Archaeology and Ethnology* 44, 3, (1954), 259–376:

> . . . it seems that brothers are assumed to be senior to sisters, and entitled to respect as such, in the absence of evidence to the contrary. (320) [Dozier quoting Barbara Freire-Marreco, 'Tewa Kinship Terms from the Pueblo of Hano, Arizona', *American Anthropologist*, n.s. 16, 269–287.]
>
> Within the family, the mother's brother, or, in his absence, any adult male of the household or clan, is responsible for the maintenance of order and the discipline of younger members. (339)

Iban

See above, page 42.

Iroquois

Lewis Henry Morgan, *League of the Ho-Dé-No-Sau-Nee or Iroquois* (New York: Dodd, Mead, and Company, 1901):

The Indian regarded woman as the inferior, the dependent, and the servant of man, and from nurturance and habit, she actually considered herself to be so. (315)

See also: Cara B. Richards, 'Matriarchy or Mistake: The Role of Iroquois Women Through Time', in *Cultural Stability and Cultural Change* (Annual Meeting of the American Ethnological Society in Ithaca, New York, 1957), 36–45; Martha C. Randle, 'Iroquois Women, Then and Now', *Bureau of American Ethnology Bulletin* 149 (Smithsonian Institution, undated).

Jivaro

Stephens presents two contradictory ethnological views of the Jivaro. One pictures a strong male dominance. The other, on which Stephens bases his suggestion that the Jivaro male is not dominant, is R. Karsten, *The Headhunters of Western Amazonia* (Helsinki: Centraltry-cheriet, 1935). I assume that the text is identical to R. Karsten, *The Headhunters of Western Amazonas: The Life and Culture of the Jibaro Indians of Eastern Ecuador and Peru* (Helsingfors: Finska Vetenskaps-societeten Helsingfors; Commentationes Humanarum Litterarum VII, 1935), in which Karsten writes:

Of the relations between husband and wife it may be proper to say that it is regulated according to the principle 'the man governs, but the woman holds sway'. (254)

Kenuzi

See above, page 42.

Kibbutzim

See note 14 on page 27 and page 35, above.

!Kung

Marjorie Shostak, 'A !Kung Woman's Memories of Childhood' in Richard B. Lee and Irven De Vore, *Kalahari Hunter-Gatherers* (Cambridge, Ma: Harvard University Press, 1976).

N≠isa's descriptions . . . of her relationship with her husband, Tashay, suggest that relations between the sexes are not egalitarian, and that men, because of their greater strength, have power and can exercise their will in relation to women. This confirms Marshall's (1959) finding that men's status is higher than women's. (277)

Richard B. Lee, '!Kung Spatial Organization' in Lee and De Vore:

The dominant impression one gets from accounts of patriocal bands is one of semi-isolated, male-centered groups, encapsulated within territories. (75)

Lovedu

Eileen Jensen Krige and J.D. Krige, *The Realm of a Rain-Queen* (London, 1943):

While under the titular leadership of a 'rain queen' Lovedu society comprises virtually autonomous groups headed by chiefs and district heads who are (nearly always) males and in which most of the decisions are made by the males of the *Khoro*.

Manus

See note 38 on page 45, above.

Marquesans

R. Linton, 'Marquesan Culture' in A. Kardiner, *The Individual and His Society* (New York: Columbia University Press, 1939):

She [the Marquesen woman] does not take the role of disciplinarian. (69–70)
  The gods were almost all male. Theoretically, women could hold the highest rank, but in practice few women were actually household heads, rulers of tribes or inspirational priests. In rare cases the eldest daughter of a chief would become a chieftainess and rule in her own right, although as a rule the chief adopted a boy if his eldest child was a girl. Such a woman might be deified, but the most powerful deities were invariably male. (184)

Mbuti (Bambuti)

See pages 35, 44–45, 52, 60, 107–111, and 239, above.

Turnbull's popular work on the Bambuti is *The Wayward Servants* (Garden City, New York: Natural History Press, 1965). His more detailed academic treatment is *The Mbuti Pygmies: An Ethnographic Survey* (New York: American Museum of Natural History Anthropological Papers, Volume 50: Part 3, 1963).

Minangkabau

E.M. Loeb, 'Patrilineal and Matrilineal Organization in Sumatra: The Minangkabau' in *American Anthropologist*, 36 (January–March, 1934), 49:

> In spite of the nominal 'matriarchate', Van Hasselt claims that the women are really the servants of the men. They not only prepare the meals of the men in their family, but they also serve them first, later eating with the children. [The material Loeb quotes from Van Hasselt is from: A.L. Van Hasselt, "Volksbeschrijving van Midden-Sumatra" in *Midden Sumatra* by P.J. Veth, (Third Part) Leiden, 1882.]
>
> The women have not the legal right to make a contract, not even to dispose of themselves in marriage. (49) [Here Loeb is writing of his own observations, not paraphrasing Van Hasselt]

Peggy Reeves Sanday, 'Gender in Minangkabau Ideology' in Peggy Reeves Sanday and Ruth Gallagher Goodenough, *Beyond The Second Sex* (Philadelphia: University of Pennsylvania Press, 1990):

> The Minangkabau are guided by a hegemonic ideology called *adat*, which legitimizes and structures traditional political and ceremonial life . . . (146)
>
> Thus, the Minangkabau make a distinction between female/weak and male/strong . . . (149)
>
> In the specifics of male and female role definition, adat ideology is decidedly androcentric. (150)
>
> First there are the *ninik mamak*, the men who have the authority to decide in accordance with *adat* law.
>
> The *ninik mamak* have authority over their nephews and nieces.
>
> [The *ninik mamak*] are the heads of the clan in the villages. (151)

Modjokuto

Stephens provides unclear evidence to support Modjokuto as 'matriarchy' (female authority in the home). Quoting Hildred Geertz, 'Javanese Values and Family Relationships', 1956 Radcliffe PhD thesis, and *The Javanese Family* (New York: Free Press, 1961), he says that the man is shown deference in that he gets the better food, must often be the first to eat, and receives 'formalized deference', but that the woman tends to have real household dominance. But Geertz states:

> The relationship with the mother remains as strong and secure as before—and lasts throughout the individual's life. While mothers are described as 'loving' (*trisna*) their children, fathers are expected only to 'enjoy' (*seneng*) them. The mother is seen as a bulwark of strength and love to whom one can always turn. In contrast, the father is distant and must always be treated respectfully. It is the mother who instructs the child in social forms, who makes countless decisions for him, and who administers most punishments. The father is usually only a court of last appeal and a model for imitation. He is expected to be, above all, patient and dignified (sabar) with his wife and children: he should lead them with a gentle though firm hand, not interfering with their petty quarrels, but being always available to give solemn sanction to his wife's punishments of disobedient children. Only during the one early phase of the child's life is this aspect of the father's role set aside. (107)

Montagnais-Naskapi

See below, Naskapi

Mundugumor

See above, pages 35–36.

Nama Hottentot

As Stephens (298) points out (quoting I. Schapera, *The Khoisan Peoples of South Africa* [London: Routledge and Kegan Paul, 1930], 251), the woman does have considerable authority in the home and over the children, but "she plays a subordinate role in matters pertaining to tribal life, and in public always walks several paces behind her husband . . ."

Naskapi (Montagnais)

Julius E. Lips, 'Naskapi Law', in *Transactions of the American Philosophical Society;* Volume 37, 4):

> Women [have] no political rights [and] cannot participate in the election of a chief. (423)

Eleanor Leacock, *The Montagnais: Hunting Territory and The Fur Trade.* American Anthropological Association Memoir (V. 36, N3; Part 2; Memoir N. 78):

> [A male] . . . is the 'outside' chief and is sharply differentiated from the 'real' or 'inside' chiefs, who are the headmen of the multifamily units. . . . (21)

In a number of her writings Leacock maintains that a non-patriarchal egalitarianism was exhibited by the Montagnais-Naskapi Native Americans of the Labrador peninsula of Canada. Robert Sheaffer, in his excellent 'Eleanor Leacock's Depiction of the 17th-Century Montagnais-Naskapi' (Usenet/Scidoc/Skeptic-Archived at various Internet sites), examined the work on which Leacock based her claim, the reports of Father Paul Lejeune, reprinted in Reuben Gold Thwaites (ed.), *The Jesuit Relations and Allied Documents* (New York: Pageant, 1959).

Now, the Montagnais-Naskapi of today are clearly patriarchal, as even Leacock's own work on the group demonstrates. However, Leacock invoked a 17th-century account by a Jesuit missionary to support a claim that this group was once non-patriarchal and lacked male dominance. Leacock's entire argument for the exceptionality of the 17th-century Montagnais-Naskapi consists of two out-of-context quotations from the Jesuit writings.

1. Leacock gives the following quotes from Father Paul Le Jeune, one of the first Jesuit missionaries to enter that region, without providing any context for it:

> The women have great power here. (*Jesuit Relations,* Vol. 5, 181)

Had Leacock quoted any of the sentences that proceed the one she did quote, it would have made it obvious to the reader that this was meant to be ironic, not literally true. Father Le Jeune was describing his attempt to persuade a man to surrender his son so that his son could be educated far away as a Christian. The man, understandably not wanting to do so, but also not wanting to offend the priest, said that he would be glad to, but that his wife would disapprove.

2. Similarly, in an attempt to demonstrate that Montagnais-Naskapi women were 'unfeminine', and that this implied an absence of male dominance, Leacock writes:

> "They have neither gentleness nor courtesy in their utterance," he wrote, "and a Frenchman could not assume the accent, the tone, and the sharpness of their voices without becoming angry, which they do not." (*Becoming Visible*, P. Lamantia ed.; San Francisco: City Light Books, 1981, 21–22)

Here is Le Jeune's statement in fuller context:

> I have never heard the women complain because they were not invited to the feasts, because the men ate the good pieces, or because they had to work continually— going in search of wood for the fire, making the Houses, dressing the skins, and busying themselves in other very laborious work. Each one does her own little tasks, gently and peacefully, without any disputes. It is true, however, that they have neither gentleness nor courtesy in their utterance, and a Frenchman could not assume the accent, the tone, and the sharpness of their voices without becoming angry, which they do not. (Le Jeune, *Jesuit Relations* Vol. 6, 235)

It is unfortunate that Leacock failed to quote the sentences that would have made it obvious that the women's lack of affect was stoical acceptance of male dominance, not evidence of its absence.

There are many other revealing passages from Le Jeune that Leacock could have quoted: *Jesuit Relations*, Vol. 7, 89:

> I observed in this place that the young women did not eat from the same dish as their husbands. I asked the reason, and the Renegade told me that the young unmarried women, and the women who had no children, took no part in the management of affairs, and were treated like children. Thence it came that his own wife said to me one day, "Tell my husband to give me plenty to eat, but do not tell him that I asked you to do so."

Jesuit Relations, Vol. 6, 217–19:

> the Savages prefer the meat of the Bear to all other kinds of food . . . the Bear being brought, all the marriageable girls and young married women who have not had children, as well as those of the Cabin where the Bear is to be eaten, and of the neighboring cabins, go outside, and do not return as long as there remains a piece of this animal, which they do not taste. It snowed, and the weather was very severe. It was almost night when this Bear was brought to our Cabin; immediately the women and girls went out and sought shelter elsewhere, the best they could find. They do this not without much suffering; for they do not always have bark at hand with which

to make their house, which in such cases they cover with branches of the Fir tree. . . . Two banquets are made of this Bear. . . . The men and older women are invited to the first feast, and, when it is finished, the women go out; then the other kettle is taken down, and of this an eat-all feast is made for the men only. This is done on the evening of the capture; the next day toward nightfall, or the second day, I do not exactly remember, the Bear having been all eaten, the young women and girls return.

Jesuit Relations, Vol. 11, 215:

Some Savages had arrived from Tadoussac on their way to war; Father de Quen and I visited them in their cabin, and, after some conversation, they told us that we should go to see the preparations for a great feast which were being made in a place that they named to us. But they advised us not to remain there long, "Because," said they, "as it is a war feast, the women will serve there entirely naked."

Numerous other passages in the Jesuit reports make clear the presence of patriarchy and male dominance. None supports Leacock's claim that the Montagnais-Naskapi are in any way an exception.

Navaho

Clyde Kluckhohn and Dorothea Leighton, *The Navaho* (Cambridge: Harvard University Press, 1946):

Formally, from the Navaho angle, the 'head of the family' is the husband. Whether he is in fact varies with his personality, intelligence, and prestige. (55)

Nayar

E. Kathleen Gough, 'The Traditional Kinship System of the Nayars of Malabar'. Manuscript, Social Science Research Council Summer Seminar on Kinship, Harvard University, 1954, quoted in Stephens, page 317:

The Karanavan [mother's brother] was traditionally unequivocal head of the group. . . . He could command all other members, male and female, and children were trained to obey him with reverence.

Paliyan

F. Dahmen, 'The Paliyans, A Hill-tribe of the Palni Hills, South India' in *Anthropos* (V.3,N.1; 1908):

Women are considered little better than animals, and are rather harshly treated and in some instances brutally beaten. (27)

Semai

Robert Knox Dentan, *The Semai: A Non-Violent People of Malaya* (New York: Holt, Rinehart, and Winston 1968):

No rule prevents women from being influential, and some women are. Most of the time, however, Semai women are primarily concerned with the petty affairs of hearth and home. As a Semai proverb puts it, "men's loincloths are long, women's loincloths are short", that is, men are concerned with major problems, women with minor ones. Furthermore, Semai women feel 'embarrassed' to take a prominent part in public debate, although a woman often exercises influence through her husband. (68)

Semang

See above, page 42.

Tahitians

Robert I. Levy, *The Tahitians* (Chicago: University of Chicago Press, 1973) makes clear that, while a woman can be a village chief, women are village chiefs about as often as they are Senators in the United States. Moreover:

For important matters in Piri the village males meet as a whole, usually in an open field toward the center of the village, with a number of politically concerned women in the background listening carefully to the discussion. (15)

Men are also in the forefront of village political activity, with the women as an interested and vocal background. (233)

Tasaday

In 1971, the Tasaday, a 'society' of 14 adults and 12 children, was 'discovered' in a remote area of rain forest in the Philippines. In the two decades that followed, there ensued a debate over the authenticity and nature of this group. At first the mass media presented the Tasaday as a 'Stone-Age culture' replete with the Edenesque qualities so often associated in the popular culture with primitive societies. By the mid-1980s, many anthropologists had concluded that the Tasaday were a hoax perpetrated by their 'discoverer'.

No one believes that the 26 people did not exist. Disagreement revolves around the issue of the nature of the group. Few if any anthropologists believe that the Tasaday have been isolated for any great period of time and many believe that they were never isolated.

All of this is discussed in *The Tasaday Controversy: Assessing the Evidence,* a fascinating compilation edited by Thomas N. Headland and published by the American Anthropological Association in 1992. The book presents articles by the leading proponents of each view. It is difficult to believe that any reader will find the arguments of those claiming the Tasaday to be of anthropological interest to be as persuasive as those who see the Tasaday as a hoax.

All of the arguments presented concern identities of individuals and genealogical, nutritional, and linguistic considerations. The early journalistic 'descriptions' of the Tasaday lead G.D. Berreman (*op. cit,* 36) to write: "Imagine anthropologists, or anyone else, claiming the description of the Tasaday as the product of research". The only reference in this book even distantly related to the issues we discuss is a journalistic reference to an all-powerful male deity (*ibid.*). The point being made by the anthropologist Berreman is that the entire journalistic description of the Tasaday is unmitigated nonsense. I mention the religious description here merely to indicate that the *only* sentence in this entire book that has even a remote relevance to the issue of male dominance speaks of a *male* deity.

Tchambuli

See pages 31, 34–35, and 41, above.

Tlingit

Aurel Kraus, *The Tlingit Indians* (Seattle: Washington University Press, 1956):

The rank of chief . . . passes from uncle to nephew. (77)

Vanatinai

Maria Lepowsky, *Fruit of the Motherland: Gender and Exchange on Vanatina, Papua New Guinea* unpublished PhD dissertation, University of California, Berkeley, 1981:

Almost all sorcerers on Vanatinai, who often exercise political and economic control over their neighbors, are male. . . . No Vanatinai women have ever been elected as a Local Government Councillor. (469–470)

Waorani

See above, pages 60–61.

Yegali

This tribe is alleged to have existed in Madagascar in Harold Hodge's introductory sociology text, *Conflict and Consensus* (New York: Harper and Row, 1971). Dr Hodges writes (personal communication) that he heard of this group from the late Donald Bender. Investigation has not uncovered any mention of this group in either anthropological or popular publications.